D1274635

MIGRATING TO OPEN SYSTEMS

MIGRATING TO OPEN SYSTEMS: Taming the Tiger

Daniel R. Perley

McGRAW-HILL BOOK COMPANY

London · New York · St Louis · San Francisco · Auckland
Bogotá · Caracas · Hamburg · Lisbon · Madrid · Mexico · Milan
Montreal · New Delhi · Panama · Paris · San Juan · São Paulo
Singapore · Sydney · Tokyo · Toronto

Published by
McGRAW-HILL Book Company Europe
Shoppenhangers Road, Maidenhead, Berkshire, SL6 2QL, England
Telephone 0628 23432
Fax 0628 770224

British Library Cataloguing in Publication Data
Perley, Daniel R.
  Migrating to Open Systems: Taming the Tiger
  I. Title
  004.6
  ISBN 0–07–707778–4

Library of Congress Cataloging-in-Publication Data
Perley, Daniel R.
  Migrating to open systems: taming the tiger/Daniel R. Perley.
    p.   cm.
  Includes index.
  ISBN 0–07–707778–4
  1. Computer architecture. I. Title.
  QA76.9.A25P44   1993
  004.6—dc20   92–32088 CIP

Copyright © 1993 McGraw-Hill International (UK) Limited. All
rights reserved. No part of this publication may be reproduced,
stored in a retrieval system, or transmitted, in any form or by any
means, electronic, mechanical, photocopying, recording, or
otherwise, without the prior permission of McGraw-Hill International
(UK) Limited, with the exception of material entered and executed
on a computer system for the reader's own use.

1234 CUP 9543

Typeset by Wyvern Typesetting Ltd, Bristol, Avon
and printed and bound in Great Britain at the University Press,
Cambridge

Contents

Trademarks   viii
Preface   ix
Acknowledgements   xi

1 Starting the journey: a general introduction   1
You cannot tame the beast until you know it   1
Objectives of this book   2
What you will be able to do after reading this book   4
Chapter outline   5

2 Open systems: the nature of the beast   7
Overview   7
Closed systems   7
Open systems   9
Open system interconnection   12
More definitions   13
Standards and standards organizations   17
More equal than others: standards for standards   23
Profiles of standards   25
Developing a practical approach   37
Conclusion   41

3 Costs, opportunities and benefits   45
Introduction   45
Tactical costs   49
Strategic costs   60
Tactical opportunities   68
Work, work item (WI) and workspace sharing   69
Strategic opportunities   79
Tactical benefits   92
Strategic benefits   100
Conclusion   106

**4 Architecture without buildings: the role of system architecture
    and other frameworking activities   107**
Introduction   107

Definition of system architecture 107
The importance of system architecture 109
System architecture in context 114
Idealism, flexibility and practicality 114
Single user versus client/server 116
Single user versus multi-user 121
Client/server versus multi-user 124
The advantages and disadvantages of different processing tiers 146
Conclusion 152

5   **Step by step: slow and steady wins the race** **153**
Introduction 153
What kind of tiger? 153
Corporate requirements 154
IT requirements 156
User-group motivators 156
The need for champions 158
A strategic plan 158
System architecture 160
Send smoke signals to your staff 161
Central technology management infrastructure 162
Optimum sourcing strategies 171
More on workgroup system building blocks 175
You, your legacy vendor and open systems 178
Off to a good start 183

6   **From paper to pilot: learning your way in** **184**
Introduction 184
Qualifying, evaluating and certifying vendors 184
Lab tests 191
IT Alpha Tests 194
Trial or pilot 194
Trials 197
Pilot projects 203
Conclusion 204

7   **Hardening the framework: building from the foundation** **205**
Introduction 205
Capitalizing on your success 205
Making trials permanent 207
Extending pilots to other sites 207
Organizing for technology management 208

Software registry concept   212
Application placement   215

8 Fact and fiction: two case studies   **220**
Introduction   220
The Transport Canada Unit Level System (ULS) program   220
Cascade Transportation   233

9 As old as the industry; as modern as the hour   **247**

Index   **251**

Trademarks

All computer vendor names used in this book, and the abbreviations thereof, are the registered trademarks of the respective vendors. For example, 'IBM' is the registered trademark of International Business Machines Corporation, 'DEC' is the registered trademark of Digital Equipment Corporation, etc. Nothing in this book is to be taken as a specific endorsement or criticism of any vendor or product.

Preface

In seeking to plan, foster and oversee the migration of an organization from closed, proprietary and vendor-specific computer systems to a more open computing environment there exists no lack of challenges. Indeed, problems and pitfalls abound. One must first try to understand the organization's business and the information it handles now; more importantly, one must address the future information management requirements. As in duck-shooting (wherein the shot must be placed where the duck *will be*, not where it is now) open system implementation means shooting at a moving target. One must also understand the technology and the vendors in relation to what they can do, what they may be able to do soon, and what they clearly cannot do (even though they may claim otherwise). Finally, one must gain a good vision of how to bring information handling needs and ever-developing technologies together. The migration process must take full account of organizational dynamics and culture.

While it will be many years before the authoritative work on this subject can be produced (there is insufficient experience anywhere in the world), this book does attempt to provide some practical guidelines and mileposts for what can be a very difficult, perplexing and sometimes hazardous challenge. It is intended primarily for prospective and actual leaders in the information technology (IT) field, but should be of assistance to anyone seeking to work with the new technology. The book provides a (hopefully) practical 'How-to' approach for a move to the next generation of computer and communications technology; a move into the era of open computing systems and open system interconnection. It includes everything needed to plan and execute a logical and incremental in-migration of next-generation technology. Included are system architecture, acquisition (planning, lab tests, field trials and pilots), implementation, training and education. The text includes examples and case studies, as well as pitfalls to be avoided in dealing with complex technologies, managing relationships with multiple vendors, quelling the reactionary behaviour of proprietary vendors and trying to change organizational culture—all at once.

However, this is more than just another book for computer specialists; it can also serve the needs of senior executives and managers who may seek to understand why their IT organizations are making the move

to open systems. All major concepts presented also include a special
'☞' paragraph, written in plain, non-technical English. These may help
form a bridge between the senior executive and the IT professional, who
often tend to speak very different dialects of the language.

The book is based on my fourteen years of experience, over half of
which has involved the implementation of challenging new technologies
within various types and sizes of organizations.

Daniel R. Perley

Acknowledgements

There are many people whose ideas and encouragement have contributed to this book. Chief among these was Mike Plouffe, my immediate superior during two-and-a-half very enjoyable years spent as a Director with Transport Canada. His guidance and suggestions, and the pressing need to develop new approaches and procedures as our acquisition program progressed, helped give rise to many ideas which have since been successfully implemented. While the efforts of all members of my staff there were little short of herculean, one of them deserves special mention; Jim Tam contributed substantially to the GX operating system concept and was a crucial participant in proving its practical viability. Gary Donnelly, a Washington-based consultant, provided no small amount of encouragement and support during the formative stages of this book.

1 Starting the journey: a general introduction

You cannot tame the beast until you know it

As a young child, I was always struck by the beauty and grace of tigers. Circus tigers, wild tigers and even the one on a cereal box. Of course, these tigers varied widely in personality, from the amicable cartoon character to the ones great white hunters used to go to India to shoot! Because of their very attractive colouring and often amicable demeanour, it is sometimes easy to forget that tigers are among the most powerful, fearsome and dangerous beasts on earth. In a flash, their docility and calmness can change to ferocity and lethality.

During my work over the past few years in helping to bring open system technology to the fields of computing and computer communications, it has often struck me that effectively managing and supporting the acquisition of open computing systems and open system interconnection (OSI communications) is not unlike attempting to tame, or at least train, a tiger.

At the outset, there is the tendency to be attracted, even consumed, by the beauty and the possibilities of the beast without a full consideration of some of its other attributes. We know, however, that professional tamers of the big cats share a steely-nerved ability to maintain intense concentration, to stare down would-be deviation from the routine and a constant, unflinching respect for the animals they oversee. For even the most confident tamers with many years of experience and a good relationship with their charges, it takes only a momentary slip, loss of confidence or turning of the back to result in a tragedy. It isn't, in most cases, that the tiger hates the master or tamer; it is just that he or she is dominated mostly by a nature and instinct fashioned over thousands of generations of survival in the wild, in a very distinct role. The distinction between a playful nudge, a playful romp and a slightly aggressive mauling may be moot to the tiger, but not to the tamer, nor to any other human. From our human perspective, to characterize the tiger as 'bad' or 'evil', except in the case of committed man-eaters, is probably unfair in the extreme. However, to fail to respect the tiger is much worse.

Open systems, as defined in the next chapter, offer the modern organization many costs, opportunities and benefits and in almost all cases these net out to a substantially positive change. They let computers of different manufacture work more smoothly together, they ease the migration of software to larger or smaller platforms from the same (or different) vendors and they allow greatly increased operational flexibility. In many cases, they will substantially revitalize and rejuvenate the organization. However, like all other aspects of technology, open systems are not a panacea and must be implemented and supported with the respect they deserve. Otherwise, they will come around behind and bite us just as surely as the inattentively managed tiger. We know from history that technology is, if anything, neutral.

Nuclear energy can be used to heat homes or to kill people, for example. While open systems usually tend not to be lethal, they certainly could be if prematurely installed in a real-time oriented traffic control or process control situation. Even where not lethal, a prematurely or ineffectively implemented open system can cause significant grief to the organization, and could greatly disrupt the careers of those responsible.

Objectives of this book

To help you define the real issues for your organization

There are few subjects today about which there has been so much discussion and debate as the application of open systems technology in the fields of computer systems and computer communications. There are those who say that systems were never really meant to be open, or at least it is not possible to make them fully open in the practical sense. There are those who say that open systems are a laudable objective but one whose pursuit is like that of the Holy Grail. Still others hold that there is a natural evolution from proprietary to open systems and that all suggestions to the contrary are nonsense. Into the midst of this lively arena many smoke bombs are cast by hardware vendors, software vendors, system integration firms, consultants, informed analysts, supposedly informed analysts, financial experts (who have appointed themselves as 'advanced technology industry experts') and many other classes of commentators. It is possible to find articles in the present trade and professional press which take all of the following positions:

- Open systems are fully viable in business environments.
- Open systems are the coming thing, they'll be viable in X years.
- Vendor A's systems are more open than vendor B's.
- Open systems are a hoax, a dream or a fraud.
- Open systems are irrelevant, it is ZZZ that really matters.

All of these persuasions, and others, have their followers and it is doubtful that there are many major religions with as many 'sects' or subdivisions as the open systems movement.

Chapter 3 sets out a substantial menu of the pure costs, the exploitable opportunities (which can turn out to be either costs and/or benefits, depending upon what *you* do) and the pure benefits of open systems. This book should therefore assist you to select those opportunities and benefits which you believe would be of most assistance to your organization and to focus on them in your planning, acquisition, implementation and support activities.

To help you manage open systems on an ongoing basis

One of the most important things I have learned about open systems is that obtaining them is not a 'one-shot deal'. In years past, you could order a mainframe or minicomputer from your favourite vendor and, if you desired, thereafter let that vendor take complete charge of the installation, operation, support and even the upgrading of your system. If you were sufficiently trusting, the vendor's salespersons (sometimes called customer engineers) would actually come and live in your building! Today, except where a commitment is made to total outsourcing, you no longer have that choice. Committing to open systems without also consciously committing to multiple vendors is like installing electricity and continuing to use gas lamps; you simply will not reap many of the benefits without 'multi-vendorism'. In moving to a multi-vendor environment, however, it is necessary to recognize that more of the components must be obtained, integrated, tested and supported by in-house Information Technology (IT) staffs or else by trusted agents not tied to any of the hardware vendors. I will seek to provide some ideas, and guidance, on how to plan and manage this technology inflow process on an ongoing basis.

To permit learning from the experiences of others

For approximately two-and-a-half years I managed a large open system acquisition program for Transport Canada (The Canadian Federal Department of Transport). A number of the examples and analogies in this book are drawn from my experience in this, and previous, roles. Others are more general and are based on what I have learned from colleagues during my participation in the founding and activities of the User Alliance for Open Systems (UAOS). A key purpose of this book is to share experiences with the intent of helping you, the reader, to learn from them.

To be intelligible

One of the most difficult things for anyone in the IT field to do is to write meaningful material about the field for those not actually engaged in it. While the primary audience of this book certainly is IT managers and their staffs, in deference to executive (and general-interest) readers, I have attempted where possible to provide 'plain English' translations of key passages, usually prefaced by the ☞ symbol.

This book also has one non-objective. It is *not* intended as a general introduction to, or a treatise upon, the concept or anatomy of open systems themselves. It is far more a treatment of how to get there from Square Zero. Rather than a map of the New World, it is closer to a chart for finding one's way across the Atlantic and into the general vicinity. For readers desiring a good general treatment of what open systems themselves are, and how they came about, I would unhesitatingly recommend Pamela Gray's book *Open Systems: A Business Strategy for the 1990's*. It is readable by a very wide audience and presents a balanced and reasonably complete and current coverage of the subject.

What you will be able to do after reading this book

If you are a business manager or executive, after reading this book you should be able to do the following:

1 Understand why viewing open systems in terms of only pure costs and pure benefits is an inadequate approach. Consideration of all of the costs, opportunities and benefits is important.
2 Understand why an unduly short-term and/or narrowly defined (usually finance-dictated) view of business planning almost always does not favour the adoption of open systems.

3 Understand why your IT organization may be reluctant, even terrified, to try taming the open system tiger.
4 Understand why linking open systems to business objectives is
important, both for you and for your Chief Information Officer
(CIO) and staff.
5 Understand the pitfalls and problems of acquiring, or being acquired
by, an organization with a commitment to open systems which is
significantly stronger (or weaker) than your own.

If you are a CIO or other IT sector executive, manager or staff
member, this book should help and, hopefully, spur you to be able to do
the following:

1 Understand the technological and operational basics of open systems
and where/how to get more information, as it is required.
2 Understand how to link open systems to business objectives in such a
convincing way that neither well-meaning supporters nor the most
wilful detractors can disconnect them.
3 Understand each identifiable cost, opportunity and benefit of open
systems as well as how to decide which relate most closely to your
organization, thence using them to build a strong business case for
open systems.
4 Understand the role of system architecture in the adoption of new
technology (including, but not limited to, open systems) and the
thornier issue of how to determine how much system architecture is
enough.
5 Be able to conceptualize, and then write, a plan which will take you
from the earliest stages right through to actual implementation of
open systems.
6 Be able to establish a technology in-migration plan which will serve
your organization well, including system specification, test, certification, acquisition, integration, commissioning and support.
7 Actually implement the plan, while maintaining the requisite flexibility. This tends to involve, as Rudyard Kipling put it, trusting
yourself while all men doubt you, but making allowance for their
doubting too.
8 Cope with doubting senior management, screaming accountants,
hostile proprietary vendors, irate COBOL programmers, confused
end-users and the many manifestations of the word 'compliant'.

Chapter outline

Chapter 2 provides a brief profile and definition of a few of the most
salient characteristics of open systems and a working vocabulary of

definitions which is a prerequisite to understanding much of the rest of the book. Chapter 3 details the major costs, opportunities and benefits of open systems in the context of the medium-sized and large user organization. Chapter 4 touches the area in which system architecture and open systems converge, and provides some hints for understanding and managing the architectural process. Chapter 5 deals with requirements assessment, future-casting, plan making and pace setting, all of which are essential to getting started. (You won't teach the tiger to dance on your first encounter, unless you are equipped with a teflon suit.) Chapter 6 puts planning into practice with some suggestions for actually getting the in-migration and adoption process rolling, while Chapter 7 contains suggestions for moving early ventures to production status. Chapter 8 shares two case studies (one factual and one fictional) and Chapter 9 deals philosophically with the challenge of coping with ongoing, indeed constant, change.

2 Open systems: the nature of the beast

Overview

The purpose of this chapter is to provide some working definitions (and additional characterization) of open systems which will be referenced in the other chapters and to provide important additional information about not only open systems but also their proponents and detractors.

Closed systems

As computer systems developed, between 1960 and 1980, a number of competitive vendors became well established in the marketplace. Each of these developed their own processors and communications technologies with their related low-level languages and protocols, which in turn gave rise to varying operating systems and high-level languages. These differences, plus additional real or perceived value added by each of the vendors, tended to make commitment to one vendor's products or even to one product line or architecture within a given vendor's overall offering a very long-term proposition. As more and more investment was made in training, operating experience, system software modifications, development of applications software and in more terminals, printers and other peripherals, it became very difficult for a user organization even to consider changing products or vendors.

☞ Computers tend to have five key levels, as set out in Fig. 2.1.

☞ The hardware includes the boxes, screens, keyboards, printers, tape and disk drives that you can see and touch. The operating system is the program that permits higher-level programs to control the hardware and which helps the computer keep track of itself. High-level languages permit a programmer to write programs which actually perform the work, manipulating data. In the hierarchical block diagram shown in Fig. 2.1, each layer depends upon those below it. For example, if you remove the hardware, the rest of the stack collapses.

☞ Computer makers each developed different hardware and operating systems. Therefore, their languages and, of course, the programs written with such languages and the data they handled could only be used on their own machines.

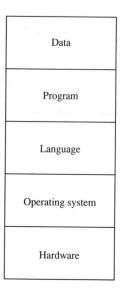

Figure 2.1   Conceptual elements (layers) of a computer system.

In general, vendors encouraged this trend as it established them as virtually the sole source of supply for a given customer, often leading to typical monopolist behaviour of, sometimes, poor service, high prices and vendor-dictated contractual terms. Only the very largest corporate and government customers, who clearly had the resources to make a wholesale switch if they perceived their vendor as unreasonable or greedy, were able to gain sufficient leverage to negotiate mutually favourable arrangements. And even these organizations frequently had to pay very high operating system licence fees on an ongoing basis, despite the very low marginal cost for the vendor to support and upgrade an installed and stable operating system. Vendors regularly introduced new processor, memory and storage technologies and generally provided upward compatibility within, but not among, their product lines. Systems conforming to the above description eventually became known as 'closed' systems because installations of such systems were, in general, closed to the hardware, software and communications products of other vendors. Conversely, systems which are closed tend to trap or 'lock in' the customer to the vendor and product line concerned.

There were, of course, advantages to remaining with a given vendor and product line, familiarity and confidence in a known level of service being two of the key ones. Certainly, a large 'plug-compatible' market evolved for the products of some proprietary vendors, but dogging the footsteps of such giant corporations was an expensive and high-risk venture. The builders of such plug-in equipment were forced to offer better performance and/or lower prices and were often perceived as offering inferior service and support. They thus tended to garner only a fractional or marginal market share and did not threaten the dominance of the vendors with whose products they sought to interconnect.

> ☞ Companies which make computers have a vested interest in arranging things in such a way that it is very hard for you to move programs from their computer to someone else's computer. This is great for the companies but not so good for the user, as it increases cost, decreases flexibility and makes the user organization a 'captive customer' of the computer company. The term used in the information technology industry for this is 'vendor lock-in' because the customer is 'locked in' to one computer vendor.

Open systems

In the US defence/aerospace industrial sector, where very extensive use is made of computer resources at all stages of product design, manufacturing, deployment and support, there was increasing irritation with this sometimes crushing dependence upon a single vendor, particularly when such vendors tended to control very high percentages of the overall computing goods and services market. This was inconsistent not only with the competitive nature of government acquisition (which stressed price competition) but also with how these firms did business. For example, a firm developing a new aircraft would have many competitive sources from which to select avionics and engines and even such sundry items as windows and toilets. The best combination of price and specified performance, where backed up by a reputable supplier, would be selected. Interoperability was also a key factor in the aviation field; a given aircraft might be certified with several engines, a given engine would be used on many aircraft and even two engines or aircraft from competitive builders would have many common, industry-standard parts. They would also be built to common engineering standards. Such was patently not the case in the commercial computer industry and even among the firms building equipment intended for scientific, engineering and technical computing.

For a number of years a solution was sought to this problem. Over time, university and other research work led inexorably to the conclusion that 'open' systems were indeed possible and practical and that the only major barriers to such systems were the welter of conflicting approaches and 'standards' already erected for commercial reasons by the computer makers. These manufacturers, in the main, had no serious interest in standardization as this could remove their self-created monopoly positions with their captive customers. Indeed, many vendors have sought to retard or even reverse the progress of open systems, usually while claiming to be doing something else, even such as supporting open systems.

An open system, as defined by the IEEE POSIX committee in the *Guide to the POSIX Open Systems Environment*, is:

> A system that implements sufficient open specifications for interfaces, services and supporting formats to enable properly engineered applications software:
>
> – to be ported across a wide range of systems (with minimal changes)
> – to interoperate with other applications on local and remote systems, and
> – to interact with users in a style which facilitates user portability.

This is a very useful definition, but I do not believe that it goes far enough. In reality, the term 'open systems' refers to two very distinct sets of standards, products, features and characteristics, as defined below:

1 Open Systems Interconnection (OSI) is a seven-layer hierarchy of communications standards, conventions and protocols which permit interconnection and, in some cases, interoperation, of similar or dissimilar computer systems. These standards are set and managed by international standards bodies and are the basis for international, industry-wide efforts to standardize the ways in which automated systems communicate with each other.

☞ OSI relates to standardizing how computers communicate with each other. It is a means of making similar or dissimilar computers use a common approach to becoming aware of each other, having a dialogue, exchanging information or working together. This common approach is defined in terms of a hierarchy of mandatory and optional ways of packaging and sending signals between the computers. Referring to the five-layer stack presented in Fig. 2.1, it lets computers with totally different layers communicate with each other.

2 Open Computing Systems (OCS) are computer systems which, through the use of common or compatible components such as system software (operating system), Relational Database Management System (RDBMS), programming language and other components, permit vertical, horizontal and forward portability of user environments, applications, data and packages. Open systems exhibit a high degree of application, data and user environment *portability*, *scalability* and *interoperability* with each other.

☞ OCS relates largely (but not entirely) to standardizing the most basic programs that computers have, the programs that link the computer itself to the higher-level programs that actually do the work for the user. These basic programs are called operating systems, often also known as system software. By running the same operating system on two very different computers, it becomes possible to transfer (port) a high-level program from one type of computer to another. Having the same (a standard) operating system on two different computers helps make things more open, although sometimes it is not enough. Using the same computer programming language also helps, as does using other software which runs on both computers. With OCS you can carry a user's program to a larger or smaller computer, as well as to a replacement computer from a different vendor, much more easily. Referring to the five-layer stack, it makes the operating system layer identical or very similar on different computers. This should, in theory, let you carry everything above the operating system layer (i.e. the language, program and data layers) between computer systems of different manufacture.

In order to maximize the positive opportunities and benefits available to you from open systems, it is necessary to have a two-halved apple. You have to have both OSI and OCS to obtain the full benefits. If you implement only OSI, disparate computers can communicate and inter-operate but user environment, data and software portability will suffer. If you implement OCS within a proprietary network environment, much of the interoperability benefits will be unavailable. This is treated in greater detail below.

An 'open specification' is seen, by the IEEE, as one which is maintained by an open public consensus process and which can adapt so as to take in new technology over time. Put simply, open systems can more easily communicate with each other and permit computer programs, data and computer users to be moved easily from one vendor's system to another.

All of the following can impact the degree of openness of a computer system:

- The selection of a processor and the development and customization of the instruction set;
- The selection and customization of the operating system including its interface with the user and applications as well as the actual services it provides to the user, the application developer, the administrator, the application and the communications environment;
- The selection and manner of implementation of software and hardware communications facilities, standards and protocols and the selection of options or choices within them (collectively such choices are known as profiles);
- The choice of high-level languages, database packages and office-automation packages which will be supported on the processor;
- The degree to which information on the above items is made available to acquisition authorities, system administrators, independent application software developers, end-users and competitive hardware vendors;
- The consistency with which customizable elements of the hardware, system software and communications facilities are modified;

- The consistency with which end-user shells and scripts are customized; and
- The consistency with which application development efforts follow the definitions of operating system interface and user interface as well as the application development method, documentation and life cycle management standards, procedures or doctrines.

It will be seen that the first five of the above factors are under the sole or predominant control of the hardware vendor, whereas the final three fall into the province of the user organization and of independent software vendors. It is thus crucial to have a clear approach as to 'how to accomplish things' in an open system environment agreed upon, and faithfully followed, by both the vendor and user communities.

An open system must demonstrate:

Compatibility—applications running on the system will be able to run on future versions of the same system;

Portability—applications running on the operating system on a given hardware platform will run on any other vendor's computer which utilizes that operating system;

Scalability—applications written for the system will run on the full range of computer architectures and sizes from micros to mainframes; and

Interoperability—applications running on the system will be able to communicate with any other computer system using the same networking protocols.

Open systems interconnection

The hypercomplexity of inducing computers to communicate with each other *within* companies and countries, much less among them, was meanwhile causing the evolution of a new set of communications standards and approaches, broadly labelled the Open System Interconnection (OSI) approach. The International Standards Organization (ISO), based in Geneva, Switzerland, which coordinates the activities of many national standards bodies working in every field from screw threads to road construction, began to focus on the desperate need for standardization in the computer field. Standards would allow diverse computers not only to be connected together but actually to communicate and work together (to 'interoperate'), would promote the distribution of applications (to bring them close to the users by having the same program run on small computers that formerly ran only on large ones) and would make computers and communications networks easier to manage. In this sense, OSI is a distinct concept, different from operating system or other commonality; although it promotes interoperability it does not allow application programs to be ported from one computer to another.

A seven-layer model of computer communications, over a network, was created as follows:

- *Physical* layer handles the encoding of data into signals able to be sent over mechanical, electrical, radio channel and/or fibre-transmission media.
- *Data link* layer synchronizes transmission and detects/corrects errors.
- *Network* layer establishes, maintains and ends communications between two nodes (and their respective computers) by establishing a logical path.
- *Transport* layer gives the user or application the 'handles' needed to control the functions of the previous three layers.
- *Session* layer oversees the dialogue between the computing systems such that each computer sends information when the other is expecting it.
- *Presentation* layer converts data for presentation to the recipient computer in a form it will understand.
- *Application* layer provides specific services which complement efforts by the applications or end-users to transfer files or to access each other's databases.

☛ This is the hierarchy of approaches to packaging (nesting) and sending signals between computers which was referred to in the last English-translation section. It is becoming very widely accepted in Europe, in North America and elsewhere.

The above is also called the 'OSI Reference Model'. Taken together, these seven layers provide a framework or model for 'slotting in' individual communications facilities and services provided by a computer, a communications node (which itself may be a form of computer) or by a private or public network. The model is vendor-independent, enabling even two proprietary and otherwise incompatible computers at least to communicate with each other. It can do even more when these computers are themselves both open systems as defined above.

More definitions

Tiresome as it may seem, we have not yet fully explored the beast; knowing that the tiger has paws without also knowing that it usually possesses claws, for example, could spoil your whole day! There are some interesting logical paradoxes in the open systems world which need to be highlighted here.

The term 'UNIX' is used in this book as a generic for any open operating system, one which runs on multiple vendors *and* multiple architectures, and includes AT&T UNIX V.3, Berkeley BSD, XENIX, SUN-OS, UNIX International UNIX V.4, Open Software Foundation OSF Version 1 and a number of others. Almost all UNIX and UNIX-like operating systems trace their heritage back to work performed at AT&T's Bell Laboratories.

☞ Operating systems called 'UNIX' and those with generally similar names, usually ending in 'IX' and 'UX', permit programs to be carried more easily from one computer to another.

The term 'POSIX' defines a family of standards developed by a group of committees under IEEE auspices which specify operating system and other *functional and user interfaces* but which do not specify, for example, the operating system itself. POSIX is important to portability but does not, on its own, guarantee portability. For example, a fully POSIX-compliant OA package running under a proprietary operating system *cannot* be carried forward to a POSIX-compliant UNIX system from another vendor.

☞ Do not be fooled, POSIX is *not* an operating system! POSIX defines the way in which users, and certain elements of the computer itself, will *interact with* the operating system, but says less about the operating system itself. Proprietary operating systems can become POSIX-compliant. That does not make them into open operating systems— in some cases it merely gives them a 'cloak of openness'. Putting a tiger skin over a bear does not turn the bear into a tiger; it merely makes it look something like one. Some computer vendors have become very excited about POSIX, hoping customers will continue buying their proprietary operating systems if served up with POSIX.

A Personal Computer (PC) is a DOS/INTEL standard-based processing system running the MS-DOS operating system, usually including a Central Processing Unit (CPU) cabinet, a keyboard and a cathode ray tube (CRT) screen. Often a printer and mouse accompany the system. MS-DOS is a proprietary operating system since it only runs on one computer architecture (INTEL's 8086, 80286, 80386, 80486 and successor processors). However, the DOS/INTEL combinations are now so widely used that they behave something like an open operating system. There is avid price competition among suppliers of hardware and software. The PC is by far the most successful component of the microelectronics revolution; it has gone a long way towards democratizing the technology, placing it in the hands of millions of users.

The term 'workstation' (WS) is generally used to describe a more powerful personal computing system based on the DOS/INTEL or another computer processor architecture. Many workstations run UNIX but some run the DEC VMS or other operating systems. At any given time, the tendency has been to use the term WS to describe a desktop system more powerful than the then-current PC. This has become very confusing since, for example, today's 80386SX-, 80386- and 80486-based PCs are more powerful than the 'power user' workstations of just a few years ago.

☞ PC and WS equipment is for a single user and normally sits on or near the desktop, although the same processing engines used to drive these systems are found in everything from factory robots to the cars they build.

A Micro-Based Server (MBS) is a system based on PC technology (i.e. using the DOS/INTEL standard) which is able to control a Local Area Network (LAN) and provide access to data, communications services and certain programs to end-users with PC or WS equipment. Usually, the MBS and the PC or WS function as a team. The MBS, which has more storage capability, runs part of a program and the desktop device runs the other part. The part on the MBS usually finds the required data (and sometimes a copy of the program logic needed to manipulate that data) and 'serves' or provides it to the PC or WS. The latter uses its own processing power to perform the required functions on the data.

☞ An MBS functioning as a server can be thought of as an overgrown PC that acts as a sort of a 'mother hen' to a number of other PCs, passing them what they need to do their respective jobs and then later taking back the results for safekeeping. While an MBS does this job very well, when the dataset grows too large, the logic becomes too complicated or the number of PCs in the brood becomes too many, problems will result. Then, it is necessary to choose between having more than one MBS or moving to a larger system, as defined below.

A Mid-Range System (MRS) is a multi-user computer which is installed in an office environment to support a workgroup with anything from five or ten to approximately 70 members. It can provide any or all of the following functions:

- Facilitate access to mainframe environment by emulating proprietary mainframe vendor terminals, controllers and/or front-end processors;
- Run Office Automation (OA) software which includes local E-mail, interchange to X.25 backbone carried E-mail among systems, word processing, calendaring, resource scheduling, telephone list management, personal 'cardfile' databases, spreadsheets and calculators;
- Run an RDBMS with third-party or custom applications;
- Run third-party or custom applications written in languages such as COBOL or C;

- Provide PC interworking by permitting PCs to employ MRS storage space as a logical/physical location for storing or backing up MS-DOS files;
- Function as a node on a LAN permitting users with PCs or UNIX workstations, and terminal users connected to a LAN terminal controller, to access the MRS as though star-wired to it;
- Operate as a LAN server providing all of the connectivity and file access capabilities of a dedicated server. This is often accomplished with a dedicated board as the LAN controller and by using other MRS resources to support the other elements of the LAN server role.

☞ The MRS is the current counterpart to the traditional 'minicomputer' but there are some important differences. Unlike the minicomputer, most MRS equipment does *not* require a special environmentally conditioned computer room (often colloquially called a 'glass house') or even a dedicated room in which to live. It can use the standard office (or even home) 110V/60 Hz or 250V/50 Hz power and its sound/heat output are compatible with placing it in someone's office or cubicle. Another important difference is that today's MRS equipment can be taken care of (administered) by a paraprofessional trained and certified for this purpose. It does not need a computer expert to look after it on a day-to-day basis.

The terms 'server', 'LAN server' or 'file server' apply to any device (be it a dedicated stand-alone MBS or an MRS) which is functioning as the controller and file server for a LAN. (Note that some LANs may have more than one file server but will have only one controller.) This server receives requests from intelligent (PC or workstation) clients and responds to them, usually transferring a copy of the requested file to the client and receiving an updated copy back from the client later. The relationship between 'LAN server' and 'MRS' is not reciprocal: while virtually any MRS can be equipped also to function as a LAN server, not all LAN servers can be equipped to function as an MRS. Most MBS class systems can only timeshare five or, at most, ten users, providing such users are not overly demanding in terms of processor capacity. Many MBS-based LAN servers have insufficient CPU power, storage or I/O capacity to serve as a true multi-user MRS. While a LAN server is primarily a file server it may also provide client access to communications services (including gateways to networks and mainframes) and single-user RDBMS or other single-user applications. Applying the term 'RDBMS server' or 'application server' to an MRS is very often incorrect since an MRS normally runs *multi-user* versions of the RDBMS, RDBMS-dependent applications and other applications. In this case the RDBMS or application is not 'served' to an intelligent client but the user merely accesses it as a terminal or emulated terminal on a PC. Likewise, calling an MRS a 'communications server' is incorrect because the server model implies intelligence at the client (user) location and single-user server-based communications applications, whereas an MRS can provide proprietary terminal and controller emulation (for mainframe access) to one or more real (or emulated) non-intelligent ASCII terminal-equipped users.

A *client/server* service model is one in which a server, as defined above, receives requests from intelligent clients and responds to them, usually transferring a copy of the requested file to the client and receiving an updated copy back from the client later.

☞ Here, each of the MBS or MRS or even a large mainframe system and the PC do part of the work. The work is divided according to its functional content.

A *multi-user* service model is one in which an MRS, functioning as a true multi-user system, permits two or more users with actual or emulated terminals to make simultaneous use of the same application or package. Locking at the file and/or record level prevents two or more users from simultaneously attempting to modify the same data. The operating system manages all user interactions and processes.

☞ Here, the MRS or larger system does all or virtually all of the work. The PC or WS may, however, package and present data for the user's inspection.

Client/server and multi-user service models are not mutually exclusive; an MRS can be equipped to facilitate either or both of them. The only absolute restrictions are that client/server architecture requires the users (clients) to have intelligent workstations, or at least quasi-intelligent terminals, and client/server also is not truly multi-user because the server deals with each client in isolation from all other clients, as if they did not exist.

An X-terminal is a quasi-intelligent reincarnation of the old non-intelligent terminal. It can do as good a job as a PC by 'fooling' an MBS or MRS into believing that it is a fully intelligent 'client', able to do cooperative two-level processing, as defined above.

Standards and standards organizations

As cited above, for a number of years there has been a drive towards standardization of computer systems and computer communications. Public standards bodies, industry standards groups, user groups and even dominant single vendors can create *de facto* (on-the-ground) or *de jure* (agreed and institutionalized) standards for almost any aspect of computing from keyboard layout to transaction processing. The nature of a user organization's business, the specifics of its intended system architecture and the state of the technology (and market) at the time of acquisition will all work to determine which standards are relevant, applicable and workable.

Progress from concept to draft to ballot, to more drafts and more ballots, and finally to an acceptance recommendation, actual acceptance and promulgation can take three to five years, longer in some cases. There is no doubt that determining a standard, particularly where systems will control or impact safety in a field such as transportation, must be very painstakingly and carefully done. However, there are also some absurd situations. The Canadian federal government and the Quebec provincial government for years perpetuated an all-out bureaucratic feud over the proper structure of the 'Canadian French' keyboard, and twice approached (and then shrank back from) a consensus standard.

There are several reasons why the standards process takes longer than most people would like:

- The consensus method used on most standards committees to arrive at a draft for balloting is reasonably, but not perfectly, well suited to standards determination—some things simply cannot be conferenced into a consensus. At one time the US House of Representatives approved a conventional aircraft carrier and the Senate approved a nuclear one; conferencing the two versions of the bill into consensus was, of course, impossible;
- Consensus building is always slower, although obviously also better in most cases, than having one person or a small group dictate the results; and
- Many vendors have had a strong vested interest in slowing down the progress of open systems standards both to allow their design engineers to catch up with competitors and to help prolong the commercial life of their existing proprietary systems.

Also important is the fact that only a large computer manufacturer or a very large user organization can afford to dedicate sufficiently expert and senior individuals to spend a fifth, a half or even all of their time participating in standards activities.

The purpose of this discourse is not to jaundice the reader with respect to standards (for without them there could *be* no open systems). Rather, it is to encourage treatment of standards as 'tiger cubs'. Embrace and adopt them if you will, but treat them with respect and do not let your guard down. In other words, it is important to know about heritage and pedigree, as well as to (at times) apply tender loving care. The following are the questions you should ask about any standard.

Where did it come from?

Was the standard first created by a single vendor and, if so, how did it become more generalized? This is, by the way, not necessarily a bad thing. After all, UNIX itself came from AT&T and until about 1990 they continued to insist on seeing the little circled 'R', meaning trade mark registered, behind UNIX when other people used it. Recently, things have been more liberal. Knowing where the standard came from may tell you something about what baggage it has picked up along the way and where it is likely to go now.

Has anyone been able to participate in the creation of this standard or has it been a 'big boys' club' with a very high price of admission to the organization which made the standard? Just who got actually to vote on the standard?

What is its present state and how did this come about?

A standard may be anything from the gleam in the eye of some influential individual (who has managed to have a standards body assign an official number to it) at one extreme to something which is a widely used *de facto* and *de jure* standard at the other. Determining where on this particular continuum a given standard sits is of crucial importance in assessing its usefulness. The promulgating body, vendors, system integrators and the trade press are all ready sources of information on this subject. They are not, however, always unanimous on a standard, particularly on its strategic significance. Also, most national governments have bodies which track (and at least attempt to catalog) standards. Be particularly cautious if the standard's name or number has a year attached to it. This usually means that the formulating committee knew of many other wonderful things it intended to include in the standard, but time or practicality considerations caused them to 'saw off' inclusion of such enhancements. Usually this means the standard is, in at least this sense, an 'unfinished work' which will subsequently be abridged. This has good and bad elements. The good part is that often early promulgation of a standard, even if it is rather basic and represents a lowest common denominator among the entities it seeks to standardize, is preferable to late promulgation. Sometimes, early promulgation is the only way to set a basic direction and prevent the emergence of a complete helter-skelter (i.e. unstandardizable) situation later on. The bad part is as follows:

- If the 'common denominator' is too low (as with the early American National Standards Institute (ANSI) System Query Language

(SQL) standards for databases) its usefulness may not justify the cost and trouble of committing to it; and

- If the formulating committee is not very careful, and/or if subsequent historical events do not cooperate, the next version of the standard may actually abrogate part of the earlier one.

In the latter case, this leads to what can be called 'Early Bird Syndrome', wherein the visionary and farseeing organization that adopted, and actually implemented, the standard in its earliest workable manifestation ends up ripping out cable, changing production operating systems or whatever.

What proprietary extensions are contemplated?

In certain cases a standard will take either a lowest common denominator (common to all existing products) or a middle-ground route (where most existing products are compliant but some will have to add functionality to comply). In such cases, most products will have existing functions which exceed the basic standard and thus, once the standard is promulgated, must be considered as proprietary 'extensions' of those products beyond the standard itself. We must address ourselves to these extensions or they will bite us!

In fairness to the vendor who created the product, what a year ago was seen as an advantageous feature which gave his operating system, language or database an edge over its competitors suddenly becomes, in the post-promulgation world, a heinous proprietary extension which, if we use it, will lock us into the product and exclude others. Often, bad faith on the part of the vendor is imputed where it does not exist. The truth is, that if we (or contractors developing application programs for us) have been using the product we may already have used this extension. Now we have an application which does not comply with the new standard. We can change the application, ignore the standard or else hope fervently that the next version of the standard may embrace and actually include this expanded functionality. This often happens. Most desirable features developed in the XENIX and SUN OS versions of UNIX, as well as the pure Berkeley strain, were incorporated into the unified UNIX System V.4 interface definition standard. Whichever of the three options we may choose, we *must* contemplate the standard and its relevance to us.

There is, however, a more sinister aspect of proprietary extensions to standards. In many cases, while a standard is worming its way through a committee (or, more often, a maze of committees) prior to its promulgation, the vendors most interested in keeping things proprietary have been quite busy. First, they may have an unspoken vested interest in cooperating to ensure that the standard is as close to a lowest common denominator as they can influence it to be. This will not only make compliance easier for each of them, letting them avoid expensive cross-licensing of technology, but it will also maximize the temptations of new users of the standard to embrace and use their proprietary enhancements. It will also tend to scare users of existing fully proprietary (non-standard) products away from seriously considering the new products based on the standard in the first place. Second, if it appears that the standard may indeed emerge with a very high degree of functionality, they may vote against each other in various sub-committees to induce confusion and slow progress. The voting records of some such committees even show members of specific companies voting against each other!

What, if anything, will known (or likely imminent) proprietary extensions to the standard do to your plans to standardize (whether across two or three regional mid-frame computers, several hundred MRS installations or tens of thousands of PCs) with a product, or a collection of competitive products, based on this standard? The simplest answer is that if you can live with the basic functionality and have the mandate and means to force in-house and contract developers to avoid the extensions, you may not need to care about enhancements. The proprietary vendors can do as they like. On the other hand, if your influence and/or authority over end-user organizations is context-sensitive, financially or operationally constrained or there is very significant purchase of business-specific, versus generic, applications from third parties, you may be unable to constrain the use of enhancements. In such a case, they can become a significant issue.

What other proprietary extensions are possible?

Unfortunately, not even today are all of the cleverest engineering minds harnessed by the large computer vendors being focused on how to make computers more open and interoperable. While virtually all vendors are moving in an open systems direction, and have stated commitments in this regard, their degrees of commitment and states of on-ground product release vary widely. Major computer firms have continued to release products which are wholly proprietary, and also products which are labelled 'open' but which require major concessions in favour of the contemplated ideal system architecture as espoused by themselves. Alternatively, their product is said to be interoperable and you can safely use their enhancements without lock-in, but if you choose to interoperate with the purportedly open product from another vendor, you find both are then reduced to a very low level of functionality. The sales brochures (and salespersons), of course, do not tell you about this. You learn about it after the sale.

Use your imagination! Be a bit creative! If you were a proprietary product vendor (be it of hardware, package software, communications or whatever) and you wanted to prevent consumption of the open system standard-based products, including your own, what would you do? If you couldn't prevent consumption of the product, what could you do to make the purchasers as miserable and unhappy as possible?

☞ In a satire by George Orwell about Communism called *Animal Farm*, it was remarked that: 'All animals are equal, but some animals are more equal than others.' Perhaps this little conceptual twister would apply equally well to the field of open systems if rephrased thus: 'All vendors are committed to open systems and all their open systems are open, but some vendors are more committed and some open systems are more open than others.'

Who promises commitment and compliance?

The answer is almost always the same: everyone! Canadian statesman Jean Chrétien, a minister in the Trudeau government and later leader of the Liberal Party during part of its time in Opposition, once stated that: 'I never met the guy who was in favour of war!' Well, I personally never met the vendor (except one) who would state that they were not in favour of open systems. They all claim to be very supportive of the idea.

What compliant products are available now?

When a standard is projected, being balloted or has been promulgated, a given vendor and/or product may have a status, with regard to that standard, which is any one of the following:

- Committed to standard unknown;
- Committed to standard and compliance projected for an approximate future time;
- Committed to release of a new version, fully or partially compliant with the standard, at a specific future time;
- Compliant product released to alpha test;
- Compliant product released to beta test;
- Compliant product released to production and now being shipped; or
- Compliant product withdrawn from market due to discovered non-compliance as found in one or more major procurements, end-user experience or otherwise or due to demise of product, vendor or standard.

Depending upon your own timing and requirements, any but the second-last may be an unacceptable current status for a prospective product and vendor.

How can I determine if a product's compliance claim is true?

Unfortunately, there are far fewer testing laboratories, certification facilities and branding organizations than there are standards promulgators. In many cases, it is very difficult to obtain independent verification of a product's compliance to a standard. Also, the language in marketing materials can be very confusing. Saying a food product is made 'of' something is not the same as saying that it is made 'from' that same thing. There is a legal difference and there is most certainly a factual difference. However, the advertiser may seriously hope that you will find the two phrases conceptually identical. Here you have several fundamental choices:

- Accept the vendor's own claim (only if you let the fox guard your chicken shed or your banker tell you where to buy your insurance);
- Seek independent verification from a recognized source engaged regularly in such activities;
- Seek to obtain information from another user organization which has recently acquired products to this standard and has itself conducted research and/or testing of its own into the veracity of compliance claims; or
- Force the vendor to prove the claim by setting your own test, perhaps with the help of the body which promulgates the standard.

Only the largest user organizations can afford the final alternative above. In some cases, it can be an absolute nightmare and end with gowned lawyers and high court justices ultimately assuming the role of research directors when vendor tester and user tester cannot agree on what the results mean.

More equal than others: standards for standards

It has been tritely, and frequently, observed by those working in this field that one of the nicest things about standards is that there are so many to choose from. As if the above issues were not cause enough for concern for the prospective proud owner of a collection of open systems, there is more growling and roaring with which to contend. There is a whole 'upper tier' in the standards world, and that is what you might want to call the 'meta standards' tier. They are the standards which govern other standards. The amalgamation of standards (like the amalgamation of governments, the merger of large organizations or the mating of the big cats) is most often accomplished only after much roaring and posturing. Consider the case of poor UNIX itself.

UNIX, as recounted above, came from Bell Laboratories and over more than 15 years many different strains of the operating system were developed by the widest range of organizations, and for as many different purposes. By the late eighties it was clear that most existing and all prospective users would be well served by a 'unification of the UNIXes'. To this end, well-meaning experts laboured intensively to unite the three most prominent streams of UNIX; these were AT&T System V.3, Berkeley 4.2 (also known as BSD) and XENIX into a single one, to be called System V.4. Just as this not-inconsiderable challenge was being overcome, came cries that various of the participants, including SUN and AT&T, were in reality feathering their own (future) nests. This caused a momentous reaction by many large vendors who, uncomfortable bedfellows though they were, formed the Open Software Foundation (OSF) to foil the unification of the UNIXes and indeed to create their own version. After the open system community recovered from its shock and disbelief, which took months, not weeks, they pushed and prodded AT&T into first leading its own *alter ego* to OSF (called Unix International) and then, after further culture shock, actually reducing its control of the Unix Systems Laboratories themselves.

At that time, as related in Chapter 8, my staff and I were preparing the specification for a major UNIX-based MRS procurement. As you may imagine, we greeted these developments with nothing short of shock and horror. Now we found ourselves embroiled in a situation almost like that in *Gulliver's Travels* wherein the Littleendians and the Bigendians were engaged in a fearsome struggle over which ends of eggs should be broken and we, of course, found ourselves caught in the middle. If we specified the UI standard and OSF won the battle, our procurement program could be ruined. Likewise for the reverse. In the event, we came up with a compromise strategy which, although moderately high risk, did work. However, we only had to do this because of the 'battle of the standards'.

In the spring of 1990 I represented the government of Canada at the second of two meetings of large user organizations which led directly to the founding of the User Alliance for Open Systems (UAOS). The sessions were attended by the representatives of many of the largest private and public sector user organizations in North America, with Europeans also present. We decided that we truly did want to work to remove the barriers to open systems, which had been identified earlier. However, when I suggested that we in the room collectively had enough power to end the battle of OSF and UI, there was a stunned silence. Undaunted, I proceeded to recommend that we collectively inform our respective vendor suppliers that we would not purchase a single new piece of equipment starting nine months or one year from that point if OSF and UI had not, by that time, merged into one organization. There was voiced immediate fear that we might encroach onto antitrust territory and that, if we were even to talk about this idea, we might be held to be conspiring to control the market. Someone then suggested that we all sign a paper certifying that we were not lawyers! I am not poking fun at the UAOS, which is certainly a worthwhile organization, but am rather stating that user groups have been very reluctant to exercise the very real power they hold over proprietary product vendors. The customer really is king, as the North American manufacturers learned when they refused to make high-quality small cars. Computer buyers have just as much power as car buyers.

At a subsequent user meeting in Canada I had the delightful opportunity to question—on one platform—the presidents of OSF and UI and promptly demanded that they justify the continued separate existence of their two organizations. After regaining their composure, they spluttered that competition among standards is healthy. Several members of the audience retorted that it may be healthy for the vendors, but not for the users.

Profiles of standards

For good and obvious reasons, many promulgated standards permit the user to select from among options of two types:

- Those which can simply be added onto the bare bones or base standard without fear of proprietary vendor lock-in; and
- Those which offer a choice of attribute or feature A or B.

While the development of profiles could itself be the subject of a book, perhaps the simplest way to discuss profiles is to provide a commentary on a family of profiles created by the Government of Canada. One caveat: the views and interpretations of the profiles discussed here are my own, and do not necessarily represent those of the authors of the profiles.

During the 1970–85 period the Government of Canada, like many large user organizations, experienced EDP costs which were rising much faster than most other classes of expenditure. Further, the large number of incompatible systems resulted in more and more information being output by one system only to be manually entered into another. Thus, many of the humans whose work was first lightened by a machine soon found themselves caught between two such machines, using much of the time 'saved' by one machine to stoke another machine. This had not been part of the promise offered by automation and was occurring not only between departments or agencies but, increasingly, even within them.

The Treasury Board of Canada (TB), which has responsibility for the good management of federal government and also for items such as the adoption of standards by government, began to see the requirement for computing standards. Whether this meant standardization of all departments (as some provincial governments were then considering doing) on one product architecture from within one vendor's offerings (for example, DEC VAX/VMS or IBM 370) or a wider form of standardization, some action was needed. As the TB became involved in national and international standards bodies working in the computing field, it became increasingly evident that there would be, over time, a movement towards open computing systems and certainly, in the more immediate future, towards open communications systems. To commit to anything less was to automatically set in place the future day when a wholesale changeover to open systems would be required, and at much greater cost than a gradual migration to open systems from the outset. The large existing inventory of hardware and applications would require a gradual or incremental transition plan; a radical or overnight transition was not possible.

An even greater problem was that in the latter half of the eighties open systems were widely talked about but not readily available. A number of vendors had introduced hardware, software and communications products which they claimed were 'open system oriented' or would lead to open systems, but these were usually based upon their current product architectures. For example, DEC introduced the ULTRIX derivative of the UNIX operating system on its VAX product line in the eighties but did not offer its popular ALL-IN-ONE office-automation product under this environment. IBM introduced the AIX (UNIX)-based RT single- and multi-user RISC-based processor, but it existed primarily as a single-user system, having limited utility in a multi-user role. Further, the AIX variants for the PS/2, RT, RS/6000 and 370 architecture machines were somewhat incompatible even with each other! Neither company went out of its way to promote such products.

By the early nineties, TB had mandated as government policy that all departments and agencies should move, as and when possible in their future procurements, towards open systems. The policy requires departments and agencies to:

- Require vendors responding to RFPs to indicate commitment to open systems (OSI in particular) as well as the availability of present/planned products and services based on OSI; and
- Ensure that preference is given to products and services conforming to standards which support OSI.

TB was certainly realistic about the difficulties this might impose on some acquisitions, particularly in the short term, and provided that such acquisitions would only need to specify the *then current* state of evolution of OSI standards while taking into account the means of transitioning (new or existing) non-conforming products in future. The Management of Information Technology documents promulgated by TB in mid-1990 also seek to provide for *application portability*. This is clearly recognized as being *separate* from, but complementary to, OSI and planning for portability is acknowledged as embracing the areas of operating system, database management systems, programming languages, data exchange, system interworking over networks and the user interface. Any coherent portability strategy must address all of these items.

☛ The Canadian government wanted to be able to carry programs among computers within and among departments. With so many kinds of computers in use, short-term standardization was not practical. It would be possible to decide what parts of what standards were most relevant, and officially to sanction them as they emerged.

The Treasury Board Information Technology Standards (TBITS) program has been issuing standards to address progressively more and more of the above-cited areas. The TBITS documents are in various stages of draft development, balloting and approval at any given time, and therefore represent a dynamic target. This section is based on a review of a selection of some of the TBITS items in development or approved as of 1992.

TBITS-0 addresses the nature of the TBITS program and provides a general overview of how the process works. As more and more TBITS requirements become mandatory, all federal departments and agencies will become increasingly involved in implementing new procurements so as to meet these standards.

☛ The first profile, not surprisingly, is a profile about the profiles.

TBITS-1 recognizes the OSI reference model as described above and provides for the selection of one or more compatible sets of options from the OSI standards to facilitate interworking of computer systems.

Collectively, such sets of choices or options, once selected, are known as 'profiles'. The Canadian Open Systems Interconnection Criteria (COSAC) project, which seeks to develop such profiles, is cited.

☞ It is important to start with OSI. OSI will help both open and closed computing systems to communicate more effectively.

TBITS-2 addresses the Structured Query Language (SQL) in both its schema definition language, used to define data and its integrity constraints, and the module language, used to define the data manipulation language in applications. This TBITS applies to all application generation, end-user-generated queries, data distribution, program libraries and distributed (data) communication systems. Its (Sec. 10.2) inclusions of where to use SQL are highly dependent upon a department or agency's *internal* portability strategy and approach to the internal re-use of software, as well as the software support model. It is relatively easy to 'engineer' a department into or out of the inclusions statements and the implications of choices made regarding RDBMS and SQL standardization must be carefully considered. The following points are particularly relevant:

- Choice of a single RDBMS which runs under UNIX for all three processing tiers—Mainframe (MF), MRS and Workstation (WS) will improve vertical and horizontal application and data portability but will cause extreme dependence upon the RDBMS vendor.
- If one or more RDBMS vendors chosen by the department make proprietary extensions to the evolving, but still very limited, SQL standards then these may restrict application portability. Most vendors do make such extensions and the choice of whether or not to employ them may be crucial to force the vendor to differentiate between those which cut portability and those which do not (such warnings are difficult to elicit as it is not in vendor interest to give them, but rather to have the user unwittingly lock itself in by use of such features in application and dataset development).

Although there is sufficient latitude given to 'tailor' the SQL strategy to departmental needs, the following must be considered carefully:

- ANSI SQL is still under development and probably will be for some time;
- ORACLE and other vendors make proprietary extensions to SQL;
- A department has essentially three choices of specification strategies:
  - Pure SQL: open to all SQL/RDBMS vendors;
  - SQL+: some restrictions—open to some SQL/RDBMS vendors;
  - SQL++: highly customized—only one vendor may qualify.

Departments may make exclusions where no off-the-shelf application software and/or SQL RDBMS meets requirements or where the application is intended for a single user. Most departments have considerable development at the grass roots (PC and PC/LAN levels) under DBASE-III and DBASE-IV. When these are considered for migration to local multi-user MRS equipment, the question of whether to compile for use under FOXBASE or CLIPPER or to rewrite entirely in the corporate standard full RDBMS will almost always arise. While most full-feature RDBMS engines (ORACLE, INFORMIX, etc.) are bulky and difficult to run on even high-powered PCs or UNIX single-user workstations, encouraging (or even requiring) new applications to be developed from the outset in the corporate standard database, once it is selected, will offer easier portability. The alternative is to allow a LAN (even one where an MRS is also connected) to become a virtual thicket of non-professionally developed, ill-documented, poorly supported and backed-up and usually incompatible personal databases, many of which contain workgroup or even corporate (not just personal) information.

☞ Relational databases are very powerful, but the ways of accessing the data (of getting it out of the database so you can *use* it) are not as standardized as one might think. If two systems are otherwise open, and even have applications performing virtually the same function on identical data, they may be impossible to integrate if the data-access mechanisms are different.

TBITS-3 addresses the character set requirements of TBITS and adopts the 'Latin Alpha #1' (CSA A243-4-87) standard for the interchange role but only at the 8-bit level. Lower-case accents are to be provided for as stipulated by the Treasury Board Circular TBC-1988-31, the official languages computer requirements circular. No conformance procedure or check approach is offered. Both the UNIX International (UI) and the Open Software Foundation (OSF) varieties of UNIX have internationalization efforts under way which will exceed TB requirements by a wide margin. BULL, DEC and IBM are quite strong in this area and it therefore comes as no surprise that OSF, although itself still in the release process, appears to exceed UI in its progress in this area. What this translates to in practical terms is the following:

- Requirement for hardware support of Canadian French (according to the Canadian Standards Association guidance);
- Requirement for a bilingual operating system;
- Requirement for bilingual documentation;
- Requirement for bilingual or CSA Canadian French keyboards (see also below).

☞ Standards for national language character sets become crucial for any business which operates internationally. Non-Latin characters present additional challenges.

TBITS-4 prescribes ANSI COBOL (ANSI X.3-23-1985) although in a somewhat restrictive fashion. Use of purely ANSI COBOL in development may reduce programming efficiency substantially. However, use of vendor extensions (even on otherwise very compatible UNIX systems) may significantly decrease portability. Also, use of CASE tools or other design/development aids that generate COBOL which goes beyond pure ANSI may have the same impact. Here again, vendors must be forced by the procuring agency to classify their proprietary language extensions as impacting or not impacting portability; in the language area, unfortunately, most such extensions must be used with extreme care or else not at all.

The TBITS recommendation (at part 9 (b)) that COBOL be used as the prime language where intervendor portability is required is at considerable variance with developments and experience in the open systems community and must be seriously questioned.

There is no doubt that COBOL is a very widely used (and easy to use) programming language; it is certainly not going to disappear in the near future and indeed many new applications are being written in COBOL at this time. There have been various attempts to develop universal COBOL versions, and some of these, from independent vendors, offer very good portability across architectures and operating systems but too frequently exceed the ANSI standard. Prescribing purely ANSI COBOL and then saying that this COBOL is the best way to promote portability could be seen as inconsistent! Whereas ANSI COBOL is so limited there will be extreme temptation to employ vendor-specific enhancements and features which will, in most cases, limit portability and reduce the ability of the department to support more than one vendor's open system at any of the three computing tiers (mainframe, MRS and PC). This TBITS fails to point out (as does TBITS-8, which covers the C language itself) that the C language has a very distinct advantage over COBOL in the open systems world.

While enhanced (proprietary) COBOL offers more features than common (fully portable) ANSI C, ANSI C in turn offers more features and functional richness than pure ANSI COBOL. This is most significant when setting the open communications (OSI), open system (UNIX) and local workgroup multi-user processor (MRS) strategies for an organization embarking upon open systems. Selection of enhanced COBOL will greatly increase portability costs. Selection of ANSI COBOL may reduce application development efficiency. Thus, the purely ANSI C language may be the least of the three evils except where an existing COBOL application is being carried to MRS equipment. Certainly, any open mainframe, MRS or MBS specification should require COBOL but it should be viewed as a supplementary language, not a primary one, in the open system strategy.

The C language and UNIX have many deep links, including the fact that the UNIX operating system itself is written in C. Failure to recognize this synergy at the outset will, at best, reduce the effectiveness of the open computing strategy and, at worst, make application portability extremely difficult. Tradeoffs among the above-cited enhanced COBOL, ANSI COBOL and ANSI C languages must be addressed both at the corporate level (strategically) and as individual applications are planned and implemented (tactically).

The TBITS correctly postulates that it will be necessary to restrict the output of CASE tools to ANSI COBOL to the greatest degree possible. Three standards levels and four options are to be recognized at debug time and this is offered as a conversion aid.

> ☞ COBOL is perhaps the most widely used computer programming language in business, industry and government. However, we cannot rely too heavily on COBOL as a means for standardization because there are so many different versions of it. Also, the C programming language is closely connected to UNIX and is more widely used in its 'purest' form. Balanced against this, however, is the fact that moving from COBOL to C involves fear and trepidation for many programmers, and forces them to think in different conceptual terms.

TBITS-5 prescribes English/CSA Canadian French keyboard standards. While Canada-specific, the principles of dealing with internationalization in open systems are well illustrated by the following discussion. Function keys are excluded and procuring agencies may wish to consider requiring the 101-key format (in English and French) for keyboards of MRS consoles, MRS terminals, PCs, diskless PCs and UNIX workstations. The TBITS adopts CSA Standard Z243-200-1988 but also with the alternate key cap layout. This is a preliminary standard which will undergo further review. Any procuring organization should also consider any specific or unique key assignment requirements it may have, once the remainder of the intended architecture is finalized. It is also positively essential that the terminal emulator software package(s) selected to emulate VT-100, VT-220/340 and/or ANSI 25 terminals for PC user access to MRS equipment be standardized not only against this key placement and format requirement but also against the requirements of the OA and RDBMS packages selected for use on the MRS. Failure to align the following items will result in significant implementation difficulties:

- Non-intelligent terminal keyboard and key assignments;
- X-terminal keyboard and key assignments;
- PC keyboard and key assignments;

- PC terminal emulator keyboard assignments;
- OA package assumptions about terminal emulator and key assignments;
- RDBMS package and application program assumptions about terminal emulator and key assignments.

Alignment of these is crucial even at the pilot or trial stage, and even more so as a full-scale open systems acquisition program is pursued.

☞ Just selecting appropriate keyboards and character sets is not enough. It is necessary to think about how all the programs accessed by a user will deal with the selections you have made.

TBITS-6 addresses the Canadian Open System Application Criteria (COSAC), providing overview and detail reference to a very large number of ISO and other standards. A key choice already made by many organizations is commitment to the Ethernet (E-Net) or ISO 8802.3 CSMA/CD standards for LAN implementations. This standard is the one most amenable to open system communication and least liable to proprietary lock-in. Agencies intending to make OSI/open system procurements are advised to obtain and synthesize the latest information, as many of the referenced standards are quite dynamic at this point. OSI is cited as being preferred to any vendor- or installation-specific architecture or approach *insofar as communications is concerned*. Recall the distinction above that OSI and OCS are two different things.

In general, COSAC profiles do not alter a standard but merely select combinations of options or choices *within* a standard and thus define a 'way of using' the standard.

It should also be pointed out that the greatest immediate or short-term value of the OSI standards is often for *inter-organizational* communication of information and interworking of systems. Conversely, it is often true that the greatest value of OCS, including the UNIX operating system and various other pillars of portability, is for the *intra-organizational* porting of applications and data and interworking of systems within and among processing tiers (for example, MRS-MRS and MF-MRS, respectively). Both OSI and OCS promote vendor competition and multi-vendor solutions. OSI, when strictly interpreted, none the less tolerates islands of proprietary computing providing they can interconnect and interwork; such islands may offer no application portability whatsoever.

In establishing an OSI network, a federal department or agency will need to be aware of several key issues:

- Choices made by TB/COSACS regarding X.25 impact the flexibility of the network.

- X.25's packet-oriented basis will, by definition, cause it to exhibit 'bunchy' or 'bottlenecking' tendencies as traffic intensity increases. This is not an argument against X.25, but is a recognition that in the medium to long term networks will probably need to progress beyond it.
- Some types of applications will find interworking over an X.25 network to be disruptive in the temporal sense and may require modification to tolerate network behaviour.

Use of booster (repeater) modems may be an issue for LAN and star-wiring implementations of MRS equipment; this should be considered for all physical *and* logical topologies contemplated at the outset. For example, if a new MRS is installed in a location which does not yet have a LAN, will a LAN be implemented at that time or will star-wiring be implemented until a LAN requirement is otherwise generated? The deployment strategy chosen may impact how the LAN and WAN interface is to occur.

It should also be noted that the transition from X.400 (84) to X.400 (88) includes additions, deletions and modifications; therefore the X.400 level is not always trivial.

COSAC assumptions about the co-location of the User Agent (UA) and the Message Transfer Agent (MTA) for X.400/X.500 purposes may have implications for any users of the communications server model (wherein a server-function-only device makes available a single-user communications application or facility to an intelligent client), as defined in the terms section above. Further, regarding local unit (workgroup) mail addressing, the 'domain' concept as set out in COSAC should be directly applicable providing one of the following two alternatives is selected:

- Specify your own requirements on pure OSI/open system basis.
- Use one or more vendors' existing mail-handling solutions providing they do not violate the OSI model significantly.

It may be possible to combine the two approaches to some degree by segmenting different suppliers' systems into separate mail domains.

Regarding security, it may be highly desirable to avoid use of black boxes as contemplated in the COSAC documents; these will greatly impede network performance and increase complexity. Use of NCSC Orange Book Level of Trust C2 may be the highest possible common level among an organization's as-installed equipment.

With wiring, the degree of intended user compliance to the profiled wiring standards will impact the flexibility of the overall network implementation. Certainly, co-installation of optical fibre and twisted pair (tp) would be highly desirable in technical terms. Installation of both LANs and MRSs will not negate the eventual requirement for 10 Mbps communications service to the desktop. The existence of the MRS in an organization's system architecture can be expected to *slow* the requirement for the growth of desktop intelligence but not to negate it. As desktop intelligence grows so too will the communications bandwidth requirement. Sometimes it is necessary to conduct a cost/benefit study of retrofitting to 10 Mbps at LAN-installation time, at MRS-installation time or at some other time, versus not doing it until hard demand is there: certainly, the recommended two sets of four tp per workstation (with optical fibre co-run and available at the rear of the termination).

The TBITS/COSAC approach permits cross-connection of telecommunications closets (essentially outside of the wide area network), and this may be useful for MRS-to-MRS connection (usually at high bandwidth) for adjacent units which need a high level of interaction between their two MRS installations. This can be achieved more efficiently on a given premise off-line the X.25 backbone. It is particularly relevant where a unit of 100 people has two MRSs installed but wants to function as one OA environment for E-mail and scheduling purposes. Most modern UNIX-based OA systems contemplate such interconnection.

> ☛ Some foreign-language expressions don't translate well into English. Neither do certain parts of the 'techno-babble' language spoken by the IT community. The COS-ACS documents provide a further set of 'ways of doing things', which reference the OSI and other standards and which are recognized in the TBITS. They provide guidance with such areas as wiring for local and wide area networking.

TBITS-7 recognizes and accepts POSIX, but it must be understood and accepted that POSIX is in fact a whole family of interface specifications/standards covering very many system elements. POSIX was developed for use with UNIX systems but nothing restricts it to them; indeed, various vendors are bringing their otherwise wholly proprietary systems into line with POSIX. Some such vendors have suggested that POSIX compliance alone, plus OSI communication, makes their proprietary system an open system, but nothing could be further from the truth. A group of fully POSIX- and OSI-compliant systems does *not* exhibit full and true portability of applications and data between systems of the same scale (MF-MF, MRS-MRS, etc.) or different scale (MF-MRS, etc.). Employing the 'Continuum of Portability' model discussed below gives a much fuller view of how to approach portability planning than the simple ratio porting to redevelopment costs proposed in the TBITS.

While TB clearly dislikes vendor lock-in, the use of OSI, POSIX and ANSI COBOL, as proposed in the TBITS, does not go nearly far enough towards ensuring a true multi-vendor environment. Certainly, individual departments and agencies are free to go beyond the TBITS in specifying their architecture and procurement specifications but this must be done cautiously to avoid the twin traps of:

1 Specifying things so narrowly that functionality is very seriously impaired, or
2 Inventing one's very own specification which subsequently becomes non-mainstream or even unique.

Failure to go beyond POSIX in specifying a supposedly 'open system' is to court significant danger of having a winner which is a 'bear in tiger's clothing'—a closed system masquerading as an open one by means of its 'cloak of POSIX'. Various US agencies are now specifying POSIX only and, as one senior official put it, 'hoping for UNIX'. This is a result of the former USAF AFCAC-251 bid in which constrained control by AT&T/SUN of the UNIX V.4 operating system was challenged by other bidders. Since then several other events have occurred:

- OSF has been formed to 'keep AT&T honest' in how UNIX V.4 was to be licensed;
- AT&T has responded by spinning off its control of UNIX's strategic direction to Unix International, a user-controlled body;
- COS, the (COS-adopted) User Alliance for Open Systems X/Open Corp. and other standardizing influences have greatly increased the pressure on both UI and OSF either to merge or at least to use XPG3 and POSIX as a middle ground as well as to behave responsibly.

These developments make the specification of 'POSIX+UNIX' a safe alternative. The X/Open Portability Guide (XPG3 and the emerging XPG4) should also be specified. Within this approach there are three options:

1 Specify only UI UNIX SVID V.4.
2 Specify only OSF 1.1.
3 Specify the functional intersection of these two and demand that UI-, OSF- and vendor-unique features at least not be required to run the system and, wherever possible, disabled or not provided and in any event not used by users, developers or administrators.

The last is the Transport Canada Greater UNIX (GX) approach which was successful in the Unit Level Systems (ULS) field trial program at providing reasonable interoperability and application portability. Vendors from both the UI and OSF organizations qualified and were approved. The approach is not perfect but it is reasonably workable, not only with UNIX derivatives (UI and OSF) but also, eventually, with other types of operating systems. (This latter capability is probably several years away at this point.) Contract work has already been carried out to begin extending GX to a 'GX2' format, embracing recent internationalization developments, On-line Transaction Processing, Real Time processing and various other requirements not included in the version released by Transport Canada in its 1989 RFP issue. Conceivably, GX could become a TBITS federal government recommended or mandatory standard, but that is not definite at present. For more information on the Transport Canada program, *see* Chapter 8.

☞ It is good to have a profile to recognize (albeit still developing) POSIX but reliance on POSIX alone to provide OCS capabilities is not recommended.

TBITS-8 correctly advises federal institutions to avoid vendor-specific enhancements to the C programming language but fails to make clear the significance of C within an overall open system strategy.

☞ Where posible, treat C as the default language for new applications intended for your open system environment and only accept use of something else (COBOL, FORTRAN or whatever) where there is a clear case that C is sub-optimal or not practical at all.

TBITS-9 concerns the ADA programming language, developed by the US Department of Defense (DOD). A major objective of ADA was to be able to link embedded and non-embedded systems. ADA is now being standardized but has a history of much user difficulty and non-acceptance, particularly in demanding or complex applications. Even in areas such as simulation, ADA has a poor record. You should clearly examine any ADA requirements you may have because specification of ADA in, for example, an MRS procurement—assuming a clean compiler is demanded—may limit the field to those MRS vendors who have large DOD/DND-installed bases. DOD has, in my opinion, changed its stance several times in recent years on what ADA should contain, leading to the release of a large number of partially or wholly incompatible compilers.

☞ ADA is not a bad language for controlling weapon systems or keeping track of army food rations like field biscuits. If your operational systems will not be open in the near term, or if you have only business systems and no operational systems at all, then you may find use of ADA counterproductive. Certainly, much recent effort has gone into improving ADA, but there is still quite a way to go.

TBITS-10 addresses Electronic Data Interchange (EDI), embracing both of the ANSI X.12 and EDIFACT standards. TB will require federal agencies to convert to any future EDI standards it chooses (from what they are then using) very quickly; i.e. within six months. Whereas some aspects of X.12 and EDIFACT are competitive, this could be a significant issue for large users.

☞ Getting into EDI is every bit as important as getting into open systems. Here again, there is the danger of Early Bird Syndrome, although the danger of ignoring EDI is the greater of the two. Developments in progress as this book is being published will help end some of the internecine feuding of the EDI standards community. Where possible, wait until 1993 to pick your EDI approach.

Developing a practical approach

While I have been critical of certain aspects of the TBITS, and have not reviewed all of them here, there can be no doubt that the profile-based approach which the British, Canadian and American governments have adopted is the correct one. Profiles allow the prospective user to 'get a leash' on certain standards in order to put them to practical use.

Let us return to the issue of operating systems. At present the Treasury Board (TB) has specified the POSIX operating system interface standard as a preferred direction, and some consideration can be given to using POSIX alone as the means of promoting portability among computer platforms. Prospective users of the TBITS (and there is nothing stopping a private firm from using them) may ultimately wish to exercise data environment, application software and data portability on three axes:

Vertical portability among different sizes of computers at the Central (data centre mainframe), Local (mid-range workgroup multi-user system) and Desktop (PC/workstation) levels;
Horizontal portability among similar computers within one level; and
Forward portability to replacement computers at any level, and probably from a different vendor.

Portability can be promoted by commonality not just of operating system but also of database environment, development tools and procedures and by user conventions. However, given the rapid technological advancement within the mid-range system marketplace, forward portability may well be by far the most important for MRS equipment. Many such MRS installations will be replaced well before the applications they run are obsolete. At that time not only the applications but also the data, the file/directory structures, the administrative scripts and control mechanisms and many other entities should be migrated *forward* to the replacement processor, which may well come from another vendor. When a given local system is replaced by a successor machine, *all* the software and data on that machine must be carried forward and commonality of operating system is thus a cornerstone of portability in general.

Horizontal portability is also very important at the local level because there are fewer opportunities for horizontal portability at the data centre levels, where fewer lateral peers exist, and much lower initial custom application software investment, with much more use simply of generic packages such as LOTUS and DBASE, at the workplace (desktop) level. It can be readily shown that use of POSIX alone would not permit this to occur. For example, if a fully POSIX-compliant but none the less proprietary office-automation (OA) system were running on a proprietary operating system (on a minicomputer) it could *not* be transferred forward to a replacement UNIX mini from a different manufacturer. Even data undergoing such a transfer would most likely require reduction to the lowest common denominator: ASCII or even binary format. POSIX specifies some elements of how the operating system interacts with the user and in certain cases with application and communication software but it does *not* specify the content or the complete function of the operating system itself. At some time in the future, when the POSIX suite of specifications is entirely complete, it may be possible to rely principally on POSIX to support application portability. In the next few years, such reliance is clearly insufficient. Indeed, it is counterproductive. Some systems vendors have gone to great lengths to assure customers that POSIX alone will be sufficient but this can produce islands of incompatibility. Thus, while POSIX has been found to be valuable and necessary, POSIX is, in and of itself, insufficient to protect portability on the *forward* axis. A common operating system is still required, and UNIX is seen as the only viable common operating system if a multi-vendor (price- and performance-competitive) acquisition strategy is to be followed. No other operating system runs on so many hardware architectures and so many vendor products.

Government and private sector organizations are making everincreasing use of IT to improve productivity and to meet management, financial and operational constraints now being faced. Such organizations have a very high—and rapidly increasing—total investment in IT and one which represents both an asset and, in some cases, a liability.

Once a given application program is implemented, with the accompanying hardware and operating system, networking, orientation and training, system and application administration, software maintenance and hardware maintenance in place, it becomes necessary to make operational and/or system-dictated changes and upgrades to the software. Over time, the cumulative impact of these changes tends to make detailed understanding of the application more and more context dependent. Combined with this is the inescapable fact that, historically, computer system vendors have tended to offer, and encourage the exclusive use of, their own proprietary hardware and operating systems.

These proprietary systems did not encourage the transfer or 'porting' of applications and sometimes even of data, not only between systems of different vendor origin, but often even between different systems from the same vendor.

The effect of increasing application 'contextualization' over time and proprietary computing environments was, and is, to anchor, mire or even trap, depending upon one's perspective, the application within its initial system environment. This has a number of impacts such as maximizing vendor-dependence and usually increasing costs, preventing otherwise logical application migration as the relative cost of processing power changes over time among micro, mini and mainframe tiers of processing. It also prevents easy duplication or cloning of the application elsewhere within the original or another organization.

The response of the IT vendor community to this problem, as expressed by users, has been to define the concept of 'open systems' which, in theory, would permit the porting of any of the application program or data elements from one computer system to another. In an ideal world, full binary compatability would, for example, permit a fully compiled program, written in a common language, to be transferred and run without recompilation on another system. Each of the 'DOS/INTEL' and 'VMS/VAX' architectures now permit this but they are in reality each a single processor architecture with all central processing units indeed coming from the same vendor. The desired type of application porting cannot, for example, be performed between an IBM AS-400 and a DEC VAX or between a SUN UNIX workstation and an IBM MVS mainframe. As a working minimum, even the ability to port language code cleanly and recompile it on another system and to readily move data would be a major step forward.

Many national and international standards bodies, in some way connected with open systems, have been established; so many in fact that just keeping track of all of them, much less participating, has been impractical for all but the largest organizations. The very existence of so many standards efforts, often with overlapping or ambiguous subject or jurisdictional boundaries, combined with the fact that hardware vendors display varying degrees of commitment to open systems, has tended to retard progress towards immediately available and implementable solutions. It is virtually certain that no one alive today fully understands all aspects of OSI and open computing systems.

The UNIX operating system, developed by AT&T/Bell Laboratories in New Jersey, has been widely heralded as offering the widest potential for supporting portability among varying hardware architectures. Indeed, UNIX is now running on computers manufactured by many vendors and offers a reasonably high degree of commonality in operating system, application interface and communications among most such systems.

A *continuum of portability* can be defined with at least the following points:

- Complete incompatibility—port by total rewrite;
- Language and context differences—port by rewriting in another version of the language (for example, pure ANSI FORTRAN versus CDC FORTRAN);
- Source code portability—port by recompiling high-level language, such as pure ANSI COBOL;
- Enhanced source code portability—port by recompiling high-level language with automatic optimization for destination host machine;
- Object/binary compatability with hardware masking—port directly but providing destination host is made 'aware' of particularities of origin host's hardware architecture and can execute relevant masking of hardware features;
- Object/binary compatability—port directly and run (DOS/INTEL, VMS/VAX, etc).

(This continuum was first set out by Mr Jim Tam, who worked with me at Transport Canada.)

☞ Depending on a program's nature and structure, and on the origin and destination computer systems, that program can be anything from very easy to very hard to carry from one computer to another.

There are a number of *pillars of portability* which must be used together to ensure future application and data portability:

- *Operating system*—use systems which run the same operating system (MVS, VMS, UNIX, etc.—only UNIX runs not only on multi-vendors but also on multi-architectures). Promote portability by using only UNIX International (UI) UNIX SVID V.4 or Open Software Foundation (OSF) OSF/AES 1.1 specifications or else a specification which addresses the area of functional overlap of the two (such as GX or an equivalent).
- *User interface to system*—use POSIX and specification of items such as Graphical User Interface (GUI).
- *Language*—force 'all' developers and maintainers to use ANSI standard implementation of common high-level programming languages (for example, FORTRAN, COBOL, C, etc.) and ensure that all code generated by CASE tools meets these requirements.
- *Database management system and SQL standards, rules and conventions adopted*—ensure that either a common RDBMS is used on all

platforms or else that all RDBMS engines comply with SQL and other specifications set out by the organization.

- *Data/media formats*—ensure that systems use similar data-representation formats and, wherever possible, that they use (or at least have access to) peripherals which permit use of compatible or identical storage media formats.
- *Communications and networking*—use full OSI reference model.

The role of the vendor is to make and honour commitments to comply with specific standards, drawn from the above, within promised time frames. The role of the customer organization is to ensure that acquisition and support authorities, system administration and management groups, application developers (in-house, contract and third party) and end-users comply with the architecture, specifications, standards, profiles and any further guidance or restrictions adopted by IT. In most cases this requires that the organization:

- Run a one-time master procurement with a single winner but provision for future competition; or
- Certify two or more vendors for each product and service to be acquired and permit competitive acquisition on an ongoing basis; or
- Permit any supplier meeting relevant requirements to supply any product or service at any time.

Many factors must be considered in determining the optimum strategy for each class of product and service being acquired. It is not a given premise that the same strategy will be appropriate for all open system products and services required within the agency.

Conclusion

There remains a fairly high degree of misinformation (perhaps bordering on the results of wilful disinformation on the part of some technology vendors) about OSI and open computing systems (OCS) issues in the technical, operational and economic realms. In a recent survey which I conducted of several hundred trade and professional journal articles, a significant number of them contained one or more of the following:

- Highly inaccurate, incomplete or misleading technical statements, widely known to be so at time of publication;
- Erroneous short-term predictions (often out by between 20 per cent and two orders of magnitude);

- Failure to recognize and deal with major issues either supporting and/or detracting from their main thesis;
- Misunderstanding or outright misconstrual of current events in the industry.

Some vendor-oriented and/or old-line MIS loyal publications and authors are still in the 'Dewey defeats Truman' mode; they think proprietary systems will never be defeated by open systems.

There is no doubt, however, that between 1985 and 1991 UNIX and OSI have come fully into their own as elements of the mainstream commercial computing field. Frequency of mention of keywords like *open system, open computing system, OSI* and *UNIX* more than doubled between the 1985–6 and the 1987–8 periods and more than doubled again as one moved into the current (1989 to present) period. The time divisions here are arbitrary but are believed reasonable because:

- The first period represents the advent of the first viable commercial UNIX systems such as the NCR Tower and similar systems in Europe and North America, while most of the computer industry continued to treat UNIX as the technical specialist (often called 'propeller nerd') operating system, viewed as unsuitable for business computing use.
- The second period represents the maturation of international cooperation of government and industry on OSI standards including POSIX, the merging of UNIX into V.4, the emergence of the OSF and UI camps, the adoption of UNIX as a commercial operating system by virtually all vendors and the beginning of the major proprietary 'backlash' in the literature.
- The third period represents the very rapid escalation of interest in open systems (both OSI and OCS) by users, a much wider consideration of *all* of the problems of UNIX (user friendliness, transaction processing, etc.) and a determination to try to seek solutions for them as well as a shifting of the 'onus of proof' from the open system advocates to the defenders of proprietary systems.

Any literature review, whether concentrating on technical, operational and/or economic issues related to OSI/OCS, would probably find the same basic temporal segmentation in the literature, reflecting (but leading by one phase) the flow of events in the real world from *initiation*, to *onset* to *saturation*. For example, the literature is now in the *saturation* phase while most actual implementations in the real world remain in the *onset* phase.

It is also worth noting that in the 1985–90 period, UNIX faced the same problem as the early cars and trucks in gaining user acceptance:

- No infrastructure (for fuel, repairs, advice, etc.);
- Lack of *long-term* operational experience induces a high degree of caution on the part of large organizations who are potential users;
- Too many small suppliers (pre-shakeout situation) gives rise to a serious confidence problem on the part of customers with all but the largest suppliers.

Most articles about open system implementations reflect whole or at least partial success stories and the fact that open systems are at the same time both far more complex to plan for and also far more operationally rewarding than closed systems. Because the vendors have provided far less support to open systems than to proprietary systems, and due to the fact that a given user can obtain open systems from multiple sources, the open system user must themself provide a greater portion of the planning and support services, or else buy them from an impartial third party.

There is increasing vehemence in the user/developer community that they will no longer tolerate delaying, obfuscating and water-muddying tactics on the part of the large proprietary vendors. User militancy, of a previously unseen kind, is definitely on the horizon. There is a strong probability, in the author's view, that 1993 will see some collective of large user organizations present the pro-proprietary vendors with a virtual ultimatum: either place a much higher priority on OSI and UNIX or face even faster degradation of market share, perhaps even an outright and publicly declared boycott. However, there is also no doubt that all vendors, even those with the greatest proprietary installed bases, are responding much more earnestly to user demands for open system products than in the recent past.

Despite many predictions, as late as 1990, that *any* serious incursions into the mainframe world by UNIX were still three to five years away, an increasing number of large- and medium-sized organizations have ejected proprietary mainframe vendors completely. While the cataloging of benefits is still far from systematic, IT professionals, who have undergone even such a cataclysmic change as ejecting their mainframe vendor, have not been slow to share information on the types of benefits they have realized. Many are still in the 'post-partem blues' phase.

At the MRS, mid-frame and possibly even mainframe levels, the order-of-magnitude, or sometimes even greater, cost reductions in processing power brought by RISC architecture are cited most frequently as the key payoff of moving to open computing systems. While scalability is seen as important, it is regarded by many as but a by-product of the fact that more and more complete product lines are RISC-based, from small MRS to any desired size of mainframe. The second most discussed and second most important perceived benefit to open systems is portability of application software (as well as data and user work environments) from one vendor's system to another. Interoperability is the third most discussed benefit and a significant portion of these discussions relate to the merging of corporations, or of units within them due to downsizing. In such circumstances, the existence of two proprietary systems usually leads to both parties migrating at least to OSI and often to UNIX as well; only where one party is part of a tiny minority or is in fact a minority of one within an otherwise monolithic proprietary environment is there a strong probability of a proprietary solution. Finally, there are many benefits to open systems when it comes to moving end-users, paraprofessional administrators and IT professionals among different types of systems. The learning curve tends to be much smaller or even non-existent.

3 Costs, opportunities and benefits

Introduction

Open systems provide greater access to information, and greater information empowerment of individuals and workgroups, than do closed systems. Leveraging the organization's environment and operational context, they create many new opportunities, both for individuals and for the entire organization, which would not otherwise exist. Where internal and/or external stimuli make organizational and operational flexibility (and rapid responses) imperative, open systems can in most cases be clearly linked to business objectives; in some cases they will even be a means of survival.

Planning for, acquiring, integrating and supporting open systems is much more complex and demanding than for proprietary or restricted systems, such as those which represent a single architecture such as VAX/VMS or INTEL/DOS. This not only leads to higher front-end costs for most elements except the hardware and software components themselves but also requires the IT organization to first reorient/retrain many of its staff and then to 'make' or 'buy' far more of the support services formerly provided by proprietary vendors.

Most observers today agree with the proposition put forward by the User Alliance for Open Systems (UAOS): it is necessary that top management link open systems to business objectives in order that the 'whole picture' be addressed in considering the introduction of such systems into the organization. Open systems must be addressed in strategic, not just tactical, terms.

At this time much of the quality North American literature on how to approach Cost/Benefit Analysis (CBA) for open systems, or even covering case studies of successful or unsuccessful open system implementations, either came from MAP/TOP and is 1–2 years old (not reflecting latest technology) or is being held confidential by those who have authored it. Much more longer-term (3–5 year) experience with open computing systems and OSI networks exists in Europe and Australia than the level that is present in North America. It is also clear that the value of the networking advantages of OSI, as well as the many new opportunities opened up by open computing systems, are quite difficult to capture accurately.

A more systematic and codified approach to CBA is certainly required, but in many cases it provides only a first-test or initial predictor of the full implications of the introduction of open systems. Rather, it can be seen as an initial means of gaining legitimacy for a proposed migration to open systems, as well as of gaining access to the Boardroom or Executive Committee with such a suggestion.

It would seem that the medium term is the important conceptual and practical middle ground between the costs of open systems, which are mostly short and medium term, and the benefits, which, except for the price advantages of competition and RISC, are mostly medium and long term. Of course, within different organizations the definitions of what constitutes short, medium and long term will differ. A workable pro forma definition might be as follows:

- Short term (less than 1 year);
- Medium term (1–2 years);
- Long-term (3–5 years).

This approach is justified because in most government and business organizations, planning operates on a basis of no shorter than a year or, at the extreme, a quarter. Reactions to external stimuli therefore tend to fall into the medium or long term as defined above. On the other hand, budgetary and operational planning tends not to use a horizon longer than five years due to the large number of environmental, business and technological uncertainties beyond that point.

Organizations outside North America, both private and public sector, have proved far less concerned about short-term (tactical) costs and benefits of open systems and far more willing to address the more strategic issues. These include comprehensive life cycle cost/benefit consideration of the degree to which systems create new opportunities for the organization to improve how it does its business.

Lamentably, many North American firms and government agencies have been hidebound not only by their huge infrastructure of proprietary systems and the entrenched supporters of same in the IT department but also by overly short-term and unduly narrow economic and financial analysis. Many of these same organizations have, as a result, failed to integrate new technology for information processing at a sufficiently rapid pace. Further, the causes of this failure, as well as the failure itself, have in turn acted to reduce the ability of the organization to import other new technology directly related to its core business. Finally, this lack of technological change combined with an increasingly demanding business environment has led a number of organizations in such fields as military armaments, aerospace, transportation/distribution and others to a place where open systems are now seen as a life preserver for which they are grasping. About the only fortunate aspect of this chain of events is that once top management comes to equate rapid, unopposed adoption of open systems with organizational survival, such adoption can proceed apace.

The already commanding advantage which UNIX-based RISC processors had over proprietary CISC (and certain proprietary RISC) systems has expanded considerably during the past two years. At the workstation and Mid-Range System (MRS) tiers, UNIX/RISC products exhibit price/performance advantages of between 5:1 and 15:1 over comparable proprietary systems, even where both come from the same vendor. User organizations do not require an economic model, nor CBA, to determine that UNIX/RISC products have a lower *initial* cost. However, many are heeding (quite correctly) the oft-voiced concerns that the total cost and benefit picture must be appreciated to place any such savings in their true context. In many cases, the UNIX/RISC savings work to get not only open computing systems but also OSI networking 'in the door'. From there, the resulting opportunities for increased worker productivity, flexibility and responsiveness are added to the benefits while the need to manage the technology comprehensively is added to the cost.

The technical risks are increased when an organization moves to OSI and UNIX at the same time but the probability of economic benefit rises faster than the risk when both are adopted at once. Perhaps UNIX and OSI tend to compensate for each other's remaining incompleteness and immaturities. OSI, and perhaps all elements of open systems, can be seen as an 'optimizing compromise' for a multi-vendor and multi-protocol environment. Clearly, it is necessary to optimize among elapsed time, risk and cost in selecting a conversion strategy for a given processing tier or for the organization as a whole.

Vendor independence can be seen as a form of corporate life insurance which protects against a number of ills and perils which can befall an organization wholly or largely dependent upon one vendor. These can include non-competitive pricing, curtailment of product lines, services or support and even demise of vendor. This corporate life insurance also increases the probability that if the organization wishes to take over or orchestrate a friendly takeover by another firm, that, at the very least, its systems will be able to interoperate with those of the other firm.

In seeking to understand the benefits of an open system, especially where these in part derive from the creation of new opportunities, it is crucial to consider the business environment, context and processes of the subject organization. Conventional, even modified, Cost/Benefit Analysis is, for all intents and purposes, ill-equipped to handle a consideration of all costs and benefits or opportunities offered by an open system, particularly where the opportunities relate to change of business strategy or tactics and/or the ability to transform the organization from a conventional (hierarchical) state to a knowledge-based (information authority) state.

In studying the business case for an open system, far more than for a proprietary system, full recourse must be had to the dynamics of and leverage available from the organization's business environment and business mission in seeking to establish the short-, medium- and long-term benefits of open systems. Failure to exploit these will almost certainly lead to understatement of the real or potential benefits.

Consideration of the implications of open systems merely in terms of costs and benefits is an inadequate approach. It is clear that in many cases open systems present new *opportunities* which connote, within themselves, their own sets of potentially positive and/or potentially negative impacts. A good example is the area of security in which open systems have long been reputed to be inferior but in which they also offer a very logical and solid foundation for high levels of trust. An opportunity offered by open systems may be used by one organization to good effect and may be ignored, misused or bungled by another. Therefore, the implications of open systems must be seen in terms of:

- *Costs* which arise from the acquisition/operation of systems which are purely and only costs or disadvantages to the organization and which, when considered narrowly, do not display any positive aspect in and of themselves;
- *Opportunities* which are situations or circumstances created or manifested by the arrival or use of open systems which offer the potential for the organization to achieve a range of results or outcomes ranging from very positive, to mixed, to very negative; and
- *Benefits* which arise from the acquisition/operation of systems which are purely and only benefits or savings to the organization and which, when considered narrowly, do not display any negative aspect in and of themselves.

Thus, costs are purely negative or disruptive, while benefits are purely positive or facilitative. Opportunities are those things which are not purely one or purely the other but must be netted out, within themselves, before being classified as to their net qualitative and/or quantitative implications. *In some cases, the positive and negative aspects of an opportunity can be reduced to internal costs and benefits, within the sole*

*context of that opportunity, and netted out; in others, such as security, a
purely cost or financial orientation simply will not work.*

This chapter considers *costs*, *opportunities* and *benefits* in terms of
tactical and *strategic* classifications, with the organizational or corporate
frame of reference used to determine that which is tactical and that
which is strategic. Most of these are given in the context of UNIX Mid-
Range System (MRS), the class of open computing system with which
the author is most familiar.

It should also be pointed out that the costs, opportunities and benefits
here are based on the results of both study and practice in the open
systems field over several years. They arise from the experience of many
organizations, as shared with me by my colleagues, as well as from my
own experience. This chapter is based largely on a paper produced in
connection with my membership in the User Alliance for Open Systems'
Business Case Working Group, presented in late 1991.

Tactical costs

Hardware

These are the costs associated with acquisition of the computer and
communications system hardware, and related items, for open computing systems and OSI networks. They include:

Main unit including bus/
  backplane, CPU, disk drives
  and tape drive
Additional CPU(s)
Serial I/O ports
Additional memory
Parallel ports
Expansion cabinets and bus
  bridges/umbilicals
Uninterruptable power supply
Console (intelligent or
  non-intelligent)
External disk drives
External tape drives
System printer (laser)
Laser printers
Matrix printers
Plotters

Modem(s)
Async terminal multiplexors
SCSI host adapter
Maths co-processor
X.25 network interface card
Proprietary network interface card
Mouse port
Remote console interface
Auto reboot
Alarm interface
Thermal alarm interface
Remote reset interface
Security access protective device
  (for example, RACAL)
Star-wire jack panel/distribution
  panel
Star-wiring and booster modems
Star-wiring connectors

LAN controller card
LAN distribution panel
LAN wiring and booster modems
LAN connectors
LAN package for PC
Non-intelligent terminal (ASCII mono)
Non-intelligent terminal (graphics)
X-terminal
Diskless PC (with DOS and communication software)
PC286
UNIX-capable workstation

☛ These are the components you can 'see and touch'. All of them are part of the bottom layer of the five-layer model presented in Chapter 2.

System software

This generally includes a variant of the UNIX operating system and other key accompanying system software. It is possible to develop a specification or 'user profile' for UNIX which bridges the UNIX International (UI) and Open System Foundation (OSF) operating system definitions, permitting certification of vendors utilizing either. Key system software cost components include:

Operating system kernel and utilities
BOURNE and C shells
Security extension to OS
System administration package
RFS
NFS
Text processors and editors
BASIC interpreters
Language compilers
    COBOL
    C
    PASCAL
    FORTRAN
Print spooler
Batch job scheduler
Real Time optional extension of OS
OLTP extension of OS
Performance monitoring and tuning tools
X.25 node and gateway software
X/Windows software
Diagnostic software if not otherwise included

☛ All of these items help tie the hardware to the performance of the work. They represent the second and third from the bottom layers of the model.

Package software

In many cases an organization moving to open systems will find that by far the most important package software is a Relational DataBase Management System (RDBMS) and Office Automation (OA) software. Package software, however, includes all of the following:

- RDBMS including:
  - DBMS engine
  - SQL interfaces
  - Data import/export facilities
  - Application and/or data manipulation languages
  - Networking interfaces;
- OA package including:
  - E-mail
  - Word processing
  - Telephone directory
  - Cardfile database
  - Spreadsheet
  - Calendar/agenda
  - Calculator
  - Text/object import and export
  - Network/multi-system interface for E-mail;
- Mainframe controller/terminal emulation (mini emulates local controllers and terminals specific to proprietary mainframe, permitting the ASCII (real or emulated) terminal user to access mainframe via mini);
- Async terminal emulation (mini itself emulates async terminal when it logs onto another system);
- PC networking module (provides PC user access to disk space on mini as a logical DOS drive);
- PC interworking module (provides PC networking and also permits execution of DOS programs on mini, running under a UNIX task);
- LAN server package (provides full LAN networking and server function from mini);
- PC terminal emulator;
- PC word processor (single-user version of OA word processor package or a standalone word processing package such as WordPerfect);
- Workstation terminal emulator;
- Workstation word processor.

☞ A package is simply a program implemented in a language which makes it easier for you to handle data. LOTUS 1-2-3 is a spreadsheet package for manipulation of numeric data. WordPerfect is a word processing package for creation and manipulation of text (and multi-media) documents.

Application software

When an open system architecture is in place, the organization has the opportunity to establish a central Software Registry (here simply called the 'Registry') which is described in the Strategic Opportunities section below. When this is accomplished, software may be sourced by any of the following methods, each of which may represent a different level of cost:

- *Registry* application used as is;
- *Modify* an application from the Registry;
- *Third-party* sourcing of application;
- *Develop* application from scratch, either in-house or with an external contractor.

☞ The term 'application software' is generally used to apply to software which is developed specifically to perform a given business function. In some cases, only a high-level language is used and, in terms of our model in Chapter 2, the software spans Levels 3 and 4. Other application software may require the presence of a database package, such as ORACLE or INFORMIX in order to function.

System installation, integration and commissioning

System integration is crucial to all advanced technology systems but doubly so in the case of open systems. Unlike the case of a proprietary vendor and a closed environment, the user organization cannot simply state that since everything comes from one vendor, that vendor itself must make all components interoperate. Invariably, the various components of an open system architecture will be sourced from their respective multiplicities of vendors. The components of system integration generally include at least the following:

Site survey
Shipping
Unpacking/checking
Site wiring
System installation
System integration
System commissioning
System approval and sign-off by functional authority

☞ These are the costs of getting the computers installed, working together, tested and made ready for the users.

Orientation and training

Experience has shown that a failure to anticipate and fully meet the human needs arising from the introduction of new technology almost always results in a suboptimal implementation; often it results in ejection of the new technology and even those who purveyed it. Because open systems are often more complex than proprietary systems and because not all of this complexity can be hidden from end-users and paraprofessional local system administrators, much less IT staff, these costs must be recognized and met at the outset. Failure to do so is to risk premature write-off of the entire investment. These costs include:

- Site course customization as required.
- Course delivery and follow-up:
    - Orientation sessions
    - User terminal emulator/OS training
    - User OA training
    - User application training
    - User LAN training
    - System administrator training:
        - UNIX
        - OA administration
        - RDBMS administration
        - Security
        - Other.
- Opportunity cost of time spent on course (lost productivity, salary equivalent or whatever).

☞ These are the costs of making the users ready for the computers.

Software and hardware support

A System Functional Model developed earlier by the author hypothesizes that good documentation is the very foundation of a good human support program for any system, open or otherwise. Equally important are the arrangements to keep each installation cognizant of ongoing developments and current in terms of versions/releases. These costs include:

- Documentation:
    - User manuals
    - System administration manuals
    - Reference manuals
    - Flipcharts/checklists
    - Technical manuals;
- Operating system licence currency fee (if any);
- System software support/upgrade contract;

- Hardware maintenance contract;
- OA maintenance fee;
- RDBMS maintenance fee.

☞ It is necessary to have professionals, or at least paraprofessionals, who know what they are doing to help the end-users when problems arise. Problems may arise from hardware, software or network failure, user error or forgetfulness, user incompetence, malice or other causes.

System operation and administration

Well before the arrival of commercially viable open computing systems such as those running UNIX, it was well established that Local Area Networks (LANs), their servers and certainly the larger mid-range systems require proactive administration, even where they are otherwise automatic. Although it is increasingly possible to perform many system administration and system management tasks remotely, this is by no means the case for all tasks. Sometimes there is no alternative but to have someone on-site. When moving to UNIX-based MRS equipment, it is in many cases necessary to institute a formal program to train and certify paraprofessional MRS Administrators (MRSAs) to oversee the operation of such equipment. For any system, open or otherwise, proper administration is required. Whereas UNIX/RISC architecture provides many opportunities and outright savings, the local line management must realize that the 'cost to get into the game' is the commitment to ensure that the corporate, workgroup and personal information held on the system is adequately managed. These costs include:

- Direct labour (salary and/or contract);
- Supplies/expendables (paper, tapes, disks, etc.);
- User relocations (10 per cent of users per year);
- Other/miscellaneous.

☞ Someone has to perform regular housekeeping of the system including making extra copies of the data now in use and ensuring that the system is expanded or that usage is changed before the system is swamped by too many users, too many programs, too much data or all three at once.

Communications and processing overhead of OSI networks

The complex protocol stack inherent in true OSI network implementations gives rise to the requirement for additional effort in planning, managing and supporting an OSI network, as opposed to traditional, closed proprietary networks. There may also, in some cases, be increased operational costs due to the same overheads, particularly where pay-as-you-go (by packet, kilocharacter, line minute or whatever) services, as opposed to dedicated services, are employed.

☞ Open systems networks are often more complicated because they require many features and capabilities in order to have a basis for compatibility with each other. This adds to the cost of buying and operating them.

Foregone features

In some cases, a UNIX/RISC-based system will be supplied with a less complete set of features than a directly competitive and otherwise identically specified proprietary system. In such cases one or both of two costs may be incurred:

- Acquiring additional third-party product or service to meet specified requirement;
- Disruption or lower level of service due to lack of specific desired or required feature.

☞ Even where open systems do not offer lowest common denominator functionality, they sometimes exclude required components expressly to prevent lock-in of the user to one vendor or approach. This is good, but the other side of the coin is that required components are still necessary, and must be bought separately and, of course, at extra cost.

Early retirement of existing proprietary system

Even though RISC-based systems may bring substantial initial cost savings and additional benefits, they may, depending upon the organizational context and situation, on their arrival force early retirement (before write-down is complete) of existing proprietary systems. In such cases the costs include:

- Disruption of extra accounting and/or audit services;
- Dollar amounts of write-off of remaining undepreciated capital amount or unrealized service value related to any hardware, software or prepaid service or licence, less any recovery on sale of such equipment.

☞ Sometimes, adopting open systems means that you must eject proprietary systems earlier than you otherwise would have, leading to early write-down or write-off.

Incremental liability insurance for untried system

Where an operational organization, or at least its customers, regulators and/or insurers, has a lower level of confidence in an untried or unproven system, there may be an increase in operational liability insurance (and/or other related insurance) relative to the operations in which newly acquired open systems are to be employed. Such costs include:

- Estimating and securing additional coverage;
- Actual incremental cost of coverage;
- Risk-weighted cost of increased deductable(s), if applicable.

☞ Insurance firms like certainty and existing, proven systems offer more of it. On the other hand, your insurance company won't insure or compensate you for the ills of vendor lock-in if you elect to stay with closed systems.

OSI product overpricing

While open systems are generally associated with lower rather than higher prices, as compared to closed products, this association is generally made more closely with open computing systems (UNIX/RISC, etc.) than with OSI networks. Software and hardware for OSI networks is often more complex than that intended for proprietary networks; sometimes the higher costs this engenders are not entirely mitigated by the competitive market. Also, some European-based vendors, aware of the lack, until very recently, of good OSI networking products in North America, have been extracting oligopolistic prices from their customers. Limited competition in North America for some of these products as well as the potential for proprietary vendor price manipulation of OSI products to make them less attractive have also had an impact. This cost includes:

- Obtaining (often all but extracting) information about open system products from vendors;
- Incremental cost of such products compared to proprietary equivalents.

☞ When something is exotic or at least rare there is sometimes the opportunity to charge more for it. Where there is a premium of this sort, it is a cost of moving to open systems over and above the cost of buying an equivalent proprietary product. Until very recently, good OSI networking products have been relatively rare. Some vendors took full advantage of this; others did not. The situation is now changing, as more and more suppliers enter the market.

Increased failure risk

This is the more direct aspect of the above-cited insurance or liability risk; it is the risk that a business, operational or even mobile computing system will fail. Both because the particular system is new—and because the technology is new—this risk cannot be ignored. The cost is:

- The probability weighted estimated net present cost, disruption and/ or other disadvantages of the single or stream of failures involving or caused by the open computing system and/or OSI network.

☞ The phrase 'stream of failures' in the above paragraph may strike terror into the hearts of many managers. However, when nothing is ventured, nothing is gained. Don't run your first pilot project with a bet-the-business application! Many problems implementing open systems have nothing whatsoever to do with any failings of the technology itself, but result from inadequate training, unwilling employees, hostile proprietary vendors or a combination of these. Close monitoring and clear lines of accountability are the enemies of the would-be saboteur.

Lower functionality at the outset

Many open systems offer lower functionality because they are either delivered in an incomplete state or the standards (or profiles) to which they seek to be compliant are themselves incomplete. Cost here is:

- The identifiable dollar cost or other cost arising from functionality which is incomplete or missing in the as-installed and as-operated system which would be present in a proprietary, closed system.

☞ The absolute or relative functionalities of otherwise equivalent open and closed products are less relevant than the funtionality you actually require. It is what *you* need that counts! Perhaps both the open and closed products offer twice the functionality you require so the differences are moot. Perhaps the open product offers only 85 per cent of what you need now but you can live with that until the next release six months or a year from now. Perhaps you can delay the changeover until then. Failing all of the above, you may have to buy the proprietary product. Realism is the friend of the advancement of open systems.

Longer implementation and learning period

Experience has shown that open systems generally require a longer system integration, orientation, training and learning curve period than closed systems. This cost includes:

- Dollar or lost productivity value of incremental time spent by employees becoming accustomed to an open system versus a proprietary system.

☞ Open systems are at least as big a change as the railways experienced when moving from steam to diesel locomotives and the airlines when moving from piston to pure jet powered aircraft. Open systems tend to turn the culture of your IT unit upside down, thereafter having a significant and growing influence on the rest of the organization. The in-migration process does not need to take a decade but it certainly could if there is no planning, and aimless wandering sets in. Remember the Israelites who wandered for 40 years in the Wilderness! In most cases, once you have started you *cannot* go back, but moving too quickly can cause your organization to trip itself up. A steady, measured pace is best.

Re-education and reorientation of your vendor

Once the organization has established an open systems orientation within the IT group, it is virtually always necessary for this group to begin acting on a more independent basis *vis-à-vis* the single dominant vendor, or few strong vendors, previously (and probably still) serving the organization. Unfortunately, this is easier stated than accomplished. Costs of re-educating and reorienting your vendor include IT's time/dollar cost of:

- Attending vendor seminars but ensuring that such vendor understands that you are *serious* about having an open system architecture drive your acquisition policy;
- Convincing Vendor X that you do *not* intend to buy all of his or her 'integration' products merely so that you can install Vendor Y's totally vanilla or basic UNIX or OSI system with the help of Vendor X customization, and that you will *not* accept Vendor X's claim that he or she is open unless Vendor Z's products can be used to integrate Vendor X and Vendor Y UNIX/RISC platforms and OSI networking products without further Vendor X products or services;
- Disruption of ejecting vendor 'customer engineers' who live at your site, and are often preoccupied mostly with a continual marketing/sales function inside your organization for their proprietary products;
- Hassle of ejecting vendor outside sales reps who refuse to accept your strategic direction and seek allies within your organization in an attempt to discourage or prevent you either from moving to open systems, or at least from moving to them rapidly;
- Withstanding any predatory pricing, disinformation or other disruption, including escalating issue up your line organization, which your proprietary vendor undertakes in an effort to discourage or prevent your organization from moving, or from moving rapidly, to open systems;
- Lost information due to less news and views coming in from a proprietary vendor who reduces the flow of information to your

organization about their proprietary and/or open systems products in retaliation for your move to open systems;

- Disruption and lost information from cancellation of subscription to publications taking an anti-open systems editorial approach;
- Any effects of IT employee dissatisfaction resulting from enforced reduced contact with their favourite proprietary vendor.

☞ Most large organizations are at least somewhat dependent upon the vendors who sold them their major computer systems. Various vendors have different attitudes towards open systems; some will help you with your migration, others will pretend to help you and others will do all in their power to prevent you from migrating. A basic cost of moving to open systems is the effort necessary to convince your vendor that you *are serious* and that, since the customer is still king, it is in their interest to lead, follow or get out of the way!

Immature UNIX mainframe cost and disruption

While UNIX mainframe technology is advancing very rapidly, it is clear that such environments, particularly in areas such as OLTP and real-time processing, are less mature than various proprietary systems. Costs could include:

- Incremental planning, implementation, management and support costs in the IT unit for such products, over proprietary systems;
- Lost business productivity due to any performance deficit or lack of flexibility imposed by very large UNIX/OSI-based systems.

☞ Most organizations do not *start* the move to open systems with the mainframe. The huge investment in existing (usually COBOL) programs, the need to reorient the systems staff and the criticality of the system all militate against it. Gain experience with UNIX MRS, MBS and workstation equipment first, then progress to mid-frames and, finally, to mainframes. If, on the other hand, you choose (or are forced) to implement a UNIX mainframe early, you can expect substantial teething pains unless your application portfolio is one befitting a textbook.

User frustration

This is difficult to quantify but it addresses any additional disadvantages to the organization as a direct or indirect result of end-user or local line management frustration (or flat-out exasperation) with the advent of open systems in the organization. Costs may include:

- Transferring employees who demand to move away from the open systems plus lost productivity resulting from such moves at both origins and destinations of same;

- Releasing employees who resign or are fired due to their desire to avoid open systems or their efforts to sabotage them;
- Recruiting, training and any additional lost productivity costs required to replace transferred or released employees.

☞ Users grow frustrated with all new computer systems, but especially with ones which have the potential to change the way they, the IT unit and perhaps even the whole company or department does business.

Strategic costs

Above and beyond the direct costs, as set out above, there are the corporate costs of creating and making available core programs which enable and/or support open systems hardware, software or communications services. As stated earlier, it is far more important in the case of open systems versus closed systems that the organization plan for, and actually incur, the costs of providing central technology acquisition and management services. Failure to do so will, at best, result in a non-optimum implementation of open systems technology and, at worst, result in mayhem and subsequent rejection of the technology.

Architecture planning and policy/standards development

For any system architecture component where it is desired to exploit the multi-supplier aspects of open systems, it is necessary to have a well-planned, coherent and vendor-intelligible acquisition program. Justice must not only be done but must also be seen to be done with respect to who is invited to bid, what is in the Request for Proposals (RFP), how questions are answered (vendor-to-you and you-to-vendor) and how evaluation, qualification, test and approval of vendors is conducted. If trials or pilots are employed, everyone must be given an equally 'desirable' site; at the very least, user acceptance or hostility must be equal from site to site. For a substantial program these costs can be very considerable and all investment must be made *before* full production systems are even purchased, much less begin to return the opportunities and benefits sought from them. Specific costs include:

- Final specifications and standards;
- Acquisition strategy:
  - Single vendor
  - Multi-vendor (limited number qualified)
  - Wide open (any vendor who meets spec);

- Ongoing technical monitoring and requirements update;
- Human development plan (orientation, training and support);
- System control, administration and support strategy:
  - Full remote control from HQ and/or Regions
  - Professional (IT) system administrator
  - Certified paraprofessional system administrator (for example, MRSA)
  - External contractor to provide on/off-site administration;
- Standard orientation and training materials;
- Course delivery framework (establish contract, etc.);
- Operations manual or guidance generic for all systems;
- User/administrator interest group establishment/support;
- Administrator meetings or conferences;
- Directory of approved products and services;
- Registry of applications:
  - Developed in-house previously
  - Modified from in-house
  - Third party, cleared for all platforms
  - Under development by in-house or contract staff;
- Master framework and specific channels for provision of:
  - Auxiliary equipment/peripherals
  - Standard application packages (RDBMS, OA, emulator, etc.)
  - System integration services
  - Development services certified for all platforms
  - Training
  - System administration
  - Technical service and support.

☞ Open systems, unlike closed systems, make you (the customer) the real king, but you are none the less a constitutional monarch! This means that you get to set the rules of the game, but once you have done so not only the would-be suppliers but you too must be bound by them. It is essential not only that you be fair to everyone (including your incumbent vendor, if you have one) but also that you be *seen* to be fair. If you know what you want, undertaking these efforts will allow you to acquire open systems without being yourself acquired by the open systems vendor.

☞ If you have not thought through exactly what you want, how you intend to make sure that you get it and how you intend to support it after you obtain it, you simply are not ready to buy. If you go to the car dealer knowing only that you want a red car, you will probably drive away in a red luxury car, whether you can afford or even need such a car or not. You are the salesman's dream customer. Automobile salespeople have an incentive to sell you what they have in inventory, and to sell you the most expensive car that the financing powers-that-be will approve. The salesperson's nightmare is the person who marches in and sets down a list of car, colour and options and says: 'Here, I would like to order this car with these options. How much off the list price will you give me for cash?' Invariably, this customer has read the consumer press, the car enthusiast press and has been to two other dealers. The salesperson has two choices: play it the way this person wants and make at least *some* commission or else lose the sale. The salesperson is *not* going to try to sell this person the red Cadillac if he has already decided he wants a blue Chevrolet Caprice Classic with Options X, Y and Z.

☛ Some of the 'open integration services' offered by computer vendors make liberal use of their own proprietary extensions to operating systems, languages, communications protocols, etc. After this brand of 'open systems integration' in which the vendor integrates his or her system with whatever else you have, you will find yourself buying future 'open systems' only from this vendor.

Operational costs

In many cases it will be necessary to *maintain* the existing network(s) for some time. The new OSI network will not replace everything now installed on Day 1. Therefore, most or even all costs associated with the establishment of a new OSI network are net costs, at least at the time they are incurred. Also, OSI network management is often more complex and expensive than proprietary network management:

- Network management:
  - Load balancing
  - Access prioritization
  - Adds, moves and deletes
  - Troubleshooting of nodes
  - Remote management of troubleshooting of LAN;
- Central system management services provided to local sites:
  - Configuration management services
  - Capacity planning
  - Remote system interrogation and analysis
  - System upgrade and migration planning support
  - System 'trade in' (used car lot function);
- Central contingency support program:
  - Spare CPUs and critical components stocks (HQ/Regional)
  - Hot standby system in regional office
  - 'Buddy system' pairing local sites for mutual off-site storage of backed-up data on tape;
- Site technical status and certification (functional authority);
- Maintain HQ and/or Regional software certification and test machines (possibly use hot standby processor).

☛ Open system network management is rapidly maturing but it would be unfair to state that it is already mature; it is in an 'adolescent' state of development. Adolescents, as you know, can be very temperamental. If you move to a two-network strategy (one open and one closed) your network management costs will certainly increase. However, you *can* counterbalance against this the fact that an increasing amount of remote system administration is possible, permitting more human effort to be concentrated on remote management of all network elements including bridges, routers, processors, gateways, etc.

Technology tracking: coping with the information overload

Once the IT staff, or at least a cadre of the same, has been oriented, educated and trained as to open systems the process does not stop. The very nature of open systems means that there is no single authoritative source, even for specifications and standards adherence. It is necessary to follow an incredibly diverse range of developments to remain current as to what is bleeding edge, what is leading edge, what is current and what is past-peak or obsolete technology. With a medium-sized or large organization, this represents a considerable challenge for the IT organization. Of course, since it is unlikely that all proprietary systems will be dropped the day after the first open system goes into production, most of these costs are over and above those of following those proprietary technologies which will remain important to the organization for several years to come. Note that these costs will rise exponentially if your proprietary vendor(s) give wilful disinformation to the IT staff. Costs include:

- Periodicals (trade and professional journals) and books;
- Subscription services (customized newsletters) and research services;
- Vendor and third-party seminars;
- Conferences, workshops and symposia;
- Employee time involved in administering, travelling to and attending the above.

☛ Keeping track of more vendors is more complex and expensive than just tracking one vendor. After all, if you have only one major vendor, you can usually turn to that vendor for most of the information you require. If you have many vendors you need not only them as sources but also people who can 'triangulate' from an independent perspective about what new developments involving one or more of them really mean.

Loss of one-stop shopping

It is almost always true that movement to open systems deprives the organization of the comfort, trust, regularity and routine of one-stop shopping with a proprietary vendor. Such a vendor may have been providing most or even all of the required hardware, software and support for some or all large and mid-range system installations within the organization. While many of the costs are counted elsewhere, there are some specific costs which include:

- Requirement to reorient senior management to the fact that a single supplier is no longer adequate to meet the organization's IT needs;
- Requirement for CIOs and their executives to maintain good working relationships with the senior and account executives of many more organizations;
- Same requirement for more junior IT staff to maintain more sets of relationships with key members of supplier organizations.

☞ Another cost of dealing with multi-vendors is the terrible burden of having to be taken out to lunch more often by many more 'account executives' to learn about their firm's latest product, service or upcoming product briefing, usually in some sunny clime. Seriously, though, senior IT management's time and attention is in short supply and if you foresee or move into a situation with several vendors being major stakeholders in your installation, dividing your attention among them is critical.

Conversion of applications and data

In many cases, it will be necessary to convert some or all of the applications now running under proprietary operating systems and/or packages to their open system counterparts. Costs include:

- Conversion planning;
- Code conversion and any inevitable re-engineering;
- Data conversion;
- Loss of application functionality due expressly to conversion, possibly from a proprietary to an ANSI language variant;
- Loss of data due to errors or accidents occurring during conversion;
- Lost employee time or productivity due to conversion.

☞ Conversion also happens when you move from one proprietary system to another and it can be just as unpleasant as moving from closed to open systems. One can argue that it is unfair to hold it up as a cost of open systems, but you *do* have the choice of avoiding this cost by staying with your existing proprietary system. None the less, if your open system program is successful, this may be the last time you will incur this particular cost for a very long time. (In this book, I have endeavoured to be conservative and to highlight *all* conceivable/known costs of open systems, so there will be no accusations of telling only one side of the story. Clearly, though, if your existing proprietary system has been dead-ended by its vendor and its demise is now on the horizon, it is unfair to treat conversion cost as a cost of moving to open systems since it is a cost of moving *anywhere* for your organization.)

UNIX technology lag

Some observers have commented upon a 'technology lag' which impacts UNIX-based hardware and software intended for such platforms. It can be argued that 'the shoe is now on the other foot' in that many proprietary systems are now falling increasingly far behind open systems in their state of technological advancement. None the less, it was true during the 1988–9 period, for example, that the OA packages intended for UNIX platforms exhibited lower sophistication than those offered for proprietary platforms, even when both came from the same vendors. (This tendency was noted in a 1988 Seybolds Report on *UNIX in the Office*, which reviewed various UNIX OA packages. My own experience also confirmed this.) The cost would be:

- Not having any feature or function otherwise available on the equivalent or competitive proprietary system.

  ☞ This is still a cost of open systems in some cases, but the trick is to put a value on the lacking function. The degree of cost or disadvantage from the lack of a function which is absent in an open system may fall into any one of the following categories:

- Nice to have but not too important;
- An irritant but survivable;
- Technically or operationally unacceptable.

Protracted proprietary vendor misbehaviour

Where the negative responses and activities of the organization's proprietary vendor(s) exceed the tactical realm and become longer term, and thus strategic, it is usually time seriously to consider ejecting such vendor(s) as soon as possible. In a free society, no customer organization, no matter how large its current investment in proprietary hardware and software, can be forced to tolerate being dictated to or bullied by its suppliers. Where the organization cannot or at least does not eject the misbehaving supplier, and where there are costs or disruptions over and above those cited at the tactical level, the costs of the impacts on the organization as a result of such misbehaviour are a part of the cost of moving to open systems. They can be qualified and quantified only in the context of organizational specifics; therefore no general statement of the nature of such costs can be made here.

☞ The only nice thing about this whole scenario is that this particular cost of adopting open systems can be avoided. Usually it can be avoided right from the outset by sending your vendor a clear message sanctioned by senior management as follows: 'We are moving to open systems whether you like it or not; cease and desist in your attempts to hinder us or we will take action you are guaranteed not to like!'

☞ This approach may be viewed as confrontational, but so is the raising of an army to defend one's own home and country when an invasion force appears. Pussyfooting and attempts at petty political solutions, such as constantly smoothing over the waters with the offending vendors or making apologies for their behaviour, only postpone the day when a firm hand is required. Usually such tactics make things worse and not better. No organization can afford to let a supplier gain control of its IT function, unless it has made the specific decision actually to abdicate that control by outsourcing the whole thing.

☞ Remember, too, that within the IT organization there will be three camps: those who support the move to open systems, those who oppose it and those who are sitting on the fence. Your IT management's resolve in dealing with the misbehaving vendor will send clear messages to each group. If you are consistent and persistent in taking this stance each and every time the proprietary vendor(s) raise another thorny issue or seek another way to foil your plans, and this can become a real battle of wits, you will send everyone a clear signal and they will respond accordingly. The first group will rejoice in your commitment and praise you for following your own policies. The third group will be encouraged to lean towards your side of the fence, even if they do remain perched upon it. Their neutrality will become more benevolent since they realize the same resolve could be turned in their direction should they be seen as obstructive. The true opponents will either side with the vendors and accuse you of beating up on them, go underground with their protests and obstructions, defect to one of the other groups or leave the organization.

Early bird standard syndrome

In very many cases, early adoption of an open system standard is synonymous with accepting a product based on a draft or otherwise incomplete standard; at worst, the standard may be in dispute between warring (mutually excommunicating) camps. There are always costs incurred when it is necessary to move to an enhanced, or even a completely different, product to ensure that the final version of the standard is reflected in the as-installed network or computer system.

☞ As cited earlier, a good hint as to whether or not a standard is an 'early bird' is whether or not a year number is attached to it. There are, however, exceptions: FORTRAN 77 is quite mature. The cost here is the cost of disentangling yourself from whatever part of the standard does not become permanent.

Software vendor lock-in potential

It has been tritely, but truly, noted that in many migrations to open systems the dominance of a single hardware vendor (or a few such vendors) is replaced by the dominance, so far as the migrating user organization is concerned, of a single software vendor. Usually, this is a vendor of something such as an RDBMS product. In general, such vendors are far smaller than even medium-sized hardware vendors and thus more subject to survival risks in the business environment. If the RDBMS or OA vendor goes bankrupt, major costs and other problems will result. Costs of an RDBMS vendor bankruptcy would include:

• Replacement of vendor's product with another;

- Major conversion of application software and stored data;
- Retraining of IT staff, site DBA staff and end-users;
- Changes to networks to accommodate new SQL networking approach of newly selected product.

☞ You can avoid this by, for example, adopting multiple vendors' RDBMS products and then using lowest common denominator (perhaps, purely ANSI) SQL access methods for all of them. However, this does not allow you to escape the cost of having to train groups of programmers and data adminstration specialists for each RDBMS. This is one of the most vexing problems in the open systems world and there *is* no one, simple answer. Most RDBMS vendors have made proprietary extensions to SQL.

☞ There is a ray of hope. Some companies have introduced expert systems which can take a very simply defined 'business process' and a dataset and thence develop fully context-sensitive procedural language code, including embedded SQL code, for a specific database. Basically, you throw the business method, the data, and the RDBMS engine into an 'arena' and out pops the application. (I am being rather trite here but surely the point is clear.) Hypothetically at least, if you used the RDBMS from Vendor A and then that firm went bankrupt, you could take your business methods and data and quickly re-engineer for Vendor B's database, providing only that the expert system had also been interfaced with that product. It is doubtful that this type of re-engineering has yet been accomplished in the real world, however, so this remains in the theoretical realm for now. (We know what happens when you put a bull, a bullfighter and a red cape into an arena. What happens when you replace the bull with a tiger?)

Requirement to restructure data to relational model

In general, the database packages used with UNIS/RISC systems are based on the relational model. Certainly, ADABAS and other non-relational products have been ported over to UNIX and are now available, but in most cases the move to a new system architecture, hardware product line and operating system will also be accompanied by a move to a fully relational data model, supporting a full RDBMS compliant at least to ANSI SQL. Like many costs cited here, moving to the relational data model is not *strictly* a cost of moving to open systems (it could also be incurred moving from one proprietary OS to another while also updating to a newer database package), it is a cost which very often accompanies such a migration. Note that although many of the costs, opportunities and benefits presented in this document also exist in a proprietary-to-proprietary migration, it is quite clear too that many of them do not. Restructuring costs may include:

- Database redesign;
- Database reformatting;
- Actual data conversion;
- Changes to or conversion of applications and job control scripts or programs necessary to accommodate the change to relational.

☞ Moving your data to a relational model is a good idea anyway, and there is little doubt that there are inherent benefits to such an effort. If you can identify data- and application-inherent benefits which exceed the cost of the conversion, then do not count any of the conversion costs against the move to open systems.

Premature discard of interim solutions

Quite apart from standards-driven issues, many open system products, or products like those employing TCP/IP tend to go hand in hand with open system solutions but are not strictly open themselves. Many such items acquired early in the migration process may be discarded before the organization reaches full operational capability with open systems. Such products may be used as bridges, patches, surrogates or other gap fillers until full OSI- or UNIX-based products are available or are practical. In most cases, such products will be discarded well before their technological lives have expired and before they have been written down by the accountants. Costs include:

- Percentage of life cycle cost not amortized normally but written off due to premature discard;
- Retraining costs associated with conversion to final product.

☞ These costs are usually a small part of the overall cost unless you are operating a gigantic network and you migrate all nodes first to an interim standard and then to a final one.

Tactical opportunities

Improve individual and workgroup efficiency and effectiveness

In most cases, open systems do more than closed systems to assist the organization to improve individual and/or workgroup efficiency and effectiveness. The savings available from open systems can be channelled in many ways but an increase in output with the same staff, a constant output with a smaller staff or even a mixture of the two can be shown in many cases. The interoperability and portability benefits of open systems (which are discussed separately below) are contributors to this.

☞ OCS products more easily serve as workgroup processors and can be more easily installed in office, operational and even mobile situations since they have reasonable environmental, heat dissipation and electrical requirements and do not usually require IT professionals to operate them.

Freed-up time available for creativity, QA or additional production

In most cases, the installation of open systems results in the freeing up of many envelopes of free time at the individual (workplace) level. Where it is undesirable or impractical to use these for increasing production and/or decreasing staff, they may be used to enhance employee creativity or work variety or to increase the quality assurance or quality control functions at the individual level.

☞ Open systems free up pockets of time which employees can use productively.

Potential for inter-tier processing tradeoffs

Where processor hardware is being planned at the same time, or at least in close time proximity, for two or more adjacent processing tiers, and/or two or more adjacent, or at least easily linkable sites, it is possible to trade off processing power, as between UNIX workstations and UNIX mid-range systems. Very few proprietary architectures offer such flexibility. The closer the implementation of two processors is in terms of time, tier and physical location, the greater the potential for such tradeoffs. Service model, security, system administration and other factors will assist in determining, for example, how much power to place on the desktop (i.e. workstation) and how much to place at a higher tier (i.e. workgroup MRS).

☞ Open systems let you decide, at implementation time, where to put the computing horsepower and give you far more flexibility in taking some away from one level (tier) of computing and putting it at another. At the planning stage, you can reallocate computing power, almost at will, among the enterprise, regional/divisional, workgroup and individual processing tiers if you are a very large organization. (Many organizations identify three or even two tiers rather than four. The most common tier structures are enterprise, workgroup and individual.)

Work, work item (WI) and workspace sharing

Because of their superior interoperability characteristics, open systems encourage the sharing of work, of specific work items or task sets and even of specific objects such as text files or graphics images. This sharing, particularly when the 'sharers' are remote from each other and thus could not otherwise share a workspace in real time without travel, is a significant value adder.

☛ Open systems provide a firm foundation for future decentralization of workers away from conventional offices. Conventional, proprietary systems do not, since most of them try to force you either to keep most of the processing in central sites and/or to keep the workers local through *Local* Area Networks.

☛ Decentralization of workers can offer environmental, energy and economic benefits of many kinds. Another book to be published by this author entitled *The Home Workplace: A Builder's Guide to its Environment, Energy and Economy* will cover the field.

Purchase decisions made on price/performance basis

The organization can, subject only to the rules set in place to systemize and regularize acquisition for a given system architecture component, make purchasing decisions on the basis of price and performance. UNIX MRS equipment exhibits approximately a 12–15 to 1 advantage over, for example, proprietary mainframe environments, even when differences in counting MIPS or other performance measures are taken into account. The same MRS products often have a 5–10 to 1 advantage over their proprietary minicomputer competitors. Medium- and high-power UNIX/RISC workstations no longer have any serious proprietary competitors in the market. UNIX/RISC is also migrating both upward to the mid-frame and mainframe world and down to the medium-power PC environment very rapidly. Frequently, however, the price/performance advantages of open systems are merely the key which unlocks the door and gets them into the organization; from that point forward their many other opportunities and benefits are made manifest.

☛ No matter what type or size computer you want to buy, you get more punch for the pound with UNIX-based open computing systems.

DOS interworking potential

OSI and UNIX/RISC products offer DOS interworking potential which meets or exceeds that offered by any proprietary system environment. In fact, it exceeds that offered by most proprietary systems.

☛ You can very effectively tie all types and sizes of open computing systems together with each other and with your PCs.

Lower system integration and support costs (after the learning curve)

Once the IT staff, and local MRS Administrators (MRSAs), LAN Administrators (LANAs) and Database Administrators (DBAs) have progressed down the open systems learning curve, the total costs to support a given open computing system are almost always lower than for a proprietary system.

☞ Once you have learned how to drive your first left-hand drive car, assuming you are British and accustomed to right-hand drive, you will find your next one easier to drive. Because open systems are so similar in their operation, learning one takes you a long way towards learning the others.

Progressivity of UNIX licensing costs

UNIX licensing costs tend to be far more progressive as one moves from smaller to larger machines than do such costs for most other operating systems. In other words, the OS and related system software cost *per user* falls as one moves to a larger machine. In most proprietary operating systems this cost stays relatively constant or even increases on a per-user basis as larger processors are required. Further, some proprietary vendors simply do not offer a single operating system extending from workplace to mainframe processors. Therefore, UNIX offers the potential or opportunity to benefit from progressive versus regressive pricing of licences.

☞ This is not an exploitable factor if yours is a very small organization. However, if you will be acquiring the larger MRS products, mid-frames or mainframes, there is a definite benefit to running UNIX on larger systems when it comes to per-user licence costs.

Security

Open systems have often been maligned for their lack of security features and characteristics. It is certainly true that the very openness of open systems is itself a confounder of efforts to make a given system secure. The saga of the ARPANET worm and the indicated susceptibility of UNIX to certain viruses, worms and other undesirables is of significant concern. Also, secure UNIX is a relatively new product. Finally, experience has shown (at least for MRS equipment) that above a certain threshold it is necessary to isolate and dedicate a system to achieve the desired security; in most cases this threshold is at a lower level (*vis-à-vis* the NCSC Orange Book, for example) than for a similar proprietary system. Certainly, all of these factors offer opportunities to have, at best, a less secure system and, at worst, a major breach, accident or even a disaster induced by a hostile saboteur, particularly where operational or mobile systems are concerned. However, the security 'coin' has two sides. UNIX, and indeed OSI networks, also offer the opportunity to build a reasonably secure system. Their logical and incremental design, inherent traceability, easy extensibility, device orientation, capability for remote management and interrogation, and good configuration control work together to provide a firm foundation for the construction by the vendor and/or the user organization of a secure system. Some UNIX systems have achieved high levels of trust. As with most open system opportunities which are technical in nature, however, much of the onus to exploit this potential rests on the implementing organization.

☞ Open systems can be just as secure, perhaps even more secure, than competitive proprietary systems. However, they usually do not come secure; you have to *make* them secure.

Qualitative and ergonomic/health impacts

Open systems and modern GUIs (which greatly enhance the effectiveness of the user interface) are mutually reinforcing technologies. Additionally, the smaller scale of UNIX/RISC-based MRS equipment in terms of heat dissipation, environmental and electrical requirements, and sound output for a given machine processing power level makes such computers good neighbours in an office or mobile environment. Experience indicates that systems supporting 50, 70 or even up to 100 concurrent users can be satisfactorily located in an office environment. Above the 100-user level, however, many of the traditional mini-computer amenities (dedicated power and room, possible computer room requirement, etc.) tend to appear. The technology continues to evolve but recent product releases make clear that even where the MRS itself can be made still smaller and less obtrusive, the size and number of storage cabinets (even for optical) for a 100–250-user system exceeds office parameters.

☞ Small UNIX workstation, MBS and MRS equipment all make good neighbours in an office environment. Their sound and space requirements are not excessive.

Maintain or enhance competitiveness

The leverage available from open systems, as it relates to the environment in which the organization does business, may be employed to maintain or enhance the competitive position of the organization. This particular business objective is perhaps the easiest one to link to open systems. With increasing pressures on government organizations to do more with less, and with the globalization of trade and commerce, both private and public sector organizations are seeking to perform their business missions in as rational, efficient and competitive a manner as possible.

☞ When open systems are widely installed they let you manage virtually *all* of your organization's information on a more integrated and rational basis. Information is easier to find, move around and extract from the computer. This can help your business be more competitive.

Maximize capability to exploit expansion opportunities

In the highly unpredictable business and financial environment of the last five to seven years, many organizations have been presented with previously undreamed-of opportunities for expansion of their business operations. Such expansions demand not only a rapid response but also the ability to 'scale up' systems, application, the IT staff and also the end-user self-support capability, to the extent that it may exist throughout various elements of the organization. Because of their scalability and interoperability—and because of their consistency and ability to promote people transferability—open systems permit an organization to exploit an expansion opportunity much more rapidly than do closed, proprietary systems.

☞ Open systems can be scaled up (or down) more quickly than proprietary systems; you can expand or shrink an existing computer's power or you can move the computer program you are using to a bigger or smaller computer literally overnight in some cases. This lets your organization respond faster to changes in the outside world. Most proprietary operating systems do not run on four or even three processing tiers but are confined to one or two. This is not a hard-and-fast rule, however, since DEC's VMS operating system can run on VAX processors from the desktop to the computer room.

Maximize flexibility and resilience in conditions of change

Apart from rapid expansion or contraction, there are many other situations in the current private and public sector environments which call upon an organization to plan and implement change rapidly. These may include budget cuts, mandate changes, demise of suppliers or customers, disappearance of whole markets due to political, economic, financial or environmental factors, reorientation or restructuring of the organization due to leveraged buyouts or takeovers or similar financial caprice, death of key officers, destruction or loss of productive facilities, strikes, boycotts, riots, revolutions, etc. (indeed, most other insurable perils and some which are not insurable). Many of these changes can be accommodated by the features and characteristics of open systems discussed elsewhere in this book; some such changes draw on another important fact about open systems. For some years, IT organizations have been actively involved in seeking to prepare for the most trying of these change conditions with 'disaster' or 'contingency' planning, often involving outside organizations specializing in providing cold or hot standby facilities and other support. A less costly means of providing for support is mutual backup and off-site storage with one or more 'buddy' sites inside or outside the organization who operate very similar or identical equipment, certainly equipment using the same operating system, packages and networking. Proprietary installations will, in the future, increasingly find themselves 'islanded' with fewer and fewer potential candidate 'buddies' available. Conversely, open system sites will find more and more potential buddy sites as the penetration of open systems, on platforms of all sizes, proceeds apace.

☞ As more and more companies and governments move to open systems, it will be progressively easier in times of peril to find people with expertise and facilities to back up your own.

Reduce response time

In seeking to respond to more routine demands made of the organization, be it to requests from the CEO, processing insurance claims, delivering model aircraft kits to retailers or moving trains over a railway, open systems provide the ability to reduce response time. The organization can better respond to all of the following:

- Changes in business environment (major change in demand);
- Changes in the regulatory environment (new compliance condition and/or documentation requirement);
- Change in product or service to be purchased or sold;
- Change in organization dictated by one or more of the above.

This is so because open systems regularize the access to information and reduce the extent to which organizational positional authority, time, space and foreknowledge are real or potential barriers to such access. If the people who have to plan or implement a change can get to and/or change the impacted information more rapidly, they can then more rapidly influence the additional information, goods and/or services intended to be involved in the change.

☞ You can move more quickly when you can find, manipulate and extract the information you want right away without waiting for your subordinates to argue over which computer contains it, whose version of the data is most accurate or who should convert or even re-input the data to get it to the place you want it, in the format you want it and when you want it.

Access more applications than for any proprietary operating system (except the single-architecture DOS/INTEL standard)

There is no doubt that the DOS/INTEL standard is the most successful computer architecture yet devised and commercially implemented. More systems have been installed, and a larger software supply/demand market exists, than for any other combination of operating system and processor architecture. The market is competitive in all aspects, except for the supply of the operating system and the processor architecture themselves: the former comes only from Microsoft and the latter only from Intel. UNIX, unlike DOS, is not restricted to a single-processor architecture and can take advantage much more rapidly both of growth within a processor architecture *and* the arrival of new architectures on the scene. In contrast, DOS could take advantage of only a small portion of the power expansion of the Intel 80286 over the 8086 and was completely overwhelmed by the 80386 and 80486 in so far as its ability to exploit hardware advances was concerned. (Indeed, that is one of the reasons why OS/2 was proposed.) Further, while all UNIX licences originate from AT&T, the unit which produced UNIX will almost certainly function in the future as though it were just as independent of the hardware vendor community as is Microsoft. The very existence of OSF has helped to ensure that this is the case.

> ☞ UNIX software is rapidly moving to the 'shrink-wrap' stage; you can buy off-the-shelf products today for UNIX just as you can for DOS. Virtually all major software producers with products running on proprietary minicomputer or mainframe computers are now also writing for or converting to UNIX. There will be no lack of UNIX software products. For example, the 1992 Santa Cruz Operation (SCO) Directory of UNIX/XENIX products contains hundreds of pages of software product descriptions. Similarly, the application product catalogs issued by RDBMS vendors such as INFORMIX and ORACLE contain many hundreds of packages which will run under UNIX and often other operating systems with their databases.

Provide the application developer with the best possible environment

The highly symbiotic relationship between the C programming language and the UNIX operating system (which is itself implemented, for the most part, in C) as well as the perfect scalability of RISC-based open computing systems allow the development system environment to be honed to the needs of the individual developer. Development, test and acceptance can be conducted on the same machine or can each be accomplished on a separate platform (perhaps varying in scale/tier) as required. Very few proprietary systems offer such flexibility in keying supplied system resources to developer requirements.

☞ Once programmers become accustomed to them, the C language and UNIX offer many synergies and capabilities not as readily available in proprietary systems. Providing vendor extensions are used with extreme care, or preferably not at all, portability of the resulting programs can be safeguarded.

Balance developer creativity and discipline

While C is a very powerful programming language it differs in a number of important ways from languages such as COBOL and FORTRAN. Once an application developer is fully competent with the C language, and accepts the discipline it often requires, there is considerable scope for creativity. Also, an increasing number of CASE tools now generate C code, with or without embedded SQL statements. A linguistic 'glue' tends to be required even for the most RDBMS-oriented applications today because many of the extended database application 'languages' offered by RDBMS vendors (such as ORACLE's PL/SQL) are *not* compilable. Use of an 'interpreted' paradigm is not always appropriate.

☞ This balance between creativity and discipline of programmers is not only an opportunity; it is a must! Failure to act in a disciplined manner can result in disorganized computer programs just as surely as in a proprietary environment. The good news is that open systems make this balance easier to achieve and maintain.

Utilize OSI to unite existing proprietary environments

Of course, OSI networking can link together and permit limited interoperability of otherwise completely incompatible 'legacy' systems. The only alternative outside the open systems realm is to buy Vendor A's complete interworking products for linking (vanilla only) Vendor B systems into his A-Network, or vice versa. Such products rarely treat the other vendor's products as true peers and usually force a reflex response to any upgrades in the system being 'worked in' to the A-Network.

☞ You can use OSI communications to tie both open and closed systems together and get them at least to exchange information, starting today. Then, as time and resources permit, you can gradually replace the proprietary systems one by one.

Faster introduction of new information technology products

Because OSI and UNIX are not tightly coupled to any specific type of processor architecture, physical communications media, front-end processor, terminal-to-terminal access, user interface or other device, they cannot be hidebound by the same. In other words, UNIX and OSI are 'technologically footloose' and can easily facilitate migration to a new and better technology in any of these areas, usually as soon as it becomes available. Conversely, a proprietary installation can move forward only if or when its own (or a plug-compatible) vendor adopts a new technology.

☞ It is easier to bring in new computers, based on new technologies, and replace existing hardware without gross disruptions when you have open systems.

Faster introduction of new technology related to organization's business area

Of even greater importance to senior and line management is the fact that the improved access to information—and better computer inter-operability—which open systems provide, allow a faster change of whatever other kinds of non-computer technology the organization uses to perform its business mission. Government defence and procurement agencies have learned that the use of open systems by firms designing and building vehicles and weapon systems permits the more rapid adoption of new technology for manufacturing purposes and/or directly inherent in the products themselves. Several oil companies were early supporters of the User Alliance because it is also true that in their (process-oriented) business, open systems permit faster adoption of new technology. In a highly competitive market, fast adoption of new operating technologies—by many types of businesses—may be crucial to the survival of individual organizations.

☞ Because you can more easily exchange information among your own computers, and with those of your suppliers and customers, it is easier to change other technology-related items in your business operation when you have open systems in service. Also, many computers used to control production and other operational processes now run UNIX so you can have them communicate more easily with the UNIX computers used by your planners or engineers.

Provide system facilities not otherwise available

Open systems can make possible the provision of facilities or services not otherwise able to be made available. Many developers of new kinds of software and new kinds of peripherals are not even thinking of developing for proprietary environments. New applications and devices simply will not be appearing as frequently on proprietary systems. There are *already* more firms developing add-on products for the open systems world than there are for any proprietary system except the DOS/INTEL standard. Of course, the latter has become so widely accepted as a *de facto* standard that it might as well be a *de jure* standard. No one supplier monopolizes the supply of *anything* but the processor and operating system itself.

☞ Open systems will over the next few years give you just as much choice of add-ons, for systems of all shapes and sizes from PC to mainframe, as you have for the IBM-compatible PC today.

Provide full UNIX transaction processing system

UNIX now offers the opportunity to provide fully proven transaction processing systems at the Unit, Area and Enterprise tiers of processing.

☞ You can now safely use UNIX computers to track and control transaction-intensive real-world activities such as reservations or banking. The real benefit from this is that it will help you integrate transaction processing with other business processes if you use UNIX on other computers too.

Integrate existing GUIs/windowing systems

Many organizations are unsure as to what strategic decisions to take regarding a choice of GUI. This issue extends far beyond the warring UNIX camps (UI and OSF) and even beyond the (now waning) debate over whether proprietary or open systems are preferable. Open systems permit an organization to put off the choice of a GUI (if indeed a single one must be chosen) for at least another 12–18 months secure in the knowledge that, whichever is the victorious GUI or family of GUIs, it will almost certainly be available for a UNIX environment and will contemplate the existence of OSI networks. However, some organizations are not in a position to wait that long because they have adopted a single OS and RDBMS and now want to move to a 'develop once for all' strategy for application development. Where an organization has selected a GUI, if another subsequently becomes the standard, open systems will lessen the disruption and 'pain' of conversion to the winning GUI. The transition can certainly be more gradual.

☞ Usually, open systems let you dither for a considerable time in your choice of the display method, whereby programs will present themselves to the user. This is important when you have trouble choosing between competing 'windowing' standards, each of which claims that only it will ultimately be the dominant one. Selecting a graphical user interface is not unlike choosing one's religious or denominational affiliation.

Improve compliance to business/industry/trade, contractual and regulatory operating requirements

In many situations, migration to OSI and/or EDI requires the adoption of at least some industry standards beyond those set by vendors of closed, proprietary systems.

☛ Here, the title is almost longer than the section, and that is no accident. This is totally context-dependent according to your business or industry. Most firms selling products to government will be *forced* to design and produce them using open systems technology to manage the process because these are the only type of systems government agencies will, in future, be prepared to interface with. The US Department of Defense Computer Aided Logistics System (CALS) activity is but one example.

Strategic opportunities

Provide three-axis data/work environment/application portability

As discussed earlier, it is possible to have portability on the *vertical*, *horizontal* and *forward* axes. This portability can extend to all of:

- Applications
- Data
- Packages (OA, RDBMS, etc.)
- User work environment (scripts/shells/directories)
- Other system architecture components

☛ You can move data, programs, files, directories and other 'non-hardware' items around among computers of different manufacture and different sizes, almost *ad infinitum*, as your requirements change. Here, we are talking about a requirement induced by the program or its users, rather than avoiding a constraint imposed by the machine.

Scalability

Scalability opportunities can be considered in terms of the present value of *not* having to undertake a major replacement of a system at a given time in the future. The avoidance of all or most of the planning/acquisition phase activities otherwise required is a part of this future-year saving. In virtually all cases, open computing systems are more scalable than those which are not. Applications can be migrated up- or down-tier as required and configuration-induced blockage or failure, and attendant user frustration, can be avoided. It is possible to change the supplied platform rapidly in response to changes in the workgroup, workload or other elements.

☞ When you outgrow a given machine, it is easier to upgrade it or to move the program to a bigger one. Here, we are talking about avoiding a constraint imposed by the machine by simply going around it.

Interoperability

Interoperability of systems which are both open computing systems is possible even without OSI, but is more effective when OSI communications are employed. Conversely, OSI networking permits at least some interoperability of otherwise closed and incompatible systems. Clearly, there is an OSI–OCS synergy. Interoperability can occur within an organization's purview or between/among organizations. The EDI-oriented business environment—even today—demands that an organization have, or at least be willing to move quickly to, interoperability. To fail to do so is to say to customers and suppliers that one is not concerned whether or not they continue to have a relationship with the organization in the future.

☞ Open systems work very well with each other and work moderately well with closed systems. Differing closed systems generally do not work as well together.

Unified configuration management

Open systems permit a much more logical and unified form of central software (application/package/system), hardware and network configuration management (CM) than do any proprietary systems, even those with the most comprehensive closed architectures.

☞ You can track and control the state of many computers, and their respective programs, more easily with open systems, particularly when the computers are geographically distributed. This is because, when using OSI networking, open systems tend to treat each other as equals or 'peers', whereas many proprietary networks are hierarchical and centralist; only the network control centre can issue commands. Remote devices cannot issue commands to each other, nor can they cooperate effectively. By analogy, open systems are like organizations populated by 'empowered' employees while closed networks are like those full of 'bossed' employees.

Remote system administration and system management

Current technology open systems permit many system administration tasks and a substantial portion of system management responsibilities to be handled remotely, even from one central site for the whole organization. In the late 1980s the prospects for remote system administration of 50- or 100-user UNIX systems did not look very good. Today, a significant role can be accorded to remote system administration, but there is still a very strong argument for ensuring there is a real person on-site who knows the machine well.

☞ This is not unlike the argument for keeping a pilot on board an otherwise automated aircraft. We have all heard the joke about the airliner flown by a robot who announces that nothing can go wrong, go wrong, go wrong.... Quite apart from daily or weekly backups, adding new users and so on (which a paraprofessional at the site can do) you need people to monitor security and usage growth (so you have enough lead time to upgrade the machine before it is swamped) and to keep track of the actual software and hardware configuration as it evolves.

Easy hardware upgrade in symmetric multiprocessing environment

UNIX symmetric multiprocessing equipment permits a very easy and non-disruptive upgrade with or among product lines. Most proprietary symmetric multiprocessing systems (and *all* non-symmetric systems) make upgrade more expensive and less convenient.

☞ UNIX generally makes it easier to upgrade the very powerful multi-processor computers.

Hone sourcing strategy to specific system architecture component

As cited earlier, the organization can plan to hone the sourcing strategy for each component or class of system to the needs of the user communities for such systems. The type of certification, the number of suppliers, the means of supply, the method of integration and the means of support can all be customized on a by-component basis. Most proprietary vendors arrange their service provision, contractual and pricing policies to discourage this sort of flexibility and third-party sourcing on the part of the customer organization.

☞ For each class of computer you buy, you can decide the best means of buying it. Where you want to benefit from vendor competition, you have the opportunity to do so. Where the time and complexity of arranging a competition is not warranted, you can buy from a single vendor.

The home workplace: telecommuting and workplace decentralization

Because UNIX systems permit the file system, and routine system administration tasks, for a home worker's UNIX workstation to be remotely managed from a UNIX workstation or MRS at an IT facility, more people can work at home more of the time without the burden of having to manage the technology actually installed in their homes themselves.

☞ As stated above, open systems and the home workplace are complementary.

Develop applications once for all platforms

Once languages, CASE tools, RDBMSs, GUIs and other 'commonizers' have been selected, it is quite possible, as one RDBMS vendor's advertisements put it, to develop applications once for use on all platforms in the organization. This is a less profound manifestation of the three axes of portability discussed above.

☞ If all computers can run the same kinds of programs, you only have to write a program once and then you can use it on any computer.

Network expandability

OSI networks can be easily, almost seamlessly in many cases, expanded without disruption of end-users and without burdensome re-initialization, reglobalization of naming or other such hindrances. X.500 expressly addresses this problem in various ways.

☞ With OSI and OCS you can make your network bigger or smaller and users won't notice the changes.

Increased potential for software re-engineering

With products such as Unikix providing a coherent CICS emulator and with Software AG porting its ADABAS and NATURAL to the UNIX environment, many IT installations with very large inventories of 'legacy systems' can move to open system platforms much more rapidly than was thought possible previously. Of course, if an organization owns millions of lines of COBOL (for example, tied to ADABAS or a similar product) the direct and indirect costs of moving through such a conversion are not trivial. However, open systems none the less increase the potential for such conversion. If such an organization were, for example, to buy a new technology proprietary system incompatible with ADABAS and NATURAL, then any application to be migrated would face a complete rewrite anyway.

☞ You can convert many of your old programs to run on the new computers. As stated earlier, you will only have to convert them once and then they will be able to run on *all* your open systems, now and in the future.

Unlock corporate information base to all potential users

This is one of the most important opportunities presented by open systems. Data can be much more easily transported, reformatted and presented to those who need it, whether this is a one-time or a continuous process, than was ever possible before. Manual re-input basically disappears and so too does the threat of time wastage and frustration (well-nigh boredom) which such re-input used to hold over those contemplating accessing such information. The dragon disappears and so does its shadow! This permits unification of the corporate information base because even when physical unification or integration is not yet complete, people start to behave as though it were complete. They are not shy about asking to have the spreadsheets from System X merged with the list from System Y, using the graphics from System Z, and all bundled onto System A for download to the director's portable PC which is to be taken on a flight tomorrow morning! They know it can be done and they are just as demanding as if a full (i.e. RDBMS-spurred) physical unification of the data had already occurred. Like *Star Trek: The Next Generation*'s Captain Picard, they are much more apt to simply and blandly request: 'Make it so!'

☞ Existing data and applications can be made available to new users and there is better, and more consistent, use of information. It is easier to get the right information to the right person in the right form at the right time. (Failing any of these 'rights', the information may be welcomed as useless or, worse, the provider may be fired. Canada's weather service, Environment Canada, once forecast and issued a weather warning for a very severe storm after it had occurred!) Better inter- and intra-organizational liaison is thus made possible and there is improved communications and understanding between/ among workers and line management in cooperating organizations.

Match technology supplied more precisely to user requirement

The platform can be more precisely matched to the user or workgroup. This substantial opportunity also imposes on IT the very substantial responsibility to do it right. The health of the workgroup can be impacted by a poor system prescription from IT just as surely as the health of the individual for whom a doctor prescribes the wrong medicine. Comprehensive and consistent planning tools will be required and it is clear that they do not now exist. IT can select the platform with the best mix of capabilities for a given workgroup and, not being confined to one vendor's product line, is not forced to 'overbuy' a system with unwanted Feature X just because the workgroup needs Feature Y. Someone else's system undoubtedly offers the one without the other. The first vendor will therefore either discount the price by the value of the unwanted feature or lose the sale.

☞ With open systems, it is easier to give each person just the right amount and type of computing power.

Wide access to open systems skills

Most colleges and universities now use UNIX at the workstation, mid-range and often at the larger system levels. Therefore, new graduates, and those existing IT staff members who are seeking to stay current, are already familiar with UNIX (usually with more than one flavour), with OSI networking, with modern X-related GUIs and with other aspects of the open systems environment.

☞ Many seasoned computer professionals, and all the bright young graduates, are learning open systems. In the future, computer specialists who know about open systems will be easy to find, and easy to move from one kind of computer to another. Computer specialists for closed systems will become scarce (not soon but eventually) and will remain hard to transfer from one closed system to another.

Utilize the same packages at all processing tiers

It is possible to run the same packages at all processing tiers. For example, you could choose to run the ORACLE RDBMS at the workplace tier under DOS and UNIX, at the workgroup tier on MRS equipment under UNIX, at the regional/divisional tier on mid-frame equipment under UNIX and at the corporate or mainframe tier under both UNIX and your proprietary system. This is also true for some office-automation packages.

☞ Users who have a PC or a UNIX workstation can run a given program requiring, for example, a database on that computer. Users who do not have a PC run the same program on a larger computer with the same database. It will run basically the same way on all the computers.

Application placement flexibility

Open systems give much more flexibility in the placement of an application among processing tiers. Some placements are obvious: in most cases a single-user and non-corporate application best resides on the desktop or an MBS server and usually a 3000-user application will go to a mainframe. Many placements, however, are not nearly so obvious, particularly when, for example, UNIX-based ORACLE and X.25

access are available at three or four processing tiers, as the case may be. The organization must decide which application placement method or approach to use:

- Implement the 'statute law approach' by endeavouring to develop a rigorous, structured and codified approach to application placement which is tier, service model and vendor neutral and which is also seen to be so.
- Utilize the 'common law approach' wherein it is accepted that a body of precedent, over successive placement decisions, will determine how applications are to be placed.
- Take no action and, by default, utilize a *laissez-faire* approach wherein IT neither intervenes nor cares where users place applications, and merely responds to capacity demands by providing more underlying processing technology and communications services wherever and whenever they are demanded.

The third approach is, of course, an almost certain means of ensuring that the CIO is sooner or later relieved of his or her responsibilities! IT will never be able to keep up with the helter-skelter chorus of demands for more of this and that everywhere and no one will be happy. Senior management won't like the cost of meeting all the demands for more systems and will wonder out loud what happened to all the alleged savings from open systems. Further, many installed platforms will be severely under-utilized while neighbouring units clamour for more processing power. Still other units will employ 'spare tire money' to buy 'spare' systems and tuck them away in back rooms for use on some future rainy day or to trade for desks or space with other line managers. (I am not speaking here of any specific organization but addressing general principles of how large organizations function, based on my experience over the past 12 years.)

☞ Open systems let you develop or buy the computer program first and decide later what size and type of computer to put it on and where that computer should be located. This is a very big advantage, since, for example, a program for a DOS PC cannot run on an IBM MVS mainframe and vice versa. However, this wonderful new freedom must be used consistently and responsibly; otherwise you will end up with many programs sitting in places where they do *not* belong and will be faced with endless demands for more computing power. You may not want to put an 80-user program on a 100-user system which it will overcapacitate in six months. Nor may you want to put the program containing all the confidential personnel records which used to live in a big minicomputer on an equally powerful UNIX workstation on a desk in an open concept office, where a summer student who also is a computer hacker may access and print them. The freedom to be creative in deciding where to put programs is also the freedom to make very serious mistakes. You need a consistent and logical method of deciding where to put programs, which addresses what size and type of computer, what operating conditions and what level of service the users are to have.

Adopt system architecture-driven approach

Adoption of open systems brings with it the opportunity, and also almost the compulsion, to move to a system architecture-driven approach. This should embrace all of:

- Planning
- System specification and acquisition
- Application specification and acquisition
- Application migration and system upgrade
- User orientation, training and education

☞ Road builders tend to let the landscape dictate to them the elevation and gradients of the roads, because vehicles with rubber tires are quite good at climbing hills. Railway builders do not bend to the landscape, because trains can only climb a very shallow gradient. Railway builders use the rules of their 'architecture' as they fashion their desired infrastructure, and where the geography does not cooperate they go to great lengths (and heights and depths) to *make* it cooperate. With an architecture, you stand a much better chance of *making* the technology do what you want, not what its vendor wants.

Framework for future expansion

Once a coherent system architecture is in place and, as maturing standards are continuously embraced and adopted, expansion of any element of the system architecture—whether in response to technology-push or demand-pull factors—is much easier than is presently the case with one or more closed, proprietary systems.

☞ If you build your tunnels and your trestles wide enough, adding a second railway line is easy. Similarly, once you have conquered the architectural battles, dealt with in more detail in the next chapter, it is easier to bring about consistent expansion of your installed computer capabilities.

Allow organization to be business-driven, not technology-driven

The organization, particularly its top management, can then stop worrying about the technology necessary to store, process and transport information and can refocus on its prime business mission. Over the past several years the only thing rising faster than IT budgets, in many large organizations, has been the amount of senior management time CIOs and their staffs have been demanding. Much of this time has been used to bombard and sometimes bombast top executives with what many of them call the 'high-tech alphabet soup' of names, acronyms and even acronyms within acronyms. It has been said, not in jest, that the only sphere of influence with more acronyms than the advanced technology industry is the Pentagon! Who provides the firm's long-distance network services and what colour logo is on the CEO's personal workstation or the corporation's mainframe will be of no more concern in the future than what colour telephone the CIO's golfing partner's secretary has!

☞ If you implement open systems correctly, the IT fraternity becomes much smaller and easier for the rest of the company to work with. *All* of the computers begin to be seen far more as tools for use by everyone in the organization and far less as a threat. This allows people to concentrate on their business, not on trying to learn yet another new computer or fighting with the IT department.

Improve organizational 'mergeability'

It has been stated in the literature that a number of recent mergers have been scuttled when convinced CEOs introduced to each other their respective CIOs who, basically, didn't speak the same language. The CIOs, like the fictional Great Lords of Blufuscu, were part of camps which 'since the time of His Majesty's Grandfather' had engaged in bitter debate among the Littlendians and the Bigendians. ... Where information systems are crucial to the business of both would-be merger partners, inability (due to technology, pride, prejudice or whatever) to merge the systems of the two companies would negate many of the other benefits of merger. All of the costs of merger would be incurred but not all of the benefits would be realized. Two vehicles, where one is wired negative ground and the other is wired positive ground, must be electrically linked only with great care, as was often learned in Canada and the UK during the Second World War. It is likely that by the late 1990s no one will want to buy out or be bought out by an organization not committed to, and indeed using, open systems.

☞ If you do not move to open systems, by the end of the 1990s other firms with which you do business (including those you might buy out or who might buy you out) will believe that you have weird and undesirable computer systems. They may avoid you like the plague.

Improve organizational 'downsizability'

There is a strong case to be made that 'fiscal responsibility' and attendant downsizing has become out of control in North America; perhaps the entire continent is not cost-justified! Nevertheless, it is clear that where there is a good and rational case for reducing the size of the organization, open systems can act as a force multiplier by reducing the cost of automating much of the organization's workload.

☞ Open systems reduce the cost of buying computers, of writing programs for computers and—in the long run—of supporting computers. In the short term, however, they tend to increase the cost of supporting computers by forcing you to make or buy more of the support for yourself and rely less on one vendor or a small number of vendors for such support. Open systems can be used to help accomplish staff cuts by letting you do more work with fewer people. Note, however, that open systems are unlikely to allow you to make big cuts in the IT department which will probably stay about the same size, but will permit you to reassign people from maintaining ancient COBOL programs to supporting paraprofessionals and end-users in the field.

Improve IT response time to user requests

With open systems, for many of the reasons discussed under the Tactical Opportunities section, IT can respond much more quickly to routine, urgent or emergency user requests. Development for open systems can often be accomplished more rapidly and far more of the hopefully very modular code developed can be placed in huge libraries for re-use in other applications.

☞ If your users are sick and tired of waiting anything from 18 months to two or three years for the IT experts to develop a small application or upgrade an existing one from a LAN/MBS situation to a larger machine, then open systems will help you. The IT people can treat more of the small subprograms they write as building blocks which can be re-used to construct most of the program a given user group needs. This speeds up development. Also, once a program is developed for one group it can be placed in a central Registry and easily carried to another workgroup's machine when called for, without any further development. In such circumstances, development time is precisely zero.

Adopt common and simpler graphical user interfaces (GUIs)

Open systems offer at least the potential of adopting a single GUI for use on:

- Mainframe and minicomputer connected terminals
- Terminals connected to modern MRS and MBS equipment
- UNIX workstations
- DOS clients of UNIX-based MBS equipment
- DOS workstations

☞ Open systems help you adopt a single method of graphical on-screen presentation for use by all users on all terminals and PCs. This means that all or most programs running on all sizes of computers will, for example, use the same key for the HELP key, have the same style of on-screen presentation and so on.

Align OSI, open computing systems and corporate application development strategy

When OSI, UNIX-based open computing systems and the various elements of the corporate development strategy (languages, CASE tools, information engineering tools, packages, RDBMS, role of software registry, etc.) are all aligned, the opportunity exists to maximize the synergy among these elements, providing internally consistent choices are made for each element.

☞ If you pick your UNIX operating system, your computers (however many vendors you settle on), your database and your development tools and languages all at the same time, and in concert with each other, you can make sure they all work very well together.

Create own customized interoperability environment

The organization can, where necessary, extend or abridge current or evolving *de jure* or *de facto* open system standards to ensure that precise internal requirements are met. This may touch such areas as GUI, transaction processing, security and others.

☞ Where outside standards do not exist, you may decide to make informal or formal interim standards inside your own organization until *de facto* or *de jure* standards emerge.

Achieve consistency in standard/profile/option selection

Once the organization has moved through the *totally inevitable* learning curve of setting a system architecture and actually adopting and using a number of standards and profiles, it is possible to strive for and achieve a consistency of approach in how a standard is embraced, adopted and subsequently implemented. Where this is achieved, IT consistency, coherence and predictability for end-users is further enhanced.

☞ The more you use standards to specify, buy and operate computer hardware and software, and communications products and services, the easier it becomes to use them in a consistent manner. With open systems, as with much else, practice makes perfect.

Increase extent to which information is treated as an asset

When information is always accessible, whether synthetically or actually integrated into a coherent whole, line managers and their end-users can treat information as an asset. Nobody is prepared to believe that something they cannot access is really an asset. Even those who keep bonds in safety deposit boxes frequently go and ask for them just to be assured they are still there and still intact. No one disputes the value of good information but, heretofore, getting hold of precisely the *right* information, in the desired form, has not been easy.

> ☞ Experts estimate that 85 per cent of the information stored on paper and filed away is never accessed again until it is disposed of. There is little reason to believe that a similar percentage does not also hold true for much of the information stored electronically over the past 10 or 15 years. Open systems help more people get at more of the information they can use more easily. If you believe information is an asset, then more use of that asset (providing the use is productive) will benefit your organization. If you do not believe information is an asset, you have wasted your money on this book.

Let IT concentrate on improving user interfaces and applications

With open systems, once a sane acquisition/support regime is in place for each system architecture component, IT can spend less time trying to match wits with technology itself (or, worse, with a proprietary vendor bent on maintaining 'account control') and more time trying to help users get the most out of what technology the organization has.

> ☞ The word *information* is more important than the word *technology* in the expression IT. No organization buys computer technology for its own sake, but rather because it helps manage information more effectively and efficiently. When the IT experts get on top of the technology they can spend more time helping the rest of your workers better manage information. Open systems help them to do this.

Provide UNIX programming benefits

As developers move down the UNIX/C learning curve, successively developed programs written from scratch and/or with CASE tools will exhibit significant synergies not possible with operating systems and programming languages more divorced than UNIX and C.

> ☞ Open systems help programmers do a better job because of important links between the UNIX operating system and C programming language.

Evolve organization from hierarchy basis to knowledge basis

Over time, it is possible to utilize open systems not only to increase the sharing and hence the value of information but also to facilitate the transition from the traditional hierarchically based (positional authority) organization to the knowledge-based (informational authority) organization. Information becomes much more important in the overall scheme of things, just as law became much more important in England after the signing of the Magna Carta in 1215. After that time, and even more with the advent of responsible government a few centuries later, the law governed everyone, even the monarch. Similarly, as information becomes more important, it has a greater effect on everyone, even a potentially capricious top management. Even top management is subject to information.

☞ The easier it is to get at and use information, the better informed and effective everyone in the organization can become. Open systems make information easier to access and use.

Change organizational culture

In almost all cases, whole or partial evolution from the traditional to the knowledge-based information will also occasion a change in organizational culture.

☞ When bosses monopolized much of the information, subordinates were often in the dark on what was happening except in their own little cubicles. When more people can access more of the information, unduly authoritarian and conservative superiors have much more trouble justifying stupid decisions and making them stick. Open systems usually increase the equality of access to information.

Provide more precise alignment

More precise alignment is needed of:
- Business requirements
- Information requirements
- Technology, communications and support provided

This is related to the linking of open systems to business objectives in the minds of senior management. Once open systems are in place, there are fewer links and hence fewer potential kinks in the chain between objective setting and actual on-the-ground performance of the organization's work.

☞ Open systems give the organization more leverage in linking the funds spent on IT to business requirements because they allow information handling needs to be defined much more generically. Again, using a *Star Trek: The Next Generation* example, Captain Picard doesn't tell the chief engineer what to bypass with what (although LaForge must be the universe's best 'bypasser'), he simply tells him that he wants more power to the warp drive, the shields, the tractor beam or whatever. He lets the specialists work out the linkages. Likewise, top management can say that we want more transaction processing capabilities because we are going to bring more of the reservations function in-house, we want more power to the desktop or we need a fleet dispatchability report every morning on the desk of the Vice-President of Operations.

Consolidate networks

In most cases, the advent of OSI networking (particularly when accompanied by open computing systems running UNIX) permits the number of networks operated by a medium-sized or large organization to be reduced, sometimes to just one. Such a network can handle voice plus all of the 'objects' we now consider important in computing and communications.

☞ Open systems networks usually grow and divert traffic from proprietary ones, once they are installed and working well. This will allow you to halt proprietary network growth and eventually to move towards one or at least fewer networks.

Optimize pace of technology adoption

This must be done in terms of:

- Elapsed time
- Risk
- Cost

The faster new technology is adopted for IT and/or for the performance of the organization's core business where the two differ, the greater the risk and, in general, the greater the cost. Open systems provide a wider range of choices in the speed of technology acquisition and implementation than do proprietary systems where the organization is quite literally at the mercy of one vendor's engineering and marketing departments. The organization can adopt *avant-garde* processing technologies which run UNIX or wait until they become mainstream. There is most often no range of *avant-garde* to current to past technologies available on the market for proprietary operating system environments; all or most products come from one vendor or from a market very heavily dominated by one vendor and represent what that vendor thinks is now the best thing to offer.

☞ You can adopt open systems as quickly or as slowly as you like. This book recommends you take a moderate pace, perhaps accelerating as you gain confidence.

Tactical benefits

Business applications

Business applications are not, of course, restricted to open systems, but there may be incremental benefits to running a given application—even for one user group—on an open system versus a closed one. In almost no cases, except where RDBMS package version features under UNIX lag those of versions on a proprietary system, will moving to open systems provide less basic functionality from the same application. To consider the benefit of running a given business application:

- Estimate time savings and productivity gains for each business application implemented during the five-year life cycle of the cost estimate — assume no benefits realized *during* the year of implementation but only beginning in subsequent year. Assumptions should be as follows:
  - Use current dollars;
  - Average fully allocated person–year costs (re: savings);
  - Five-year life cycle for all costs/benefits.

☞ Open systems give you a much wider choice in where to get your business applications in the first place. Once stabilized, they will also let you run the applications with fewer interruptions due to system upgrades or replacements. Thus, they permit each application to provide slightly more benefit than the same application would running on a proprietary system, assuming only that availability and consistency of service from the application are worth something to you.

Office automation

One organization learned, through an extensive series of OA trials, that, on average, an OA system can bring about time and material savings worth approximately $10 000 per worker per year! These have been well documented. Platforms that can be placed near the workers, and which reliably deliver OA, occasion very significant lifetime benefits. Again, there are fully and partially proprietary platforms capable of delivering OA and they too can offer benefits of this magnitude, but they do not offer the additional opportunities discussed earlier. To consider those items which are always OA benefits:

- Assume that OA, where utilized, is implemented at the outset of system life and is made available to *all* information workers connected to the system;
- Savings estimated on a per-person basis at up to $10 000.

☞ A key phrase above is 'near the workers'. If you run OA on a mainframe to offer services to all of your workers, including those in field offices, you will incur very significant network communications charges. At an office thousands of miles from the mainframe, when one worker sends an electronic mail message (E-mail) to a colleague down the corridor, they both end up communicating with that central system. Further, there is probably absolutely no requirement for either of them to check the agenda of someone who works in another field office and uses OA on that same mainframe. They therefore do *not* need to share an OA work environment with that person. Using UNIX-based multi-user MRS equipment to deliver full function OA at the workgroup level, with peer-to-peer connections to the network, is far more efficient in terms of communications and hardware costs. In other words, it takes less installed equipment and communications services to deliver the same service to the same user. Also, that user will usually have to wait less time for a response each time the <RETURN> key is touched.

☞ Certainly, you can install workgroup OA with a proprietary MRS but you cannot get the degree of interoperability you have with an open system. If proprietary systems from another vendor are installed at other field offices, E-mail exchange becomes more complicated, even where full OSI networking, X.400 and X.500 are in place. It is possible to make this approach work, but this extra hassle is avoidable with open systems.

PC support by MRSA or LANA

Where the arrival of the sort of multi-user and/or client/server platform which UNIX/RISC makes practical for a workgroup brings with it a trained/certified administrator, there are benefits to the existing PC users at that site:

* Estimated to save each PC user 10 hours per year in seeking outside help with packages and applications and each mainframe application user 5 hours per year by providing more readily accessible local support for frequently used mainframe applications.

☞ It was really the UNIX MRS vendors who pioneered and commercialized fully office-compatible multi-user systems able to support substantial numbers of users. While some minicomputer vendors had low-end office models in the early 1980s, they preferred to have you accommodate demand growth not by cloning the small system but by growing up to their bigger minicomputer. The latter was usually much more expensive, even on a per-user basis, especially when operating system and third-party software licensing and support costs were considered.

Increased access to mainframe

In most organizations, mainframes will *not* disappear but will gradually (in some cases abruptly, if the mainframe vendor is forcibly ejected) cease to be logic processors and serve as corporate data/information repositories, indexes and servers. Therefore, where a new technology UNIX system (MRS or MBS) can facilitate better and/or more access to the mainframe (and the information held there) it confers an additional benefit. Open systems, as discussed above, do this much better than closed systems, particularly those which come from a different proprietary vendor than the proprietary mainframe. To assess these benefits:

* Estimate any time-saving value of increased access to mainframe applications for those who can benefit from it—less contention for

existing dumb terminals, more convenient access from PC on each desk, etc.

- Take note, however, that this is only a short-term benefit while the mainframe remains proprietary and thus requires that either its own dedicated terminals and controllers be provided or emulated by the accessing workgroup members—once an OSI or OSI-like network is in place all users everywhere will automatically expect to have access to whichever systems they may from time to time require.

☞ Open systems help users of a given tier of computing get access to the computers on another tier more easily.

Future disruption avoidance

In the future, it will be possible to employ open systems to avoid the types of disruptions often encountered in a proprietary environment. In general, open computing systems minimize the potential cost of disruption due to upgrade or expansion. Such costs can include:

- High conversion costs (to new hardware and operating system);
- Vendor dies leaving product and installation 'stranded' and with no choice but a 'panic conversion', usually to whichever vendor will come in and assist;
- Vendor product line constrains growth (no larger machines are available and cloning is undesirable or impractical);
- Vendor has porting constraints within and/or among product lines, often leading to an almost total rewrite on porting.

☞ Moving to open systems can be quite disruptive, but it could be your last major computing disruption for decades if you do it correctly. All disruptions cost you time and money. Fewer disruptions in the future will cost you less time and money; this is a benefit of open systems. Proprietary operating systems and their underlying processor architectures usually have a life span of 10 years or less, although some have lived to the ripe old age of nearly 20. UNIX lets you jump from one processor architecture to the next with *élan*, unfettered by conversion problems.

Net installed benefit of improved price/performance

A few years ago, North American car manufacturers stopped publishing the gross horsepower of their engines and changed to SAE Net Installed Horsepower; how much power the engine generates in the context of a given installation in a given vehicle. Much the same thing is now required to rid the industry of mountains of marketing and sales hype about MIPS and many other measures of 'power'. None the less, once this has been accomplished, it is certain that the net installed power of

UNIX/RISC systems will still cost far less on a 'pound-for-pound' basis than that available from *any* proprietary processor architecture, RISC or otherwise.

☞ Even after you filter out all the hype and the disagreements about computer power, open computing systems are still provably more powerful for the price than their competitors.

Lower LAN administration costs

In general, open systems are easily integrated with Ethernet and Token Ring LANs, and even to pseudo-LANs. This usually simplifies and thus lowers LAN administration.

☞ You can choose the LAN you want with less fear of vendor lock-in or entrapment.

UNIX/OSI/Ethernet synergies

When used together, the UNIX operating system, OSI networking (particularly for wide area networking within/among organizations) and local Ethernet LANs exhibit considerable synergies. It is no accident that many UNIX workstations are now supplied with built-in Ethernet capability.

☞ UNIX, OSI communications and Ethernet LANs work very well together and you may wish to consider Ethernet as your default LAN specification unless you have a specific reason for not doing so.

Better access to external communications

When OSI communications are employed, it is easier to establish from-scratch basic communications, EDI contact or even complex application interworking with a previously unknown organizational partner.

☞ Increasingly, interorganizational communications will be via OSI networking. In the future, if you don't speak OSI, you will not be able to communicate.

Faster intra-organizational communications

The existence of fewer networks (or even one network) cannot fail to improve and speed up intra-organizational communications.

☞ With fewer networks there are fewer gateways between them and therefore much less can break and there are fewer chances for messages to get scrambled along the way by malfunctioning devices. The Canadian bush pilot's axiom is: 'What you don't have, cannot break!'

Lower cost data transfer

There is lower cost to transfer information over an OSI network, despite the overheads, because the total amount of 'conversion' is less, particularly where open computing systems exist at both ends of the communications transaction.

☞ OSI networks can cut your data communications costs, but not until they are mature and working well.

Better information connectivity (cut re-input)

With better information connectivity fewer person hours are wasted taking the output of one machine and turning it into the manual input for another.

☞ You can get your workers doing more productive things than taking data from one computer and entering it into another.

Improve communications channel/circuit utilization

OSI networks, again despite their often weighty protocol overheads, frequently create situations allowing network managers to improve utilization of existing or new channels, be they virtual or actual, packet or otherwise.

☞ OSI allows network managers to make better use of available communications channels, again saving money.

Permit worker co-function with audio and information (text/graphics) shared workspace

Open systems can fully interoperate, allowing workers to share one or more objects in a common workspace where either (any) of them can impact such object(s) in the full view/cognizance of the others. Of course, the workers need not be together; one might be at Office A, one might be on Vehicle B and one might be sitting at home, near his or her pool.

☞ With open systems, it is easier for workers to work together on the same item even when they are in different places.

Improve people transferability

Once an end-user, site application specialist or DBA, MBS/LAN or ULS Administrator or IT staff member has been trained on a given aspect of OSI or UNIX they tend to be directly transferable to products of other vendors with little adjustment. Conversely, vendors such as IBM and DEC differ right down to the level of how information is encoded and stored in the machine!

☞ Once computer specialists understand one type of open system, it is very easy for them to learn and work with another type.

Reduce software support and upgrade costs

With a systematized means of software planning, acquisition, recycling and support it is possible to reduce software support and upgrade costs substantially. Develop once and for all usually also connotes 'support in one manner for all'.

☞ There is less unique software in your organization (since more of it gets recycled) so it is easier (hence less costly) to support the software.

Lower external support costs because support can be competed

It is not necessary to buy System Integration (SI) or professional support services from the same vendor who provided a hardware or software product to the organization. If original supplier support is unavailable in some geographic areas, is insufficiently comprehensive or quick or costs too much, the organization can generally seek support elsewhere. Even otherwise 'liberal' open system vendors may be confounded by such a practice, but it is undeniably a benefit of open systems. Competing such services will almost always lower the costs, even if the original source vendor wins the bid.

☞ There are more people in the market who can support your software and hardware so you can competitively acquire support services. You don't have to rely on one or a few firms.

Make efficient use of (underlying) heterogeneous communications

It is indeed possible to run OSI communications over certain proprietary networks, although usually with great 'fuss and expense' and only after buying pallet-loads of 'adaptation' products (usually called 'OSI for Network X' or something similar) at very high cost. However, the benefit is that once these are in place, the underlying proprietary network can be treated as though it were truly part of the open systems world. In many cases this makes much more efficient use of the existing network than any other possible strategy.

☞ You can, if required, *force* open and closed networks to live together, even on the same circuits or channels, although the results may be rather like cohabiting a tiger and a bear.

Support highly autonomous workstation users

These workers, be they physically and/or operationally autonomous, have a subset of the requirements of the home workers discussed above. If open systems can well serve home workers they can very well serve the non-standard, and usually highly demanding, autonomous users, providing they will tolerate connection of their workstation—on a continuous or periodic basis—to the network.

☞ With open systems, people who need very powerful desktop or deskside computers can be more easily accommodated. You can meet almost any conceivable requirement of a power-hungry single user with a computer not much bigger than a 29-inch television. Such a box can have much more power than a mainframe which five or six years ago filled hundreds or even thousands of square feet in a computer room.

Multiple applications share the same data

Multiprocessing and distributed processing will permit multiple applications to share the same data coherently without the chaos this would otherwise connote. No proprietary system is at present making the types of advances regarding coordinated distributed processing now being made in the open system community.

☞ Only open systems are making real progress in the challenging field of figuring out how to let multiple programs manipulate (a single copy of) the same data at the same time.

Collaborative application development among organizations

With open systems, different organizations can collaborate on application development without being forced into establishing joint pools of money to hire third parties, and therefore not requiring the involvement of the finance and accounting disciplines. They can do this by simply dividing the work into coherent processing and networking 'chunks', letting each IT shop develop its own piece to form/fit/function specifications and then assembling the result for all to use and enjoy. This process, it might be added, generally also excludes lawyers, another source of complexity, delay and frustration in interorganizational dealings related to cooperation of any kind but particularly to cooperation involving computers.

☞ Open systems let IT managers from different companies 'gang up' on a problem, divide it into chunks and each do their part to solve their respective chunk. They can then assemble the results into one program, of which they can all obtain their own copy. Previously, the odds were almost certain that some of them would have had incompatible systems, meaning that the easiest way was to hire an outside firm to write the solution for everybody, in a lowest common denominator programming language such as purely ANSI COBOL.

Strategic benefits

Lower network investment

With or without consolidation, OSI technologies will, over the medium to long term, almost always result in lower network investment due to less duplication, fewer gateways, fewer pallet-loads of 'OSI for Network XXX' conversion/interface products, etc.

☞ OSI and OCS make networking cheaper, but it takes a while.

UNIX has an inherent network orientation

UNIX has a well-proven inherent network orientation which no vendor 'extensions' have yet managed to dilute, frustrate or ruin.

☞ UNIX and OSI networks were almost made for each other.

Vendor independence as corporate life insurance

As discussed above, being independent from one or a few dominant vendors is a significant advantage for any medium-sized or large organization. Having two or more vendors for a given system architecture component effectively protects the organization from all of the following:

● Wilful disinformation by a chosen vendor to IT staff so as to bias them in its favour;
● Strategic (architectural) or tactical (sales/support) action by a chosen vendor to preserve 'account control' and/or to prevent price/

service competitive acquisition of hardware, software, communications or support services;

- Decision by a chosen vendor to discontinue product, operating system, whole architecture and/or support for any of these;
- Radical change in price or support policies of a chosen vendor, usually 'up' in the case of prices and 'down' in the case of level of support;
- Technical obsolescence of chosen vendor product line with insufficient or even *no* further investment by vendor in a technical update or refresh;
- Merger of vendor resulting in one or more of the above;
- Demise of vendor due to bankruptcy or insolvency.

☞ Moving to open systems protects you against many perils for which you cannot buy any other type of insurance. As Rudyard Kipling put it in his classic poem entitled 'If': '...Neither foes nor loving friends can hurt you.' The most reasonable and cooperative proprietary vendor, even one who will genuinely help you move to open systems later but upon whom you have decided to continue depending for the next five years, can always go out of business. If this happens, your organization could, almost overnight, find itself either with no support or discover that one or a few firms have visited the receivers, bought up everything and are now practising what economists politely refer to as 'oligopolistic behaviour'. In other words, you can double or triple your support budget.

Multi-vendor networking

UNIX and OSI promote the networking of different vendor products together better than do any proprietary systems.

☞ Proprietary vendors only interface their products with other proprietary or open systems when market pressures force them to do so. Open systems are, by definition, interfaceable and networkable to a much greater degree.

Select network channel and component providers competitively

With OSI, network and channel as well as component providers can usually be selected competitively. In the future more and more private and public communications carriers will offer OSI services. Fewer will continue to offer services keyed to the needs of proprietary networking—at least this will be the case after about 1996.

☞ As with UNIX products, OSI products and services can almost always be competitively sourced.

Move IT applications unit *out* of maintaining geriatric applications

As a large-scale commitment is made to open systems, IT can determine what to do with each existing geriatric application running on a legacy system:

- Port to the same environment (for example, ADABAS) under UNIX;
- Convert to a relational format and run under RDBMS/UNIX;
- Leave application 'marooned' on existing system and provide palliative care until application dies or users move out of frustration to a newer platform and a new application is demanded; or
- In exceptional circumstances, use draconian measures and take a hard (usually unobtrusive) look at just who is using the application for what, approach swiftly, secure top management support for your compelling business case that the application must die or else be converted as above, and then shoot the application dead.

In most cases, the total number and aggregate lines of code of the applications subjected to the first (port with baggage) and second (convert) options, plus the last (murder) option, will vastly exceed the total falling to the third option above. This means that, by definition, the number of geriatric applications receiving even half-hearted support from IT will fall and most will pass to the new regime via other portals. This rather cold-hearted and Machiavellian approach is often the *only* way to use a move to open systems as a means of cutting the application maintenance burden, which has all but 'hogtied' many IT organizations.

☞ If your IT shop, and the rest of the organization, are going to endure the disruption of moving to open systems anyway, this is obviously also the logical time to submit doubtful applications to 'trial by fire', 'trial by water' or whatever process best suits your organization.

Improve leverage available from being a knowledge-based organization

Even without full and utter conversion to a knowledge-based organization, even a partial migration in that direction will yield organizational, productivity and worker satisfaction benefits. Organizations ruled by information are less likely to be ruled by tyrants (petty or otherwise) just as this is the case for countries ruled by law.

☞ There are, as yet, to my knowledge no published theorems on the 'Rule of Information' as opposed to the 'Rule of Authority' in organizations. Open systems are too new and their abilities to homogenize and democratize access to information have yet to diffuse widely enough. When they do, however, there is no doubt that many PhDs will be earned addressing this issue.

Improve senior management visibility and control of business processes

When the information systems work more like the telephone or lighting systems, senior management is less likely to be floundering in a fog of IT-generated 'alphabet soup'. Nor is it likely to be hostage to IT's oft-recurring demand that a new mainframe be bought, usually for millions of dollars, about every 18–24 months. Water finds its own level; additional required technology finds its way to the users without pain or chaos. This permits senior management to see more clearly not only the information but also the business processes which act upon such information, upon clients and upon whatever else the organization customarily touches, be it bombs, trains, chemicals or stuffed toy animals.

☞ Using open systems, senior management can more easily see the information itself, as it actually exists and as it is manipulated by business processes. Previously, their view of information was dominated by the technology within which, somewhere, the information was buried.

Improve IT staff efficiency and effectiveness

When the IT staff is not matching wits with the marketeers and engineers of enthroned or pretender dominant vendors, it can focus much more on how to *use* the technology, versus how to buy it or what to call it. This lets the IT organization be more effective in meeting user requirements. Yes, there is a learning curve and yes, having more vendors does mean there needs to be a vigilance of a new kind, but this is a manageable problem. Having the bankruptcy of your legacy vendor make obsolete not only most of your systems but also most of your IT staff's skills is no longer a tenable or a tolerable situation. Open systems are the *only* real protection against that.

☞ Once they get used to them, the computer specialists can do a better job meeting your organization's technology and support needs with open systems than with closed systems.

☞ If you don't believe that a big computer vendor could ever go bankrupt, consider that the Pennsylvania Railroad for many years referred to itself not very modestly as the 'Standard Railroad of the World', and was one of North America's largest corporate conglomerates. Many other railways aspired to be as big and prosperous as the 'Pennsy'. Management inflexibility and unwillingness to face, and deal with, change resulted in its ultimate undoing; the Pennsy is no longer with us. Even merger and government handouts didn't manage to save it.

Achieve IT 'predictability' for end-users

When the IT department uses technology the way electricians use wire or plumbers use pipes, the IT staff become much more predictable for end-users. An end-user line manager who requests a private toilet for their office knows this will involve carpenters, new walls, plumbers and pipes and . . . eventually the toilet itself and probably a sink. Later still, interior decorators will show up to ply their trade. He or she does not care who made the toilet and probably are little concerned with its colour, as long as it is not purple or pink! However, over the past 15 years, the same manager has summoned the IT professionals to solve a problem (true, too, when they were called ADP, EDP, MIS or whatever) with absolutely no idea what rabbit (or newt) they might pull from their collective hats. They might recommend a PC, a group of PCs, a group of connected PCs, the mainframe, two mainframes, a mini-computer or something else called by a newfangled name the manager doesn't even understand. No real connection could be seen between what went into their ears and what came out of their mouths! Often the latter could not even be understood. A general contractor who behaved as they did might have installed the toilet under the desk or even suspended it from the ceiling! There can be little wonder that to this day many line managers who we in the IT fraternity politely call 'non-computer literate' are flat-out terrified of the entire IT profession.

Once established and stabilized, an open system architecture is actually capable of being represented in user-understandable terms to the same line manager, who by now almost certainly has a PC on the desk, even if it is seldom or never used. In the future, when the manager calls for our help, it will be expected that we will first try to understand what the manager wants to do and who/what it needs to be done to, and then seek to find an application program in-house to solve the problem. Failing that, we will try to modify one now owned by the corporation. If that fails we will shop externally, and only as the last resort will we prescribe our own services to write (or oversee the writing of) a custom program to meet the manager's needs. Having decided where the program will come from, we will then proceed to figure out where it will run. If it is too big for a desktop workstation and/or is client/server or multi-user in nature, we will consider very small and small mid-range servers and multi-user systems and possibly larger gear. Considering all relevant things, including those relevant to *the manager* and *the staff*, we will 'let the application find its own level'. Just like water. Then we will see if there is enough technology where it is to be placed; if not, we will add some. No wizardry, no eye of newt and no rabbits! In fact this is very much like the manner in which an employee is added. First the manager figures out what the person will have to do, next internal and external candidates are considered and one is selected. The manager must then figure out where to locate them, and finally, someone is told to make the arrangements while the manager gets on to something else.

> ☞ In the future, open systems will de-focus us from the technology itself, allowing the users and the computer experts to talk almost the same language. They will be able to talk about the information and what is to be done to it. No more will the council of experts sit around diagnosing the problems of the users like so many medical doctors, using their own language which is almost completely incomprehensible to the poor end-user.

Increase the flow of new product releases available

With more vendors, there will almost certainly be more product releases to keep the organization's technology base current. Do not get so excited about new products that the system architecture is forsaken, but update the architecture as required by changing technology.

> ☞ Not even a huge vendor is likely to release as many products of a given type per year as 20 or 30 medium-sized vendors or hundreds of small ones. Open systems give you choice and price competition.

Acquire products in a competitive market

Competitive markets lead to better service and lower prices, and nowhere is this more true than in the advanced technology field.

> ☞ See previous comment.

Increase product/version installed life

If new technologies are chosen carefully, and are upward compatible, existing products and versions placed 'atop' them in the architectural/ system functional hierarchy will usually be undisturbed for the remainder of their intended lives. This is possible in some proprietary environments but only on a uni-vendor or plug-compatible basis.

> ☞ It is now clear that many UNIX-based software products you buy today will undoubtedly outlive by many years the hardware you first run them on. You can change the underlying hardware, even the operating system version, without disturbing the package and program software resident on them.

Develop application components on a distributed basis

Within, as well as among, organizations, decentralized collaborative development is much more practical when open systems are used as the development engines and open networks link the development sites together.

☞ If you have programmers located in different places, it is easier for them to work together if you have open systems.

Provide any amount of processing power at any processing tier or physical site location

Like electricity, technological 'power' can be supplied in almost any amount to almost any location. However, unlike electricity (in its current context), there is *not* a requirement actually to produce or generate all of the power in a central location. As we will doubtless do in our future electricity grids, you can put little 'generating stations' where you require them.

☞ This flexibility is of very great value as your requirements change, either suddenly or gradually, since it will allow the IT unit to respond gratifyingly quickly when senior management calls for help.

Reduce the number of distinct network and operating system environments

The fewer environments your organization has, the fewer your people have to learn, track and support. The fewer you have, the lower the costs. Of course, large organizations may have speciality requirements and/or huge legacy systems which simply cannot be eliminated or even converted in the short term.

☞ By the mid-1990s you can conceivably run DOS on the desktop PCs and run UNIX both on the desktop and at all other processing tiers for all or virtually all of your computing requirements. If you run more than two operating systems now, and can eliminate the others in the meantime, fewer operating systems will mean less cost and complexity.

Conclusion

It is necessary to make your own determination of which costs, opportunities and benefits most directly relate to your organization, but the following categorization may be of assistance. You may want to identify those items which are:

- Relevant mostly to your IT planning, management and operations;
- Useful mostly for selling the idea of open systems to senior management;
- Useful mostly for selling open systems to end-users.

4 Architecture without buildings: the role of system architecture and other frameworking activities

Introduction

This chapter addresses the role of system architecture in planning and implementing open systems. It is intended to provide only that information necessary to the overall *management* of the inflow of open systems, not a comprehensive treatise on the subject of system architecture itself. A number of the major architectural issues, as they relate to open systems, are none the less covered in some detail. These include the current issues relating to client/server versus multi-user service models as well as to the choice of various sizes of computer system for different purposes.

Definition of system architecture

Webster's Dictionary defines the word 'architecture' as follows:

1. The art or science of building, especially for occupancy.
2. Frame, style, structure and workmanship involved in the construction of a building.
3. A building of approved design.

Most modern architects of buildings would probably find this definition a bit too restrictive, but I purposely chose to use a several decades-old (1963) edition of the dictionary to make a point here. While architectural students (and others) have been studying Greek, Roman and the more recent 'architectures' for many years, it is only since the mid- or late 1960s (in my personal view at least) that we have developed a more holistic way of looking at a particular style of architecture as a comprehensive 'practice' or characterizable collection of ways of doing things. When most of our parents were attending school, architecture was seen as the study of the characteristics of the 'as-built' environment. The actual methodologies, practices and beliefs which went into such edifices were secondary to the structures themselves. Of course, there have been many architectural 'revivals' in which a past set of practices was once again taken up and fervently pursued, but here again the aim was the result (i.e. the beautiful, awe-inspiring completed building ready for occupancy), not the practice. Once the building was occupied, the architects would disappear, usually for ever. Only their brass plaques would remain. No one would think about them again until the building came to be studied as a heritage property, a classic, the harbinger of a new trend or whatever.

In this regard, applying the conventional definition of architecture to the computer systems world would be like having conventional architects practise their profession on a beach, with sand as the only building material. The winds and tides would soon lay waste to their finest creations.

All technology, especially the hardware technology underlying all of the other technologies related to 'computing' as we know it today, is 'shifting' almost as rapidly as sand on a beach. Ironically, the silicon from which it is made even comes from sand! Further, open systems themselves aid and abet this process by making it easier to slide hardware out and replace it with the latest creation. How can you have an 'architecture' when the building materials or components cannot be counted upon to be static, and are indeed now becoming almost inherently dynamic? Few architects of buildings have chosen fudge, styrofoam or papier mâché as their building materials. Hard-shelled creatures able actually to move themselves (such as armadillos) have never been used!

However, suppose you wanted to construct a building out of a highly energy-efficient material, but one which had to be replaced every 10–15 years! In such circumstances, the architect would be forced to design the building so as to contemplate period updates to its exterior and interior non-loadbearing structure and surfaces. Indeed, many modern buildings are designed for periodic cosmetic upgrades as well as mid-life replacement of their heating, ventilation and air conditioning systems.

Far more than conventional architecture, system architecture must therefore be seen as a process. Accepting this, let's recraft the above definition in the light of the fact that we want system architects to erect a framework for how we will 'construct' our system environment but we also want them to help us, or to help us help ourselves, to go on recrafting or at least fine tuning that framework as both requirements and technology continue to evolve.

System architecture is therefore:

1 The art *and* science of applying a unified and consistent practice to build a conceptual and planning framework into which individual computer hardware, software and communications components can be fitted to create a coherent and holistic computing environment.
2 The style, structure and workmanship involved in the actual as-implemented planning framework created according to paragraph 1 above.
3 A planning framework created according to paragraph 1 above, reflecting the nature and quality of the process which created it.

☞ Put more simply, system architecture is the practice and process of establishing, and maintaining, a plan or map of what kinds of computer and related technology are appropriate for what kinds of uses. It also addresses where as well as how the various technologies will be linked and will work with each other.

The importance of system architecture

Just as generals would have trouble fighting a battle without good maps, and pilots of aircraft would have even more problems, CIOs cannot be expected to guide their organizations' IT futures effectively without a good road map. While different flavours of system architecture have different priorities and produce many different views (logical, functional, physical, etc.) of the situation, it is reasonable to consider the physical view as being similar to an urban planner's set of staged maps. Such maps show successive views of a new housing estate or industrial park at intervals, perhaps extending from its natural (undeveloped) state through until completion. For example, the first map might show only fields, the second might include the services (water, sewer, roads and electricity), the third might show the first few buildings and the tenth include everything in the development plan.

A system architecture is no different; it shows you where you have been, where you are now and where you are trying to go. In many of the flavours of system architecture, there are three key planning time references, as follows:

Baseline—the way things were or at least should have been at the earliest time of interest to the planning process; where open systems are contemplated, this is most often the original, all-proprietary state in which only 'legacy' systems exist;

Current—the way things are right now, which includes all changes and additions to, and deletions from, the baseline; and

Target—the desired eventual situation which we want to reach.

Even if your organization has absolutely no intention of moving to open systems, you can still benefit from the practice of system architecture. Most proprietary system vendors offer their own architecture which relates only to their family of interoperable products based on that computer family. For such systems, you can still use an architectural approach to map where you are now and what functionality and capacity you expect to add in the future. You can also incorporate technology updates as they are released. Without at the very least knowing your current and your target architectures, it is impossible to know for sure whether a given change, whether proposed by someone inside the IT organization or, more likely, demanded by users, will be consistent with what you have now. More importantly, you will not know whether it will take you in the direction you want to go. Suppose you operate DEC VAX/VMS equipment on some desktops, for workgroups, for divisions and in the corporate computer room. Now a user group says they cannot live without a particular application program which only runs on, for example, the equally proprietary (but very different) IBM AS-400 MRS. Consider these three alternative scenarios when the CIO and the user department head cannot resolve the issue and, in each case, it is elevated to the Executive Committee.

1 No system architecture

The IT organization may, at once, recoil in horror at the thought of having to have its support people learn a new operating system, but the user may be very insistent and extremely influential with top management. They may declare that a vital business function cannot be continued without Package X, which someone has convinced them they cannot live without. While the IT unit may have good reasons for its declared and implemented preference for VAX/VMS, the user group couldn't care less about that. (Of course, supporting it will be IT's problem, not theirs.) However, if IT cannot show that it has a solid, and well thought-out, direction that keeps the organization on the VAX track, the users will likely prevail, even if the thing is escalated to a very senior council. They will bounce the ball back into IT's court and wonder out loud whether IT is too friendly with DEC or whether IT is simply unwilling or unable to support the AS-400. IT can play this game too and suggest that the users themselves support it but this can be self-defeating for IT. If anything goes seriously wrong with the support or vendor relationship, IT will be called to the rescue later, no matter who said what to whom at acquisition time. In the end, the user case will almost always prevail since the IT unit has only the most vague ideas and concepts about the desired state of future computing to put up against the *now* argument.

☞ Without a system architecture in place it is very hard to tell users that any particular thing they might want to buy won't fit in. There is nothing with which to check the fit. Users tend to end up buying whatever they want, often resulting in dozens of different kinds of PCs, workstations, MBSs and MRSs.

2 System architecture based on DEC VAX/VMS with open future

In this scenario, the IT unit reminds everyone that it has recently created a system architecture based on the VAX/VMS products from DEC, with intended future migration to open systems. These products are reliable and expandable and have been serving the organization well for almost a decade. The users like them and everyone is happy with DEC's support. There is also the important fact that since VAX systems can also run the ULTRIX operating system (based on UNIX) and since they work with DEC's own Ethernet variant (DECNET), as well as with pure Ethernet, VAX forms a very plausible foundation for future migration to open systems. The users respond that they care not a whit about all that, but they must have Application X *now*! The CIO insists that open systems are important to the organization's future. The users counter that Application X is crucial to the organization's business *right now*! As a fillip, they add that IBM says the AS-400 can run OSI communications right now so it is an open system anyway. Further, IBM's support will be just as good (and this is no doubt quite true).

Now the IT unit takes a different tack. The CIO tries to point out the difference between OSI and OCS to the Board of Directors. Everybody gets totally confused and the President suggests a five-minute break. Taking the full five minutes to lobby the President, the CIO points out that users were fully consulted during the creation of the system architecture and they should have to abide by it. Also, the AS-400's communications are open but its processor is even more closed than VAX since it won't even run UNIX.

The meeting resumes with lots more hyperbole but, finally, seeking a compromise, the President suggests that for the IT experts getting half of the open systems apple is better than nothing and at least the AS-400 will be able to *talk* to the VAXs. So he and the VPs approve the acquisition right over the CIO's head. While IT loses the battle, the good news is that, since OSI is part of the target architecture, IT now has a firm reason to start implementing it now. ISO is necessary if the DEC and IBM machines are going to be expected to work together, which, of course, they are. The acquisition of the AS-400 is a partial departure from the plan but it is one that IT actually can work around, however grudgingly.

☞ Sometimes the users are smart enough to hit IT over the head with its own architectural stick. Phased or half-hearted commitment to, for example, a move to open systems can often be turned around and shot back at IT when push comes to shove. Few organizations can afford to throw out all existing legacy systems nor tolerate the gross disruption of moving to open systems overnight; therefore virtually all migration plans are at least somewhat phased. However, if IT believes that both OSI and OCS are important parts of open systems, the phasing should be clear as in 'After Date T we will not approve any more proprietary processors unable to eventually run UNIX'. The 'VAX now and open systems some day' commitment of the IT unit is the stuff DEC (and other vendor) marketing people's dreams are made of. This sends the vendor the signal that the migration is not tied to temporal milestones and may be influenceable in terms of timing and degree. While DEC might not welcome the arrival of the IBM AS-400, they might still prefer to see IT stay with this partial commitment to open systems.

3   Solid commitment to a phased open system architecture

In this scenario, IT has really done its homework. It has not only created a system architecture with baseline, current and target manifestations but also consulted users liberally along the way. There are specific conditions in which exceptions will be given. During Phase 1 a non-OSI and/or non-OCS system can be approved under certain circumstances. During Phase 2 only a non-OCS system can be approved so any new system during that phase *must* be OSI. In Phase 3 systems must meet both OCS and OSI requirements.

VAX/VMS systems are fully compliant during Phase 1 and can continue to be purchased, on an exemption basis during Phase 2, when most such purchases were upgrades or second processors for existing installed systems. Unfortunately for the user group now screaming for Application X, we have just entered Phase 3. VAX/ULTRIX systems with OSI communications implemented (DEC has a quite good command of OSI) are fully compliant. However, so are DG/Avion systems running DGUX, Hewlett-Packard HP-9000 systems running HPUX and also IBM RS/6000 systems running AIX. These too have been certified by IT for MRS and larger installations. The IBM AS-400 (running OS/400), however, is not since it cannot, and apparently never will, run UNIX.

The users present all of the *now* arguments and tell in detail why only the chosen software package will do. The CIO draws his line in the sand and declares that, if necessary, he will lie down in front of the train; only over his dead body will the declared architectural approach be so flagrantly violated. There is no point in having a target architecture if steps are taken to move the organization in another direction. The commitment to open systems is either serious or it is not. Ditto, the President's previous statement (after the computer planning retreat led by the CIO) that he accepted the importance of linking open systems to business objectives. The user group must understand that it is the greater good of the whole organization which must prevail. Otherwise, there will *be* no standards present, the open systems opportunities will never appear and the open systems benefits will never be realized.

After much agonizing debate, the Board sides with IT and tells the users to convince the third-party software vendor to port to UNIX, find another supplier or else have IT write a similar package for them from scratch.

☞ Here, the organization is learning, albeit slowly, how to let its technology base become 'architecture driven'. In other words, just as no one is above the law, so no computer is above the architecture. The system architecture determines what is and is not acceptable at a given time and in given circumstances. Like English common law, it is not totally static and can evolve over time, but only in the most draconian situations (such as those involving the protection of life, property or the very integrity of the business) will gross exceptions be made. In such cases, IT itself will see the need for the exemption and will not contest the issue, but should include the caveat that an open system replacement will be acquired as soon as a practical candidate becomes available or at least when the non-conforming system is replaced. This is not unlike municipal zoning. If the land under your house is zoned commercial you can keep your house there but if you tear it down you cannot build another one; the 'existing non-conforming' use is thereby extinguished.

In order to be effective, any system architecture *must* have top management's gold seal of approval plastered all over the cover. Otherwise, the wags down in User Group A will say to each other: 'Oh that's just the latest fad in the IT shop; we can find a way around it. We'll buy the computer out of the slush fund and not tell them until after we get it. Then it will be too late for them to do anything about it. Besides, I can get one cheap because my cousin owns a computer store . . . and his son is a great BASIC programmer.' Any system architecture must have active senior management support but this is especially true for one which will, albeit phase by phase, move the organization to a very different computing environment. Certainly, there are many carrots which IT can use to try to persuade individual user groups not to fight a move to open systems. However, many of the opportunities and benefits are medium to long term and are dependent upon all *other* workgroups also going to open systems. Benefits from internal software recycling are a good example. This concomitancy of opportunity benefit is hard to explain to an exasperated line manager who keeps asking: 'Why don't you guys just go away and let us do our own thing?'

System architecture in context

Some organizations use the term 'system architecture' to apply to the frameworking of *all* technology related to the handling of information. Since the advent of open systems, however, there has evolved the ability to see the application environment and the underlying technology environment as somewhat separate entities. As we have seen, this is because the technology environment can be more easily (and in future may be more frequently) upgraded or even replaced outright than the application environment, in which far more is invested. In such cases, system architecture is divided into two components as defined below:

Applications architecture, including the user interface, application development, test, certification, distribution and support for legacy-confined, migratable and *de novo* (hence open) application residency plus all of the components required to provide an applications platform for information (to be managed as a corporate resource) and for end-users; and

Technology architecture, including the hardware, system software, communications and all other components required to provide a system platform for the applications architecture.

When these are seen, as they sometimes are, as completely separate disciplines, there arises the need to consider a third discipline which is more management-oriented but no less important than the first two:

Technology management, including the generic identification of the types of technology to be acquired, identification of the implications of such acquisition and the establishment of both the requisite senior management commitment and the optimum procurement and internal support strategy.

Idealism, flexibility and practicality

Above, it was implied that the IT organization may sometimes find itself brandishing the system architecture document, or rolled-up charts derived therefrom, like a stick. This is, hopefully, a rare and last-resort situation. After all, the IT organization is there to assist and facilitate users in their attempts to adopt and effectively use computer technology, not to issue technical 'diktats' from high upon the ivory tower. Nowhere is the Prayer of St Francis about changing the things you can, accepting those you cannot and having the wisdom to know the difference more relevant in the IT field today. In crafting your system architecture in the first place, you must ensure that you understand as much as possible about the current and future functional requirements of your user groups. You have to include lots of large, juicy carrots. Stress the short-term and workgroup-oriented benefits (from Chapter 3) which relate most closely to the workgroup you are talking to at any given time. You needn't feel guilty about this because, unlike politicians who promise different things to each group (and frequently deliver nothing to any of them), you are in a position to use open systems to deliver to each group the benefits most relevant to them. Clearly, different workgroups in your organization would rate the opportunities and benefits in Chapter 3 in different preference orders and this is quite natural. A thornier issue than who gets the opportunities and benefits is who gets stuck with the costs, and when. In most medium-sized and large organizations, the flow will be something like this:

1 Corporation invests in the *strategic costs* and verifies the architecture, technology in-migration and support plans and any required organizational realignment within IT. Usually this involves any or all of lab tests, pilots and trials.
2 Divisions and workgroups incur *tactical costs* and progress through the learning curve of actually using and providing limited local self-support for open systems.
3 Divisions and workgroups begin to take advantage of *tactical opportunities* and begin to obtain *tactical benefits*.
4 Corporation begins to take advantage of *strategic opportunities* and to realize *strategic benefits*.

☞ First you have to pay to put the framework in place. Then individual workgroups and workers can acquire open systems as they need them. They get opportunities and benefits locally, but later the whole corporation will be better off as well, as a larger and larger community of open system users develops.

Here are two other questions you ought to ask about system architecture:

1 How much system architecture is enough? How will I know when we have reached that point?

Depending upon the size of your organization, and the structure of your IT unit, you may elect to make or buy system architecture services or to take a blended approach. In any but the 'make' scenario, you should appoint separate individuals who are nominally called the 'Quality Assurance (QA)' officers for the process, but whose real job is to decide how much system architecture is enough. A number of years ago, I built a snowmobile house but my father-in-law, who was a master builder, found one corner out of square and declared that the entire structure should therefore be torn down and re-erected with a more accurate plan and under his personal supervision! Your plan needs only to be as detailed or accurate as your real requirements dictate. For a snowmobile house, plans on one piece of paper were more than adequate, but obviously not for a house, a fire station or a school. If your organization has only 100 people, it would probably be foolish to spend more than $10 000 on your system architecture. (Note also that it would be foolish to spend nothing.) The degree of complexity of your system architecture will be dictated by the size of your organization, the criticality of your various business and operational functions, the degree of variety in individual and workgroup functions (as across the organization chart and/or across geography), your overall technological direction, the role and structure of your IT unit and similar factors. Ultimately, you will have to use your own good judgement in deciding whether the QA officer is right in declaring that this much is enough. There is a useful acid test, which you may wish to consider using. No matter how complex your system architecture is, it is *absolutely essential* that it be readily translatable into a simple, one-page diagram which portrays the whole thing in terms users can understand. If you cannot produce this, you have gone too far or not far enough.

2   What kinds of issues can we expect system architects to address?

If they are highly paid outside consultants, they will address everything in sight if given the opportunity. You must therefore carefully craft terms of reference, setting out the scope and objectives of your system architecture project. A blended team of outside and inside specialists is often the best approach as it can make on-the-fly changes to these items without re-scoping the entire effort. The following sections provide a tour of some of the major issues of discussion in practice of system architecture today, as it relates to open systems.

Single user versus client/server

This is a widely discussed and debated architectural issue. Basically, what it boils down to is whether to have a shared system do all or most of the work or to farm a significant part of it out to single-user processors located at workers' desks, workbenches, home workplaces or wherever. Here are some of the relevant factors.

CPU

The single-user (WS or PC) environment offers only a single tier of processing whereas the client/server environment provides the choice of performing all processing at the PC level or dividing it between PC and server. Excessive uploading of processing will, however, not only under-utilize the PC's CPU but may overload the server. None the less, the server's CPU power can in most cases be more readily extended than can that of the PC. In this environment the PC will usually run DOS (or possibly OS/2), thereby relegating the server OS to a background role, being not usually addressed by the end-user.

☞ Using an MBS, not just a simple PC, gives you a bit more growth potential to accommodate your computer program in future.

Memory

The memory situation is similar to that of the CPU; the addition of the server offers the possibility to offload some (but not all) resource requirements from the PC to the more flexible and more expandable server system.

☞ MBS equipment also offers better memory flexibility.

Storage

The client/server environment allows upload to the server of files too large to manage easily on the PC. The server offers not only more space and faster access time but also involves the user (client) in contention among users, applications and processes for such access. The PC is more limited in its space and slower in its access times but, where DOS is used, there is virtually no contention for access. Even with a UNIX-equipped workstation, contention is quite limited. The effects of contention are, of course, a factor of the number of contending agents, their resource access requirements, their time concentration and system capacity.

☞ You can store much more data on an MBS, but the PC users may bump into each other and have to queue up for it when they want their data back.

Input/output

Client/server operation permits sharing of printers, plotters, scanners, optical disks and other such devices. A single-user PC either cannot share such resources at all or is limited to a 'take turns' form of access (as dictated by the LAN operating system and/or physical switching logic). Beyond such basic access, the server can act as an intermediary for each 'served I/O device' or else each device can—from one perspective—act as its own server. The latter approach, however, introduces some conceptual anomalies which are discussed in the Commentary section of the Client/Server versus Multi-User section below.

☞ An MBS can access and share a lot more peripherals, more easily, than a PC alone.

3GL applications

Neither of these service models is optimum for running conventional 3GL applications. The PC will be completely tied up by such an application except for those very restricted cases where it can be run under a separate (background) DOS image without undue contention for key system resources. Note that virtually all PC286 and most PC386 equipment suffers significant limitations in this regard due to system resource limitations and basic bus architecture. The latter constraints also impact the same equipment even when running UNIX. Larger, more powerful workstations reduce these constraints but cost significantly more per user to buy and support. Conversely, most PC-based servers (and even an MRS-class platform configured expressly as a server and *not* as a fully capable multi-user system) implicitly assume that a significant proportion of an application will be PC-resident. Where each of a group of PCs seeks to upload, for example, 75 or 80 per cent of an application's logic workload to the server a central constriction or overload will result. Only where the server passes the data to the application and the application runs on an exclusive or near-exclusive basis wholly or largely on the PC will the client/server environment effectively support 3GL applications.

☞ PCs can often perform only one main task at a time whereas servers can 'seem' to be performing several related tasks at once.

Office automation

The PC can host single-user personal productivity tools but these do not permit work sharing, much less workspace sharing. Data is usually moved by transferring disks from one PC to another. The client/server model supports a 'pseudo-multi-user' form of OA which permits E-mail transmission and the transfer of other types of files.

☞ PCs on their own provide an unduly compartmentalized, and restricted, type of office automation. MBS equipment is a little better but it does not permit full work sharing.

RDBMS

Applications written for an RDBMS can be more readily distributed between the PC and server. In such cases the PC runs an element of the RDBMS engine, and the application logic, while the server runs the primary engine and processes calls from the application, usually over a LAN. True two-level processing can occur in client/server mode with a possible (perhaps optimal) division allowing no more (and often less) than 50 per cent of the combined application internal logic processing and RDBMS call processing workload to be performed on the server. Various authorities and experts disagree as to the optimum percentage in various situations, although most indicate that the division should be a function of application logic complexity, data record complexity, call complexity, PC and server capacity, LAN capacity and DBA/security requirements. Full DBA/security management for an RDBMS is beyond the time, skills and patience even of the more sophisticated end-users. The client/server environment provides the opportunity for more sophisticated (and hopefully better) DBA and security management, although download of sensitive data to the PC (where it is actually stored on the PC and not immediately written back up to the server after processing) connotes a significant weakness of client/server architecture.

☞ MBSs permit better management of database programs and data than do PCs alone.

Local and extra-tier communications

Communications within the workplace tier and to other tiers of processing are generally improved when a server is present. The server can provide access, as a gateway, to open or proprietary communications services. Here again, however, while 30 clients can be served by five or ten access logicals on the server, contention will result in some circumstances.

☞ The MBS helps tie PCs to each other and to larger computers.

Support

The presence of not only a basic LAN but also of an active server will almost always connote the presence of a LAN Administrator (LANA).

The LANA will provide more immediate and attentive support than a more distant micro support coordinator.

☛ With an MBS you usually have a local network linking it to the PCs. You will need someone to spend part of their time looking after this network.

Cost

Regarding capital cost, only where the client/server environment is planned from the outset (and users are thus provided with less powerful workstations than they otherwise would have received) is there a potential for a direct cost tradeoff. In a pure client/server environment there is less to be gained than in a true multi-user environment from running UNIX on the workstation, at least in the short term. As discussed below, UNIX does in the latter case permit more active tradeoff of system resources between, for example, MRS and UNIX workstations. If basic functionality can be provided to a user with some proportion (say, 50 per cent) of it being server-resident then, conceivably, a less powerful desktop device, such as a diskless PC or an X-terminal, can be utilized. Wherever the server is added later it is almost certain that total costs per user will increase since the addition of the server may free up PC-resident resources but will be unlikely to lead to their removal and subsequent decapitalization. Operating costs also rise where a full service LAN (and hence a LANA) is present.

☛ Don't count on saving money by moving users who have a PC now to something less glamorous when you install an MBS or even an MRS. It is very hard to take a PC away from someone who is using it now. They will resist vigorously!

Commentary

Many RDBMS vendors, particularly the suppliers of highly resource-consumptive ones, argued throughout the second half of the 1980s that microcomputer Millions of Instructions Per Second (MIPS) capabilities were much less costly than those on other processing tiers. There have been rapid changes in microcomputer, and MRS, price/performance in recent years. While it may be true that on a MIPS-alone basis a micro is less expensive in some cases, particularly when compared to a last-generation mini (for example, VAX) or a mainframe (for example, IBM 370) it may not be less expensive compared to an MRS. This is highly context-dependent. There is little doubt that on a MIPS-alone basis an MRS is far more cost effective than a larger proprietary system. However, when *all* the required resources to provide a given capacity are considered, progressive efficiencies are sometimes still exhibited with larger system size. This is true from PC to MBS, MBS to MRS, MRS to mid-frame and mid-frame to mainframe, where all are UNIX-capable and the comparison is thus apples to apples.

☞ For UNIX computers, the cost per horsepower often goes down when you buy bigger systems. Note, however, that this is not necessarily an incentive to buy only large systems since there are many other things to consider.

Single user versus multi-user

The following sections provide similar treatment of another issue: the tradeoffs which exist between single-user and multi-user service models.

CPU

A PC286, PC386, PC486 or fully equipped UNIX workstation has a very clear limit to CPU expandability based not only on potential swap-out CPU upgrades but also on the increasing limitations imposed by bus and device I/O data rates. An MRS (or larger system) exhibits not only a less bus-restricted and less I/O-restricted growth path but also the ability to mix and match processor slot assignment much more flexibly than do most single-user systems. Mid-frame and mainframe equipment is almost always fully modular, with bus extensions or umbilicals and additional cabinets able to be added as required, within very broad limits. Where the PC runs DOS, CPU tradeoff between the PC and the larger system is distinctly limited. Where both run UNIX a tradeoff can be made. Most optimally, this tradeoff is exercised between PC (or WS) and MRS where star-wiring or LAN connection imposes minimal communications overhead among applications or processes.

☞ Multi-user UNIX computers are always easier to expand than single-user UNIX or DOS computers.

Memory

As with CPU power, multi-user systems facilitates much easier (and larger) memory upgrades with less distinct limits than single-user systems.

☞ See above.

Storage

Most comments related to PC versus server also apply here.

☞ See above again.

Input/output

With UNIX-to-UNIX interoperation, such UNIX facilities as Streams and Pipes can be used to permit parallel access to I/O resources on the behalf of users, applications and/or processes. These can embrace client/server requirements, as a subset of multi-user requirements.

☞ Multi-user UNIX computers can help many different users and programs to use different printers or communications ports at the same time, cutting down waiting time for everyone.

3GL applications

These can be run in foreground, in combined mode or entirely in the background in a multi-user environment with little or no degradation of local PC performance and no tie-up of PC system resources.

☞ Users can run two or more programs at the same time on a UNIX multi-user system.

RDBMS

A full multi-user RDBMS engine provides file and record level locking on a full and partial basis and true sharing among users of all RDBMS resources. It permits concurrent access to datasets, full OLTP where appropriately equipped, and full DBA and security management. It provides better physical security than a desktop-resident RDBMS in virtually all cases and usually affords better overall security. The RDBMS has to be installed only once and application logic need only reside on the central system. Where vertically integrated applications are desired these can be accommodated, most readily with a UNIX–UNIX environment but even in a DOS–UNIX environment, subject to the limitations discussed earlier.

☞ Database programs can be more efficiently handled in a multi-user environment. UNIX is particularly good for handling many such programs at once.

Office automation

The multi-user system provides the end-user with a very powerful and flexible OA environment which is not only a direct extension of the personal environment but which introduces features not relevant at the personal system level. It provides full work and workspace sharing, co-editing and 'co-working' on shared work items which may themselves be complex objects (spanning text, graphics, image, etc.). A full multi-user system also permits meaningful interworking of the OA package and

RDBMS applications as well as the development of hierarchical security and user-specific customized top-end (initial post-logon) menus. A fully timeshared OA system can serve as a master front-end for the end-users, while an OA system which is 'served' out to clients by a conventional server often cannot. A personal productivity system on a PC can serve as an omnibus front-end but it offers access to far less capability.

☛ Users can fully share agendas, calendars, documents and other items when the system is true multi-user. Security is also better than for single-user or client/server situations. The OA and RDBMS packages can also work together.

Local and extra-tier communications

A multi-user environment offers the widest possible range of conduits or channels for accessing other tiers. For example, a PC-equipped user, connected by LAN to an MRS, can easily toggle among simultaneously executing connectivity facilities as follows:

- X.25 hosted logon to a larger UNIX or proprietary system;
- Access to an IBM SNA network as an emulated 3278/3174 to a remote IBM host;
- Access to DECNET by emulation of DEC network interface equipment;
- X.25/X.400/X.500 mail transfer (direct or via an OA package).

☛ A UNIX MRS can allow PC users to communicate easily with almost any other type of computer which they may need to access. It can perform much of the communications 'leg work' on their behalf, and invisibly to them.

Support

Since the lowest form of multi-user system is usually an MRS (although dedicated 30-client MBSs might occasionally host two to five timeshare users) access to multi-user facilities almost always connotes the presence of a fully trained/certified MRSA, whose user-support capabilities are a large superset of those of a LANA. As discussed above, a single-user system connotes less immediately available local support.

☛ With an MRS you need a well-qualified, trained and certified administrator. Once he or she is on-site, they can support PC and other users.

Cost

Where a user requires a given level of computing capability, and this can be provided solely by an MRS or larger system, and with an X-terminal on the desktop, the larger systems will always present a lower total capital cost/user. Of course, in most cases any existing desktop capacity (i.e. the PC286 the user has had for the last two years) will most likely not be withdrawn and decapitalized when connection to a multi-user UNIX system is accomplished. The issue of joint or overlapping costing therefore arises. There is also the issue of the time cost of delays. If a multi-user system is far distant and thus requires a complex logon, much access contention and inconvenient output must somehow be taken into account.

☛ Multi-user systems almost always cost less per user than other systems but they may offer less convenience, particularly if located far away. Also, as cited earlier, you cannot really take away most users' PCs just because they are now also connected to a multi-user system.

Commentary

Multi-user systems often offer improved cost performance (even when joint costing is considered, unless the total workload is trivial), a minimum of resource expansion constraints and better support, administration and physical security. Single-user systems offer none of these advantages. However, when an application is small and primarily local each unit of resource used by such an application does not involve user contention for logon access, application access, multi-user system resource access or user support from the MRSA or IT professional. Thus, while a multi-user system can better handle some of a user's single-user needs where an application may have resource requirements which exceed or unduly tax those of the PC or WS and can certainly better handle *all* of his or her workgroup-related activities, it is not a perfect substitute for the single-user system. In this respect, the single-user system and the multi-user system are at least somewhat complementary.

Client/server versus multi-user

Here is another hotly debated area. Some experts believe that the client/server service model which allocates the work between the PC and the larger system will become the *only* way to operate in the future and point out that many new applications are being developed to work this way. Others think client/server is overrated and that there will continue to be significant use of the multi-user model for many years to come.

CPU

True multi-user systems have much higher CPU power requirements than pure dedicated servers. Of course, the server's resource requirements are directly related to precisely what it is to serve. If the server is to run two concurrent RDBMS server images for 30 clients it will have much higher resource needs than a server which merely serves flat or similar files out to the same number of clients. In general, experience has proved that with a certain RDBMS an MRS configured to run a full multi-user engine for 30 timeshare users will require two to three times the system resources of a PC-based dedicated server running that same database in a pure data server role for 30 clients. In the latter role, the server merely answers SQL and other calls/commands sent by the PC client application. Where the client becomes more demanding (or, more precisely, where many clients become more demanding) the workload imposed on the server may soon exceed its rating, offering only four choices:

- Accept degraded level of service (users will be unlikely to tolerate this strategy for very long);
- Clone server (this opens a thicket of new problems discussed below in the Commentary section);
- Upload to MRS and go true multi-user (possibly with required changes to application);
- Upload to mid-frame or mainframe (under the same conditions as MRS but with an additional imposed network penalty, particularly on complex, multi-part commits and joins).

☞ An MRS running a full multi-user database program which does most of the processing work itself requires more power than an MRS running a server program which merely passes data out to the PCs for them to work on.

Memory

See above discussion of CPU resources.

☞ See above.

Storage

In general, the true multi-user model will require less total (PC- and larger system-based) storage because:

- Images of data used by users or applications will generally be lodged in the shared system's near or far memory rather than being transferred not only to the PC's live memory but also to its disk;
- Executable application logic need only reside on the shared multi-user system and does not have to be replicated on each PC or WS.

☞ Multi-user MRSs usually make better use of storage for database programs than do client/server systems of the same size.

Input/output

Both client/server and multi-user service models contemplate the sharing of I/O devices and other resources. However, the multi-user model gives the PC or WS end-user access not only to OS interworking and/or background tasking but also, where required, direct or shell-driven access to the shared UNIX OS running on the multi-user system. A user could thus, in theory, directly (by entering commands), via an application, a chron file or by invoking a script, launch parallel sets of processes in *both* his or her WS-resident UNIX where so equipped and—fully in parallel—in the MRS-resident UNIX or that resident on a larger system. Whereas many applications today are I/O bound this can result in higher application workload throughput when the user is working to a deadline and trying to accomplish several things at once, such as paginating and printing a file, printing a calendar/agenda page, locating and printing a name from a phone contact list while also accessing another document. Windowing front-ends accommodate this sort of parallel work where users are avid enough to perform it, but server-based systems impose more limitations between the WS and MRS OS images, even where both are running UNIX.

☞ Users can get more computers doing more things at once when they have access to UNIX on a desktop and on one or more larger systems. They can become veritable taskmasters, causing multiple tigers to jump through multiple hoops all at the same time.

3GL applications

The multi-user system offers the best environment for 3GL applications which can be run in the background. When these are in the background they can be invoked by chron scripts at various times without the PC user even making a direct intervention. In most client/server cases, PC users will have to become clients and wait for the servers to 'serve' them the application before it can be run on the server, the PC or a combination of the two.

☞ The multi-user UNIX MRS is perhaps the best place to run programs written in conventional programming languages.

Office automation

A multi-user system provides a true, versus a synthetic, shared workspace to the OA end-user. The server-based system, by its very nature, seeks to provide a separate copy of any file (and hence workspace) to each client. In OA, true shared co-working demands true shared access to the same text document, calendar, image or whatever. Also, multi-user E-mail is more efficient as it can simply place a pointer to a file in the traditional UNIX manner in each person's in-box rather than either initially, or later on user demand, copying the text file to each user's PC storage space. Further, delivery to the user's E-mail space is immediate and is not segmented by when users happen to power up their PCs and/or next become clients. If the server crashes before all clients have logged on and have been 'served' their mail messages, reconstruction may be more complex than in a true multi-user system, where all deliveries will have been at the same completion status level at the time of the crash. On a multi-user system, an OS or OA error which generates a huge amount of spurious E-mail to all end-users, such as unwanted print spool status notifications, will *not* overload, and potentially crash, the end-user PCs. It may crash the central system but its impacts will usually end there unless the end-user has implemented unprotected UNIX–UNIX links between the MRS and desktop systems. On the other hand, a server system can and will crash both itself and the PCs in such a circumstance.

RDBMS

The distinction between client/server and multi-user is, at its most basic level, that between dividing the workload into distinct parts (each of which is executed on a separate machine) versus apportioning the workoad on a fully interoperative basis, according to predetermined static or dynamic factors. A multi-user system therefore offers the end-user (who will in most cases have a PC286) a much greater potential for vertically distributing the application across two or more tiers. Also, as cited in the OA section above, a server can sometimes, especially when malfunctioning, make highly undesirable and obtrusive use of the end-user's private PC resources. A malfunctioning relational database operating under the client/server model can, for example, generate immense amounts of file writing to the limited hard-disk space of a PC, thereby corrupting the end-user's entire environment and rendering it useless, indeed usually unbootable. This is not to suggest that there is no role for the client/server RDBMS model; it is merely to state that the choice of model among single-user, client/server and multi-user must consider all relevant operating factors.

☞ If the database server on the MBS or MRS gets out of control, it can wreak havoc with the PCs, putting them out of commission for hours or days. Database vendors and LAN vendors don't tell you that.

Local and extra-tier communications

In virtually all areas of capacity and performance, true multi-user systems offer advantages over server-only systems. Where UNIX exists at the WS, MRS and higher levels, this will ease background communications and vertical integration of applications.

☞ With multi-user UNIX, you can write a program and have different parts of it doing different jobs on computers of different sizes, all at the same time. Further, the various program components will keep talking to each other and will all know what each other are doing at all times.

Support

Multi-user systems will virtually always be accompanied by at least full MRS Administrator (MRSA) support. Larger equipment is directly supported (at the OS, DBA, OA admin and end-user support levels) by professional IT staffs. The increased power and complexity of such systems (over PC-based servers) warrants such support.

☞ As stated earlier, putting an MRS into a workgroup also almost invariably means putting an MRSA there too. This person will help the PC users with many things related to their PCs, the MRS and larger computers.

Cost

Multi-user systems supporting the same number of users as a client/server system will virtually always cost more to acquire and operate, where comparisons are made on an intra-tier basis (MRS versus MRS grade or MBS class equipment, for example). However, they also provide more power, flexibility, redundancy and operational robustness in most circumstances.

☞ An MRS configured for multi-user service costs more than one for client/server service, but the former is more capable. You get what you pay for.

Commentary

The range of alternatives open to a local workgroup for their business computing is considerable and can be represented as a continuum between the 'pure server' and 'pure multi-user' extremes where each of these is viewed (only for purposes of constructing this continuum) as being mutually exclusive and uni-functional. The continuum can be characterized as having at least the following points shown in Table 4.1:

Table 4.1 Alternatives available to workgroups

SP	SLP	MSLW	MSLP	MLP	MLD	MX	MT

They are defined as follows:

SP	Micro-based file server—PCs star-wired to server
SLP	Micro-based file server/LAN/PC
MSLW	MRS(multi-user/server)/LAN/UNIX workstation
MSLP	MRS(multi-user/server)/LAN/PC
MLP	MRS(multi-user)/LAN/PC
MLD	MRS(multi-user)/LAN/diskless PC
MX	MRS(multi-user)/X-terminal
MT	MRS(multi-user)/terminal

Many organizations have already decided that their primary means of interconnection will be the Local Area Network (LAN). Thus, whenever an MRS or MBS is installed, a LAN will usually also be installed if one is not already present. Note, however, that there may be some workgroup systems which are isolated and/or where users have minimal non-workgroup-oriented desktop (personal) computing requirements; in such situations, star-wire connection of PCs to a dedicated server or such connection of PCs, UNIX workstations, X-terminals or even standard terminals (for example, VT-100/220/3XX) to an MRS may be adequate.

For purposes of this discussion of tradeoffs, several points were considered in selecting which configurations to place at either ends of the tradeoff continuum:

- Our hypothetical organization has mandated LAN connection for most users.
- It has also mandated a minimum of a PC286 system for most users.
- LAN is seen as a means of interconnection, *not* a processing tier.
- All configurations listed above are 'workgroup' systems in that they are shared by and serve a workgroup. However, because they are not all multi-user capable, true dedicated MBS installations represent an anomaly—they are part of the workgroup processing tier but *not* equal in performance or standards-adherence terms to an MRS.
- Where MRS combined client–server/multi-user and MRS multi-user (only) solutions are considered, this anomaly disappears but so too does much of the basis of comparison, since one system is basically a superset of the other, although it is recognized that MRS equipment is configured differently for pure server and pure multi-user roles.

- The client/server model is usually (but not always) associated with the provision of a PC-based dedicated server device sized for that particular role, usually an MBS based on Intel 80386 or 80486 processor architecture. Conventional client/server architectural thinking suggests that demand growth be met by addition of more servers (the so-called 'server-cloning' approach) rather than progressing to a larger system.
- The multi-user model is usually, but not always, associated with the provision of a more powerful fully configured MRS with considerable surplus processor, memory and storage capacity, from product lines increasingly reliant on RISC technology.

Thus, it can be seen that the SLP configuration best captures the essence of the client/server model and that the MLP best captures that of the multi-user model, while holding all else constant. Therefore, these two configurations were selected for the client/server versus multi-user tradeoff discussion. Note that in the case of MLP, the LAN is used as a means of connectivity only and *not* to support a true client/server service model for RDBMS/applications nor for OA. In the SLP configuration the LAN is used not only for basic connectivity but also to support the client/server service model for RDBMS/application and for OA.

User mode data are presented in Table 4.2 for a stand-alone dedicated X.25 gateway, an SLP configuration, a second server device for an SLP configuration, two MRS configurations and, for comparison purposes only, a larger UNIX system. Below, several of these are considered in more detail as options for the system architect in various circumstances.

SLP option

The SLP Primary Server will act as combined LAN controller/file server, will provide X.25 gateway services and will run LAN-version (client/server-oriented) RDBMS and OA products. Each user must have an intelligent client (PC). Secondary Servers, where added, would use the same basic technology but would not provide the LAN controller nor the X.25 gateway function. Note that there exists a small (reserve) multi-user RDBMS capability in the SLP configuration. I am assuming here that your organization has ruled out for MBS use any variant of the OS/2 operating system family member. Even if this reserve capability was omitted (and the requirement for *any* true multi-user capability was thus deleted) there are several reasons why OS/2

Table 4.2 Configuration data

System name	Gateway	SLP	SLP-B	MLP	MLP	Larger
Description	X.25 gateway	PC-based primary server	PC-based secondary server	MRS 20-user	MRS 50-user	Mid-frame 120-user
Nominal users						
• Client/server role only		30	20			
• Gateway only	30	5	–	5	12	30
• Multi-user						
– Total	–	3		20	50	120
– OA				4	10	24
– RDBMS				10	25	60
– MF access				5	12	30
– Other				1	3	6

should not be considered as the operating system for the SLP configuration:

- OS/2 cannot be extended to multi-user operation in the future should this be desired for any other (non-RDBMS-related) reason.
- While OS/2 can offer DOS under a task, it does so in a more restricted, less capable mode than UNIX.
- OS/2 offers multi-tasking, but does so at a greater total overhead per user (where the administrator may be forced to run multiple images of the OS) than does multi-user UNIX.
- OS/2 offers a less open computing environment. If a full specification for an MBS as in the SLP configuration were to be derived from an MRS product line running UNIX (with appropriate reductions in CPU power, memory and storage as set out in Table 4.2 but maintaining the degree of openness and standards-adherence which MRS vendors have now proved in the field), an OS/2 candidate solution would *not* be the operational or standards-adherence equal of the UNIX system.
- Security, On-line Transaction Processing (OLTP) and distributed computing system enhancements specified for UNIX (both the OSF and UI flavours) have not been announced for OS/2.

The SLP approach offers a number of important benefits and advantages:

- It is the lowest-cost option because the incremental equipment to be added to existing PCs is quite minimal and because it allows low-cost addition of secondary servers at any site which requires one, possibly even from a vendor other than the supplier of the primary server.
- There is the potential for wide-open competition for the supply, integration and support of PC-based server equipment if that is desired; this is a very fast-growing and competitive sector of the computer systems market.
- At an individual site, it may be particularly practical to source both the server and the desktop workstations from the same vendor.
- Even if a 'pure server' architecture is implemented, there still exists the possibility for very limited multi-user access to a PC-based server, providing OS/2 (or WINDOWS NT) is not employed as the basic operating system. This could be used to support occasional or temporary users by star-wiring five or fewer non-intelligent terminals to the server.
- For very small sites (those with five to ten users) a PC-based server may provide adequate performance, even where occasional and limited multi-user use is made of the server.

- Possible future migration of the desktop standard to 386 standard or higher, and to UNIX, could allow creation of a more integrated computing environment within the local unit, and would allow limited tradeoffs in future processing power placement between the server and client systems.

This option offers considerably lower direct hardware and software costs, for the PC-based servers, the operating system and for any related peripherals, than for an MRS installation at the local site; typically a 386- or 486-based device will cost $15 000–30 000 whereas an MRS performing the server role but configured for moderate multi-user operation will cost $80 000–100 000 for small systems and $100 000–200 000 for larger ones. Further, it is not necessarily practical, for example, to run OA in client/server mode for 20 users and to concurrently run it in multi-user mode for the five or less which such a system might be expected to support. Thus the service model should be, by necessity if nothing else, relatively heterogeneous.

☞ MBS class equipment in server mode offers a low-cost and easy 'startup' way to get into workgroup computing while you begin your move to open systems, but it also has significant limitations. Even for MBS class equipment, OS/2 is a very poor choice if you intend to move to open systems. UNIX offers more capability and far less chance of vendor lock-in.

However, this option also offers many disadvantages. True multi-user applications (for all or most users) almost certainly could not be run, although local inter-PC E-mail and limited OA services could be provided on the existing or another server. True multi-user sharing of agendas, text documents or other objects is not possible since a pure server does not 'timeshare'. Two users can each have a copy of a given file served to them if no protective locking is employed, but neither can have confidence that the other has not modified it in some way. Nor are they both looking at the same actual workspace. Vendors are working to address these problems but they are by no means fully solved.

Running a true multi-user RDBMS on the primary or secondary servers is not practical under this option due to both system capacity constraints and the inability to tightly interwork multiple RDBMS images when workload expansion forces addition of more such servers. Database operations which cross more than one server usually require full SQL networking capabilities on the part of each client *and* each server. There are also serious system capacity difficulties with running a full copy of the RDBMS or even a major subset of it on each PC where it is required. This is certainly true with 80286 PC equipment and arises from the limited ability of DOS to take advantage of the power of the processor and the extensive power requirements of RDBMS products.

Note, however, that some RDBMS vendors, such as ORACLE, have released client/server-oriented packages which could be used in this option and would reduce PC workload somewhat. This does not, however, address the issue of interworking multiple devices each running its own copy of the RDBMS, be they PCs, dedicated servers or a mixture of the two. Such interworking will greatly complicate application execution, *ad hoc* user-initiated SQL queries and local database administration (DBA).

☞ True sharing of the data managed by RDBMS or other programs running on an MBS is very difficult, especially if users want to share the data while the program is actually running. This is a big disadvantage of MBS class equipment and the client/server model.

At many sites, the use of a new-technology RDBMS for most business applications provides the opportunity to develop a comprehensive 'client file' covering all aspects of the unit's involvement with each external client managed by the unit. Such a file would, of course, be accessed by more than one RDBMS application. However, as *more applications* are situated at the site, not only the total logic but also the total common data items (the client record structure) acted upon by this logic could be expected to expand. This is readily possible with a current technology relational database. However, simultaneous growth in *record size* and *dataset size* could, on the basis of raw on-disk storage requirements, seek access times, contention for disk access or other factors in and of itself lead to the addition of secondary servers. Certainly, growth in the number of active or semi-active human and/or inanimate clients being managed by the unit would increase dataset size as well, and this factor too could increase the likelihood of the need for secondary servers at unit sites merely on the basis of storage requirements.

☞ It is very easy to outgrow the MBS as your database programs, your data and the number of users of each program all grow.

In a recent UNIX implementation study conducted for a large client organization, it was my finding (and also that of the RDBMS supplier consulted during the project) that possible distribution of the key dataset(s) across multiple 'RDBMS servers' would increase network and storage space resource use. It could also complicate DBA and reduce the possibility of any true shared logic (even for small numbers of specialized users) being successfully resident on the PC-based servers. The differing distribution patterns of such data at different sites due to hardware, software or operational factors locally could further complicate application distribution, integration and operation. Such growth, if not accompanied by server cloning, would virtually force the organization to place most (certainly, far more than 50 per cent) of the locally executed logic on desktop PC equipment. If this requirement exceeds the PC286 (or even PC386) capacity/performance level, then very significant and widespread workstation upgrade costs will be experienced, users will have much of their PCs' available time/resources 'invaded' by the server or both developments may even occur simultaneously. Finally, the auxiliary but very limited multi-user access to the RDBMS contemplated in Table 4.2, i.e. the alternative of putting even three- or four-user (shared) RDBMS application logic on the 'server', may not continue to be practical at all as the logic, data comprehensiveness and dataset sizes all increase over time.

☞ With MBS and the client/server model, growth in any or all of programs, data and numbers of users can overflow the MBS, swamping the limited resources of the PCs and forcing you into complete upgrades.

Full replication of the application logic at each desktop 286-based PC may not be an optimum use of the collective hard-disk storage and CPU resources of the desktop and intermediate systems which is provided to the local workgroup unless response time or other considerations make the application of shared logic (on a true multi-user machine) to shared data impractical. If the logic is substantial then it may force an upgrade to PC386 equipment, negating some of the savings of having selected the MBS in the first place. Alternatively, the mere addition of more secondary servers will do nothing helpful, other than provide additional space to distribute datasets; it will complicate database access, add to LAN traffic and will not address the issues of user, application logic and operating system process interworking such as:

- Two or more users seeking to deal with the same record;
- Two or more users who need to *cooperate on-line* to perform a given work item;
- Dataset records resident on different servers;
- Logic and data which reside on different devices, be they servers and/or PCs.

If this system runs UNIX it can provide DOS (running as a UNIX task) to a non-intelligent terminal connected to the LAN via a LAN terminal controller, should this be desired at a later time.

☞ Coping with the above-cited swamping can mean more MBSs, bigger PCs or both. This can cost as much, or even more, than starting out with an MRS instead of an MBS in the first place.

Whereas the PC-based server (MBS) is optimized in its CPU, disk storage, I/O and other parameters for use as a server, it would not be an appropriate platform for running a *multi-user* version of an RDBMS or OA package. Specifically, it will not possess sufficient CPU, memory, bus data transfer capacity, on-line data storage capability or I/O capability to support true multi-user application programs dependent upon the RDBMS. In terms both of expanding the raw power dedicated to the server function as well as providing true multi-user services to more than three to five users, a PC-based server offers limited expandability for future requirements. It may be possible to run very simple multi-user applications written in high-level languages and hence mounted directly on top of UNIX provided the number of users is absolutely minimal. If the number of timeshare users grows significantly (i.e. above four or five) I/O and other constraints may impact server performance for the clients served.

For the PC-based server and for all MRS options, the system can provide a primary or secondary gateway to an open network and any proprietary networks which may exist. For all options, it is necessary to preselect the maximum number of users which will be permitted to use simultaneously the small system as an X.25 or similar gateway to the mainframe (or a gateway to another network or whatever). You must then configure both the MRS and the mainframe's definition of the emulated local network access controllers/processors for this number of 'logicals', although increases to the number of logicals usually only involve software changes. Thus, the Primary Server can provide full proprietary terminal emulation on behalf of the actual or emulated ASCII terminal of the end-user. Note, however, that under this option non-intelligent terminals (should it be decided to purchase them later for occasional and temporary users) can only be connected by means of a LAN terminal controller or by direct star-wiring (in very limited numbers) to the Primary Server.

Alternatively, dedicated (virtually stand-alone) communications boards can be placed on-board the PC-based server such that these are accessed in the so-called 'communications server' model, probably but not necessarily on a one-user-to-one-board basis. However, such an arrangement may impose hardware limits to the number of users and/or logicals, which could itself in turn be impacted by the overall number of available number of card slots in the PC-based server. Note that MRSs too have limited numbers of card slots but, in general, they are more expandable in this respect than PC-based servers. Expanding the number of users able to be piped through the server may thus restrict other functions or future system capacity growth.

The SLP option generally requires that between 10 per cent and 20 per cent of a person's time during a year (here called a Person Year or PY) be allocated for a LAN Administrator (LANA) at each site where a PC-based server is installed. While a significant cost, this is a necessity for basic user support and system administration. There is the benefit that the LANA can also provide immediately accessible support for purely PC-based applications. The LANA will have some surplus time available (beyond server, LAN, client/server application and PC support) to devote to other work.

☛ Even an MBS is large and complicated enough that it simply cannot be installed and left unattended. Someone is required to look after it.

The following paragraphs summarize key concerns with the SLP option.

1 Workgroups will be provided with much lower capability for group work (for interworking together) than with a multi-user system. This has both qualitative and quantitative aspects and touches the opportunity cost of *not* sharing data downloaded from corporate applications, not having full function office automation, not having truly shared RDBMS applications for local use and being unable to obtain and mount other potential multi-user applications.

☛ MBS equipment offers a workgroup restricted capabilities.

2 The distribution of each of one or more client datasets across multiple RDBMS servers is believed to be less than optimal and it may be difficult or impractical to have any server-based logic act upon such data, should this later be desired.

☛ Running two or more MBSs in client/server mode for one workgroup can make things very complicated and exposes you to a significant failure and disruption risk.

3 With full capability record level (or even partial record) locking, it is probable that download of a specific database record to a specific user will prevent another user from performing similar or unrelated functions to the same record. This is so because the server(s) will not be cognizant of the update status of a downloaded record, of when the client (user) intends to upload the updated record or of whether the two clients are seeking to make conflicting or complementary updates.

☛ It is harder to have true sharing of data with an MBS.

4 Any significant expansions to local server capacity will be by 'cloning', simply adding another server to the network. This second device may then offer considerable excess capacity (being in many cases a bigger 'jump' than a chip or even a board upgrade on an MRS) and will certainly complicate attempts to run database applications across two or more devices. It will also complicate and hence increase the cost of system administration due to the basic overhead requirements of each machine from the operating system, LAN node and RDBMS perspectives.

☞ Adding more MBSs for one workgroup frequently causes more cost and trouble than having moved to a full MRS in the first place.

5 Within UNIX, most 'multi-user' licences begin at approximately eight users. If the PC-based server runs UNIX but has only a very slight multi-user capability (i.e. supports 30 PCs as a pure server but can also host two or three timesharing users at maximum) then you will be overbuying capability with respect to site licences for any multi-user applications in terms of the number of simultaneous (timesharing) users actually able to be supported.

☞ If you run UNIX on an MBS you probably are not taking advantage of the full capabilities of the UNIX OS. (You are, however, at least avoiding vendor lock-in.)

6 Whenever business information is downloaded to a PC there exists the possibility of a more easily acommplished security infraction, even if the user is provided a way to 'lock' the local application and its data. Such a lock is much easier to overcome than one implemented on an MRS or even a PC-based server.

☞ If you download important data to a PC and leave it stored there even for a little while, it is easier for people to access or steal than on an MBS or MRS. Someone can even walk away with the whole PC if they want the information badly enough. MBS and MRS equipment is larger and has enough wires hanging out of it that people, if they see the thief, will really wonder why anyone is taking home such a big machine.

Where a site views the selection of a PC-server/LAN combination as a permanent exclusion of MRS, you must also consider the user satisfaction and corporate cost implications of any and all small regional or local multi-user applications being automatically 'kicked upstairs' for development on larger UNIX mid-frames or mainframes (or even a proprietary mainframe) for no other reason than the lack of a true multi-user system at or within easy reach of the local site. This cost impact includes:

- HQ staff reviewing and approving the small applications;
- Consultation with regional and/or local site;
- Application development, test and implementation;
- Application support.

(Some of this cost and effort may be decentralizable but not necessarily all of it.)

User concerns with this process may include:

- Feeling they are being 'spoonfed' by IT and not allowed to buy or contract for locally needed applications within the established functional guidelines;

- Frustration with the length of the typical application development life cycle when many players and approvals are involved;
- Concern that corporately oriented IT staffs may seek to broaden the application to meet needs of other sites while reducing its ability to meet some of the requirements it was originally intended to meet locally;
- Concern over the cost of centrally developed versus locally developed or purchased applications.

MLP option

This option replaces the PC-based server with a MRS/LAN/PC (MLP); a UNIX mid-range system running multi-user applications under an RDBMS package presumably with a full multi-user office-automation package and also functioning as a file server for a LAN, including DOS/INTEL disk-equipped PC286s running both single-user applications and terminal emulators as well as LAN node software. This option provides an MRS configuration which is very powerful and flexible and which in virtually all cases will have been defined to permit significant and painless growth as user needs grow. It exhibits few of the restrictions of the SLP option due to the full multi-user nature of the MRS. LAN server functionality is maintained (but merely for file serving, not for running an RDBMS or an OA package according to the client/server model) as is the ability to perform the LAN controller role if required. Alternatively, the MRS can simply serve as a key node on a LAN controlled by a dedicated device.

A full-function MRS, even when used in a pure server role, offers the ability to deliver much more computing power than even a top-line PC-based server because:

- In the 'base product' either a CPU with more power than the 80386 or 80486 is used, provision is made for multiple CPUs of INTEL manufacture or the workload is functionally divided among CPUs of this or another type (one acts as main processor, one as I/O processor, etc.).
- Memory has significantly higher upper limits, typically two to five times that of a top-line PC-based server, even where the system is specified for the same number of users as the pure server.
- Bus transfer speeds can be five to ten times greater.
- Storage is typically measured in multiples of GB, not MB.
- I/O capability is almost linearly expandable with little degradation of the performance of other system resources except near the limit.
- The MRS typically contains many more slots and is available with a wider variety of startout chassis sizes and configurations.

Thus, the key advantages of an MRS over a PC-based server are:

- It can begin hosting true multi-user applications running under an RDBMS or under UNIX alone at installation time or at any future time; it is not totally, or mostly, restricted to the pure server role.
- It allows smoother and less restricted growth of the server function, the true multi-user function or both.

☞ The MRS is more powerful, more expandable and more flexible than the MBS.

Current-generation RDBMS packages were developed and proved on multi-user systems such as VAX/VMS environments, where they enjoyed stable operating system environments able to create large numbers of processes effectively and also to support many users simultaneously. They were, of course, first optimized to such environments. More recently, their vendors were subjected to two distinct market pressures:

- To offer current version products on multi-user UNIX platforms;
- To offer full or at least as much as possible of the functionality in a LAN client/server environment for organizations wishing to treat large or intermediate-level processors as 'pure servers'.

Meeting the first demand was relatively straightforward. ORACLE, for example, has moved to replace VMS with UNIX as its key porting base; some RDBMS vendors actually started out under UNIX. In general, RDBMS engines perform as well or better on UNIX platforms as they do on proprietary operating system platforms once they are reoptimized.

With regard to the LAN client/server requirement, RDBMS package vendors were required to substantially reorient and redesign some parts of their products to obtain full (or even some) functionality on a much less powerful processor, by offloading workload to the PC. However, this required both the presence of some software from the RDBMS vendor on-board the PC as well as considerable networking capabilities (SQL networking, etc.) which were *overlaid* on top of the LAN's existing software. Also, some RDBMS products make very substantial resource demands even of a 386-based PC. In an RDBMS client/server model, much of the application logic resides on the PC and the server RDBMS software can, for example, initiate searches of disks on many PCs seeking a single file or record. Although usually graceful, this activity can disrupt the work of many PC users. In a true multi-user system, disk searches are private as between the current user, the application, the RDBMS and the MRS's own disk(s); no one else and nothing else is involved. A key advantage of using an MRS as the LAN server is that the inherent multi-user capability frees the system from the *necessity* to use the RDBMS client/server model; use of the RDBMS client/server model is still possible (although not optimal) in this environment. While the option of client/server RDBMS operation remains, the MRS favours use of the full multi-user RDBMS model and offers no particular advantage for use of the client/server approach. Indeed, use of this model requires much more extensive software for PCs and the LAN than will likely be required otherwise. It also more fully taxes the LAN and PCs with little benefit returned for this extra imposed workload.

An MRS permits any or all of the following three RDBMS processing models to be employed:

- PC user employs terminal emulation to access true multi-user application running under RDBMS on MRS.
- PC user employs terminal emulation to access application running cooperatively on MRS and mid-frame or mainframe (this assumes the same or at least compatible RDBMS on MRS and larger systems).
- PC user runs a cooperative application which runs partially on the PC and partially on the MRS. Application can be divided between the two processing tiers in any way convenient to the developer. This does not necessarily connote a client/server model as, for example, most of the source data could be PC-based with most of the processing occurring on the MRS and with results stored on a mid-frame—this does require some PC-based RDBMS software.

In the first and third models above, the users are employing the system as a *work group* and can, where desired, make maximum use of RDBMS flexibility as to file and record level locking, interapplication communication, seamless use by applications of multiple (and overlapping) groups of datasets and other similar features.

☞ Databases and the programs written for them can come much closer to achieving their full potential on a computer which offers full multi-user capabilities. If you want to move to open systems, the smallest such system and the one best suited to workgroups of five to above 100 persons is an MRS.

Similarly, most office-automation packages including shared calendaring, word processing, E-mail, etc., were conceived for multi-user machines and initially implemented on and optimized for such equipment. By definition, 'office' automation or 'workplace' automation assumes that there exists a workgroup; otherwise why would anyone want, for example, to send E-mail to anyone else? No one sends E-mail to themselves! As with RDBMS vendors, OA vendors saw some of their customer organizations seek to decentralize processing without the benefit of true multi-user systems at the intermediate tier using devices which were 'servers' in name and pure servers in fact. They too faced demands for 'LAN versions' of their applications. The inherent difficulty with this was that, conceptually, an OA system on a server is like an office with glass cubicle walls which employees cannot penetrate; they can each access the hallway or the gangway above but not each other. There is no conference room and no meeting place.

Existing and planned LAN OA systems can transmit mail, either by assigning server storage space to each user or by responding to real or deemed mail delivery requests from the client and sending a copy of the mail file. For person A or his or her assistant to check person B's agenda on a client/server OA package often implies double or quadruple the amount of network traffic required for the same function with an MRS running full multi-user OA. Authoring a document on a PC and uploading it to the MRS for review by five others is much more efficient under multi-user OA than client/server OA because:

- With server OA the source client or server must either send one copy to each recipient's PC or else the source client must send a message to all five recipients and the server must then await and honour five individual 'fetch file' requests as clients ask for the mailed (or, more correctly, 'sitting on server and ready to mail') item.

- With server OA no two (or more) of the five can be allowed to capture *and edit* a copy of the file simultaneously or there may be a subsequent attempt by them simultaneously to perform a conflicting update.

Sending a copy of the E-mail message to each of five machines is a poor use of the collective communications capability and the collective storage space allocated to the unit (total of disk space on MRS and PCs combined) and also creates potential reconciliation problems. An MRS offers the option of either sending a copy to each person's file space directory or else, as do some products including OA products introduced by some RDBMS vendors, simply making one copy of the E-mail text file and creating a reference to it in each person's E-mail *in-box*. A middle-ground strategy is to insert a notice of the E-mail in the *in-box* but only to transfer a copy of the file when the user actually reads *and decides to save it*. Also, sequential use of the server-based file by five PCs still involves ten transmissions of the *entire file* over the LAN (five from the server out to the PCs and five from the PCs back to the server). Conversely, and depending upon LAN structure and operations and what part of the MRS multi-user OA file a PC user wishes to edit, only a few pages of, for example, a 100-page file might need to be transmitted to and displayed on each user's terminal-emulating PC. Even if the user displays *all* 100 pages, most of this material is transmitted from MRS to PC only once and not in the other direction at all, except where actual edits are involved. Even where such edits occur, the amount of data transmitted from the PC to the MRS is dependent upon whether the OA package designer and/or user have selected character, line, page or block level editing. Except where the PC-MRS channel over the LAN is absolute (as opposed to virtual) the multi-user model thus renders much better overall communications resource use. In all cases, it renders less use of and less wear and tear on collective hard-disk resources, since fewer conventional file transfers occur in the multi-user model.

☞ MRS equipment, working either with PCs or terminals, runs office-automation software more efficiently than MBS equipment combined with PCs.

Further, a UNIX MRS operating in multi-user mode can permit an appropriately configured OA system to allow simultaneous access and editing of a document by two or more users. This is the shared work-space concept which pure server-only LANs do not support at all. In reality, workers don't organize their work around 'files', neither card-board files which computers variously call 'folios' or 'folders' nor around documents or other items which computers call 'objects' but humans call 'things'; they organize it around 'work items' or tasks, any one of which may involve three people and four files. LANs and their servers are 'file' and 'facility' oriented, serving these facilities out to client PCs. A full multi-user MRS, with at least minimal integration of OA and RDBMS packages, or with a common user interface/work flow or 'handler' application on top of both of them, can allow the work-group to define work item content and relationships on a basis much closer to that of real life.

☞ An MRS can let two or more workers edit the same document at the same time. This is harder to accomplish with an MBS.

A current technology MRS strategy is not a conventional 'mini-computer' strategy which connotes the use of only non-intelligent ter-minals or, worse still, relegates more expensive 386 PC equipment to the dumb terminal role. The role of the PC in an MRS/LAN/PC environment can include all of the following:

- Run stand-alone DOS-based applications such as WordPerfect and LOTUS as well as any other user-desired specialized applications.
- Run a DOS-based terminal emulator (non-intelligent or X-terminal) to gain access to the MRS as a timeshare user.
- Upload file created under WordPerfect or LOTUS to the multi-user

version of this software running as an integral part of the OA package—this can be done as a timeshare user or a client of the MRS in its server capacity.

- Co-modify an uploaded file with another user.
- Transfer a file, via the LAN, to another user.
- Download data for processing at the PC and upload the result.
- Undertake a joint review of a record with another user while discussing it by telephone with that user—both view it at once and one or both may have modification authority at that time.
- Invoke an application which involves vertically integrated processing involving MRS-based data and logic based at both the MRS and the PC levels.
- Access the MRS as an emulated ASCII terminal to invoke proprietary terminal emulation to access a proprietary mainframe.
- Invoke a true multi-user RDBMS application on the MRS which acts on various records of one or more datasets.
- Invoke a true multi-user application on the MRS which does not utilize the RDBMS engine.

☞ Even with an MRS present, it is worth giving most users a PC since there are many productive things they can still do with it without duplicating what the MRS does.

Where end-users have PC386 or true UNIX WS equipment, it will be at least *capable* of running UNIX. This would allow users to obtain significantly increased performance from their 386-based PCs since UNIX makes much fuller use of system resources than does DOS. The possible future inclusion in this architecture of PCs running UNIX provides the opportunity to offload some processing from the MRS, allowing specification of a less powerful, and hence less costly, initial MRS configuration, *if the decision to migrate is made at the same time as the MRS acquisition made at that site*. Of course, the PC286 or PC386 equipment will have limits to memory and storage expansion and any such expansion at all will increase costs beyond initial projections. However, specifying five upgraded PCs to run UNIX faster and 20 standard PCs all running UNIX (together with a smaller MRS) instead of 25 standard PCs all running DOS and a larger MRS may bring significant savings. Therefore, a direct tradeoff of processing power between the MRS and workstation levels exists and must be addressed in planning the initial configuration (and growth path) for each site should PC UNIX migration be contemplated.

☞ If you buy or at least contemplate UNIX-based MRS and UNIX-capable PC or workstation equipment at the same time, you can tradeoff processing power between the two levels.

The coexistence of UNIX-based MRSs and workstations and Ethernet (E-Net) would permit maximum ease of UNIX–UNIX communications and provide the optimum environment for implementing vertically integrated applications. It is expected that UNIX-optimized CPU replacement cards for some PCs, based on advanced 386 and 486 processors, will become available from many vendors in the near future. Such cards will almost certainly run DOS as a UNIX task and have firmware permitting them to function with PCs equipped with moderate I/O and disk resources. This would permit you to take maximum advantage of the availability of such products, upgrading PCs at a given site as the processing requirements of individuals evolve.

☞ Soon you will be able to upgrade some of your PCs to UNIX by adding or replacing processor boards. Where you are also using Ethernet LANs you can reap a number of additional benefits.

The principal concern with respect to an MRS strategy is that of cost. To provide even basic server functionality to a group of 30 PC users while preserving the future option of full multi-user operation, acquisition of an MRS will involve approximately two to three times the cost of a PC-based server. For this extra you are buying:

- A member of a product line which extends far beyond the 30-user range and which thus allows growth in resources and facilities for the server role, the multi-user or both *without cloning*;
- Superior X.25 and other open system networking capabilities;
- True multi-user capability available from the outset;
- The ability to mix and match star-wiring and LAN-connection of users according to local site requirements;
- The experience, support capabilities and commitment to software and product development of a major computer vendor.

Except for PC-based servers from the major MRS vendors, most other PC-based servers come from much smaller firms with little or no experience building and supporting true multi-user systems. Most major UNIX-based MRS vendors such as UNISYS, BULL, AT&T/NCR, DEC, HP, DG, Motorola, IBM and others have been selling such systems for a number of years. They also sell MBS equipment.

Apart from the higher initial product costs, you will also face increased software support and hardware service costs for a given site if an MRS is specified. OA and RDBMS package software for use in a multi-user situation is normally more costly than that intended for purely client/server use, even where the same number of users are involved. You may actually elect to procure software which has both capabilities; in most, but not all cases, true multi-user software also offers some client/server capabilities.

☞ MRS equipment is considerably more expensive to acquire and support than MBS equipment.

The advantages and disadvantages of different processing tiers

Later, in Chapter 7, we will discuss how to decide on which tier applications should be placed. Here we will consider some of the inherent attributes of the processing tiers themselves. I have chosen to consider a four-tier topology here involving mainframe, mid-frame, MRS/MBS and desktop equipment, but you may amalgamate the first two if you wish to consider a three-tier architecture.

CPU

In terms of system capacity and performance resources, PC/WS equipment is far less restricted now than even three or four years ago in so far as tailoring a system to end-user needs is concerned. Normally such systems will run DOS or UNIX; OS/2 should be used only with extreme caution, given an open architectural direction, for the reasons elaborated above. The MRS offers a very efficient and cost-effective platform for user groups of five to about 100 users. However, practical support overhead limits may limit most installations to the 20–70-user range. As user ratings move towards 100, especially for a machine capable of supporting 50 simultaneous RDBMS users, the MRS begins to look more and more like a small computer room machine in terms of power requirements, heat load dissipation, noise level and support requirements.

Certainly, a 100-user system requires an exceptionally well-trained MRSA or else an IT professional. Mid-frame equipment offers fair to good price/performance but far fewer configuration options and far fewer suppliers, particularly if dynamic repartitioning of UNIX and a proprietary operating system such as MVS is required. From the end-user perspective, distant mid-frame or mainframe equipment will impose a network overhead for *all* user-, application- or process-initiated transactions. Mainframe equipment offers virtually unlimited expansion ability and, of course, the ability to co-host UNIX and, for example, IBMs VM or MVS or DEC's VMS operating system.

In cases where it is desired to write applications which simultaneously impact old (DBMS) and new (RDBMS) data, recent product announcements offer considerable potential. Software AG has announced that ADABAS and NATURAL will be available for various UNIX variants and these are now being released. This, combined with the recent release of fully capable CICS-emulators, permits existing IBM mainframe applications to be ported from the MVC/CICS/ADABAS/ NATURAL environment directly to the UNIX/UNIKix/ADABAS/ NATURAL environment, with only low or moderate difficulty. In accomplishing such porting, the supplied porting tools can automatically outfit the original application for OSF/Motif and/or Windows GUIs, if desired.

☞ With UNIX, you can select any size processor you need. Some large processors can run both proprietary operating systems and UNIX at the same time. Generally, the bigger the box you buy, the more expandable and flexible it is. Recently released products let you migrate, for example, many existing programs running on IBM mainframes directly to new UNIX systems of mainframe, mid-frame or even MRS scale.

Memory

PC and WS equipment remains relatively limited, at least as compared to large MRS and mid-frame or mainframe equipment, in this area. Also, adding memory cards to a single-user system tends to carry a higher opportunity cost in terms of precluding other add-on features than it does on MRS or larger equipment. MRS equipment offers very good memory upgrade potential but at relatively higher cost per MB compared to larger UNIX-based equipment.

☞ All sizes of system, except PC, can have significant memory upgrades with little opportunity cost or impact on their other characteristics.

Storage

The ability of the end-user to expand PC/WS desktop or under-desk storage is usually physically limited. However, the rapid increase in disk capacities from 20 to 40 MB a few years ago to several hundred MB today and newly introduced optical storage systems reduce the space/ heat penalty. MRS class equipment now offers upgrade paths on a par with those of mainframes of just a few years ago. For example, UNISYS recently released for the U-6000 MRS product line storage systems offering hundreds of GB of capacity with cabinets which indeed dwarf the actual MRS itself. With new-technology UNIX mid-frame and mainframe equipment, storage limitations tend to be only those imposed by facility raised-floor space.

☞ In most circumstances, open systems permit you to add as much system vendor or third-party storage as you like.

Input/output

Internal bus and port expansion limitations restrict all PC and many WS systems as to I/O growth. Most MRS products are expandable to communications needs well beyond those of their rated user groups. Larger UNIX equipment possesses virtually unlimited capacity, from the perspective of the individual end-user in terms of channel, process and device access.

☞ For MRS and larger UNIX systems, input/output capacity is no longer a significant limitation.

3GL applications

As cited earlier, these applications tend to tie up completely all but the most powerful UNIX-based desktop system, thereby preventing the user from pulling out someone's telephone number from a personal productivity tool or accessing a spreadsheet while the application is running. This is due to the inherently single-tasking nature of DOS. Even on a UNIX-based WS the application may still consume considerable basic system resources when running in background and may thus degrade the user's foreground application response time. On an MRS, 3GL applications can be run with equal facility in foreground or background and can, where necessary (and practical), access parallel processing and parallel I/O. When running such applications on larger UNIX equipment, the only real issues are any use made of the network to first reach the distant system, allocation of sufficient prime system resources to the user and the scheduling/prioritization of the application. As discussed above, even a conventional COBOL or C application could have embedded calls to DBMS and RDBMS engines running on the same or another networked machine.

☞ Conventional programs run well on most UNIX systems. However, workstations can still be bogged down by them, so selection of an MRS or larger platform will usually be desirable.

In general, applications developed for the PC/WS (especially those developed in-house and locally) tend to be both relatively inexpensive and also easy to port (DOS/INTEL- or UNIX-based) but offer only moderate benefit or utility on the new user's target system. Where necessary, they can be carried to higher-level systems providing they are written in a clean (ANSI) variation of a known programming language

Table 4.3 Application portability characteristics

Tier	Portability	Peers	Utility once ported	Investment
Mainframe	Fair/poor	0	Poor	High
Mid-frame	Good	1–10	Good	High
MRS/MBS	Excellent	10–500	Excellent	Moderate
PC/WS	Excellent	1–10 000	Fair	Low

(but not BASIC) or are implemented under UNIX. MRS applications are more costly to develop, offer excellent portability (particularly horizontally to other MRS equipment) and offer good utility to the receiving workgroup, although some logical (business process) modifications may be required. In general, legacy (i.e. non-open) mid-frame and mainframe applications have tended to be very expensive to develop and highly system- and context-dependent. This will probably also be true, at least to some extent, of new applications developed expressly for mid-frame or mainframe equipment. Moreover, there are few peer systems to which such applications can be ported where they are too large to move down to MRS. Most organizations have a distinctly limited number of mainframes (they are very expensive, even the UNIX varieties) and relatively few mid-frames. Also, many mainframe applications, even if written for UNIX, will be non-portable to smaller machines due to their logic size, number of users and/or scale of data regularly addressed.

Table 4.3 summarizes these application porting characteristics, which must be borne in mind when considering four-tier processor tradeoffs both *within and among tiers*. It will thus be seen that application porting *within* (and possibly also to/from) the workgroup (MRS/MBS) tier may offer the best optimization of application investment, portability and on-target utility.

> ☞ UNIX porting (carrying programs between UNIX machines) gives you more value per dollar than porting to, from or within proprietary operating systems. In general, within UNIX, porting horizontally (between computers of the same size) is easier and more cost effective than porting vertically (among computers of different sizes). Horizontal porting among MRS machines appears to offer the highest yield of all.

Office automation

True OA cannot be run on a PC or WS, although single-user productivity tools certainly can. By definition, OA is multi-user in nature. The MRS is the lowest-level and lowest-cost processor which can offer true workgroup OA including full E-mail, shared workspace and, if desired, automated telephone dialling through wide area telephone, Centrex, PBX, keyset or trunk interlink. In many cases, OA can also be delivered effectively with larger UNIX platforms. However, consumption of network resources will be considerable where many of the users are located far from the system. These larger UNIX machines are best used for OS only where:

- The specific user group is distributed or decentralized (is, in effect, a diasporatic workgroup, such as a group undertaking temporary field work) and has an MRS back at the office which cannot be conveniently accessed;
- The immediate user group is larger than appropriate for an MRS;
- The user group will use the large UNIX processor only as an interim device and will later download their OA work environment to an MRS as soon as they can acquire one.

☞ It is best to deliver office automation on an MRS. Use a larger platform only where you really have to do so, and even then only on a temporary basis, if that is possible. Make permanent use of a large UNIX system for OA only when the user group is too big for an MRS.

RDBMS

A single-user PC or WS is subject to very specific capacity limits in hosting an RDBMS, offers little physical or system security in most cases and is limited as to the record size, dataset size and application size it can tolerate. Also, the end-user is the DBA. In client/server, and more so in multi-user mode, an MRS offers the ability to allow an RDBMS to be provided with all required system resources and communications services, with these being made parallel or fully duplicated (redundant) where required.

For most workgroup applications, the MRS will prove the optimum logic processing platform. While the MRS offers better system and much better physical security than the desktop systems, this will only be as effective as the MRSA is effective in the DBA role. Where performance requirements outgrow the ability of the workgroup to justify MRS upgrades or the ability of the MRS even to *be* upgraded without outgrowing the MRS/MRSA service model, the application can be uploaded to a mid-frame.

The mid-frame can also serve as an emergency standby and/or backup processor for critical MRS-based applications and can host applications or databases which are, *ab initio*, too large for the MRS environment. Also, the mid-frame is supported by a professional IT staff, one of whom may act as a DBA for a significant part of the time. It may also be selected where a distributed group of users requires workgroup style access to an application/database.

In other cases, the regional or divisional focus of the application or the database may point to a mid-frame as the tier of choice. The mid-frame may also be used for a regional data repository and/or dictionary, and/or to support periodic audits or reviews of MRS-resident data.

Note, however, that large-system users will be subject to contention for (and any capacity or service limitations of) the Wide Area Network (WAN), large-system I/O and large-system prime resources. Time zone and day/week/month factors entirely beyond the immediate ken and control of the user community may have effect on system loading and hence application performance. Applications with very large datasets, those requiring high-performance OLTP or those serving a very wide group of users may be optimally located on the mainframe. The main-frame usually has a full-time and rigorous DBA and can also act as a corporate data server for mid-frame and MRS equipment. It can pro-vide extreme circumstance backup of data but slower restoration servi-ces than mid-frame equipment due to both the greater corporate processing (and IT professional service) workloads and the fact that corporate-level staff will be less familiar with a given workgroup's requirements than will regional or divisional staff operating a mid-frame.

☞ Above the workstation tier, you can, in most cases, put data, databases and database programs where you like. Do not be shy about upgrading to a larger machine when workgroup or other requirements so indicate! Be aware, however, of the network overhead implications of longer-distance connections for the users!

Local communications and extra-tier access

At the PC/WS level, local communication of data is by transferring disks by hand, by pseudo-LAN or by an elementary LAN offering only con-nection services and no true central hub or server. At the MRS/MBS level, a wide range of local and wide area communications is facilitated. Once a user or application reaches the higher tiers, wide area access has in most cases already been achieved.

☞ With OCS and OSI, getting at the data is no longer a problem.

Support

PC/WS equipment is normally supported partly by its user and partly by external or IT staffs or local paraprofessional specialists. The PC user is partially self-supporting and partially dependent upon the resources mentioned above. The MRS user is directly supported (as to PC and MRS OS, communications, packages and applications) by the MRSA, who is the intermediary between the end-user and the professional IT community who provide central support and operate the larger systems.

☞ The bigger the system, generally the better and more comprehensive is the required (and available) support.

Conclusion

This chapter may have been difficult for readers who are not IT professionals, but it is hoped that the '☞' sections have provided at least some relief. Now that we have considered what open systems are, their potentially positive and negative characteristics and the framework in which they are planned, we can finally progress to a consideration of how actually to implement them.

5 Step by step: slow and steady wins the race

Introduction

This chapter addresses the first steps you will want to take in your move to open systems, both OSI and OCS. It will help you to deal with your corporate, IT and user and technology management requirements and to set in place the planning mechanisms, and actual planning, to launch your open systems program. It will discuss the central human and hard infrastructure you will want to establish as well as some of the early problems likely to be encountered.

What kind of tiger?

If you were to go to India to procure a tiger, you might first want to have some idea of what you intended to do with it. If you merely want to make it into a great rug or stuff it for display in your front hall, the only two criteria may be that it be *dead* (quite provably dead, in fact) and have a good coat of fur. Many Great White Hunters have been killed by a tiger who was apparently, but not actually, dead. The skinners and/or taxidermists can take care of the rest. If you are considering keeping it for a personal pet (seriously, a certain singing star had his very own pet giraffe) you may look for bright eyes, youth and (for a tiger) a good disposition. You will also, of course, want to look for a sturdy cage. If it is to be trained and then placed in a circus or on some sort of similar display, you will likely emphasize good health, intelligence and other qualities.

Similarly, if you as an IT executive just want to be a bit trendy and are looking only for a 'rug tiger', any vendor will give you lots of very complex and profound-looking wall charts about open systems. You can use them to good effect to convince your boss, your colleagues and your users that you are at least thinking about moving in the open systems direction. Or if you are intending to import open systems on a very limited basis, perhaps just for one application or for one class of users, you can afford to ignore much of the advice in this or any other book. Specifically, you can set your own agenda for dealing with the caged beast. However, if you actually intend to climb into the cage with the tiger, to train it, you will want to know more about the tiger, the training tools, the desired eventual (trained) state of the tiger and even about yourself before you proceed. Otherwise, your first visit with the tiger might turn out to be your last! I am reminded of a question on a spoof aeronautical engineer examination encountered many years ago when serving as a civilian employee of the Canadian Department of National Defense. It went as follows:

> You, one round of twenty millimetre ammunition and a dissembled M39 cannon will be placed in a locked dark room. Seven minutes later a starved Bengal tiger will be admitted. Take whatever action you feel appropriate, being prepared to justify your decisions and methods (*Flight Comment*, May–June, 1975).

Corporate requirements

The User Alliance for Open Systems (UAOS) has correctly stated that it is crucial to link open systems to business objectives, especially in the minds of top management. A good way to get this process going is to run a short (one-day or weekend) retreat for key senior managers at which you provide a general, and not overly technical, introduction to the concept of open systems. You will also want to highlight some of the tactical opportunities and benefits (from Chapter 3) which you believe are most likely to be palatable to them.

This process is not unlike fishing. Most fishermen, even very experienced ones, do not well understand the psychology of the fish. Sometimes, in identical conditions, the same type of fish will prefer a particular type of bait over one used the previous day or week. We really don't know why, but even inexperienced fishermen know enough to change bait if the first one tried does not work and the fish are literally jumping out of the water. The psychology of senior management can be just as difficult to understand. Some months they are very enthusiastic about cost-cutting and at other times they may be concerned about cutting response times, making employees happier, or even basic survival. Like your five-year-old, senior management's attention span is often quite brief. If you are unable to captivate them immediately with a particular idea or concept, do not flog it but move on to the next one.

However you elect to proceed, you should ensure a good attendance at the session by pointing out that your suppliers, customers and competitors can all be expected to adopt open systems soon and that failure to consider such a strategy could leave your organization flat-footed in the near future. You might want to add that open systems will, over time, reduce costs and put more computing power in the hands of the user. If all of that fails to light a spark in their eyes, suggest that you are also trying to move the computer-acquisition strategy out of the control of your largest proprietary vendor! The latter is almost guaranteed to get their attention.

After the session is over you should be able to:

- Identify which tactical opportunities and benefits can be exploited in the short term and prioritize them;
- Identify which strategic opportunities and objectives can probably be exploited in the medium to long term and provisionally prioritize them.

Also, your retreat has been a failure if you have not been able to link at least some of the strategic opportunities and benefits to the business mission in the minds of the top managers. Perhaps open systems will help gain an edge on your competitors, help improve customer service or facilitate downsizing. Perhaps all three are equally important. Perhaps they will just make your company more profitable or your government agency more efficient. At the other extreme, outsourcing the mainframe and putting more computer power into the hands of workgroups may save you millions of dollars and help stave off receivership.

It is interesting to make your own private pocket list of which opportunities and benefits will be most important to senior management and then compare it to the actual ones after the meeting. However, you should not let your personal biases and views jaundice the whole process. You are giving them a *smorgasbord* of many delicious foods, not imposing the preferences of your tastebuds on them.

You must also keep them realistic, once they begin to get excited. At a truck electronics conference I attended, the Vice-President Maintenance of a huge trucking firm told us he wanted a truck on-board computer with 50 different functions which he enumerated ranging from tracking driver hours and stopping time to monitoring the temperature of a refrigerated trailer, and which would last ten years, be totally modular and cost no more than $500. I replied that my firm (a large aerospace/defence firm) would be pleased to deliver it if he could promise to get his friends at General Motors to provide me with a Trans Am which would go 200 mph, hold six people, get 80 miles per gallon and cost only $5000. His request was simply beyond the technology power curve at the time.

You have very valid cause for concern if they start saying things like: 'This is great, can we convert all the mainframe applications next month or latest by the end of this quarter?'

Finally, there is also the issue of costs. You will want to let them know that open systems, unfortunately, also have costs. These need to be placed in a reasonable perspective and discussed *after* they have prioritized the positive opportunities and the benefits.

IT requirements

Even if you have a very trusting management, which loves you and leaves everything about computers to you, approving all your requests for funds as soon as you submit them, you still need to go through the above process. You have to get senior management on board.

Then, you have to be just as good to yourself and ensure that you yourself are on board. You may want to consider what the IT organization will gain from the move to open systems. Perhaps your existing systems are so old that a total collapse is imminent, so it is a case of moving to *something* before the walls fall down. By corollary, your favourite vendor may have informed you that soon he won't be supporting your system any more or that support costs are going to triple. Perhaps you are losing a lot of staff because they want to work in a more modern environment. Maybe you are tired of a senior manager from your largest proprietary vendor frequently taking your own Vice-President Operations to lunch to try to get him to request or, depending on your organization structure, perhaps to order you to buy his latest gizmo. Maybe you realize that demand is rapidly outstripping the resources of the computer room and you simply cannot go back and ask for yet another mainframe upgrade, running into the tens of millions of dollars. Maybe users are busily commissioning the writing of totally undocumented local database applications by self-proclaimed programmers, summer students or whoever and you know these will outgrow small MBS equipment very soon. Perhaps PC and workstation usage is reaching the saturation point and users are just now discovering LANs; they are popping up like mushrooms and there are no acquisition and support standards or procedures in place. In some cases, virtually all of these motivators may be acting on you at the same time!

User-group motivators

Why would any presumably sane line manager ever want to become involved in an information management project in the first place? This is the fundamental question which must be borne in mind not only by line managers and their end-users but also by the professional IT staffs who assist the manager in considering, planning and implementing such a project.

1 In principle, the line manager wants to maximize his or her unit's or workgroup's efficiency in managing information. Information is to be managed as a resource, and on a life cycle basis. Advanced technology clearly has the potential to increase their leverage in accomplishing this. However, it must also be considered that counterbalanced against this is the tendency for many end-users and line managers to view the professional IT field as a thicket of incomprehensible acronyms, rules, devices and curious causal interrelationships, not to mention constant, sometimes almost frantically paced, change. Often, a manual or an existing (past-generation technology) solution will be retained far past the economic and operational crossover point (from which point forwards the new solution is provably better) due to factors of inertia. A project will launch and keep progressing only when the initial perception, and the continued perception throughout the project life cycle, is that not only will marginal benefits exceed the marginal costs but also that the project can be realized without unduly stressing the workgroup. Clearly, this is a perception on the part of the intended *end-users* and their *line management*. The fact that IT staff or the client staff think the project is wonderful means little if local end-user and hence local line management enthusiasm wanes. Local line management must not only continue to believe in the cost/benefit usefulness of the project but also its continued 'doability' within the administrative and operational structure. The onset, or advent, of budget cuts, reduced or increased downsizing targets, the end of the fiscal year and other factors can influence this. There is thus a 'political economy of project doability' which must be borne in mind by IT management and combined IT/user-group project team.

2 Where specific business applications are concerned, the workgroup may want to obtain an application to fulfil one or more of the following functions:

● Handle common business information and processes in which groups of end-users will share on a sequential and/or simultaneous basis;

● Permit new (and/or more) business information to be handled, thereby increasing productivity if all other things remain equal.

3 The application may replace a manual system or a combination of manual systems and existing automated systems. It may be desirable

to bring down to the workgroup level a process now performed on larger mainframe equipment where it is essentially a local process, or is one which could benefit from local enhancement. If the latter, the application may have started out on one or more PC platforms and may simply have outgrown the single-user (possibly even the client/server) model.

4 There is also the case of an application prepared by a client headquarters group, such as corporate personnel, which is then provided to the local workgroup with the expectation that they will run it. Where this is provided as a PC/MS-DOS application, the providing department in most cases expects target user individuals to have a PC available. In future, the department may similarly expect a workgroup to have a client/server (or even a full multi-user) UNIX system available. Where the application thus provided to the unit is none the less the first application to require such a platform, it will require provision of such a platform if it is not already present. This is the same as the situation where a principal provides to his or her executive assistant a spreadsheet package which is required to be run under DOS. If the assistant currently does not have a PC, it will now be necessary to acquire one.

The need for champions

In each of the senior management, IT and user communities it is necessary to secure staunch supporters (here, called champions) of the move to open systems. Clearly, there will be champions of remaining with the status quo in each camp so, if you don't have supporters for the change, it will be hard to bring it about. You need one very influential user group, or preferably several, or else a very large number of less powerful ones behind the basic idea. Failure to gain this support will at the very least hinder your planning and implementation of open systems. In extreme circumstances, your incumbent proprietary vendor may sense the potential for a user revolt and defend their position by actually going out and fomenting one with the express objective of getting you to back off, or even getting you fired.

A strategic plan

Depending how ambitious you were, and how well the senior management retreat went, you may have finished the weekend with the skeleton of a strategic plan for open systems already in your head or even up on the whiteboard. In any event, you will have to write or hire someone to write such a plan forthwith.

The plan should first address your kind of business, your business mission and the specific business objectives which your adoption of open systems is intended to help achieve. It should then discuss the types of information managed in your organization and highlight those which will soon (and later on) be impacted by the new systems. Then it should discuss the current and anticipated future business applications which will manage such information, followed by the packages (RDBMS or whatever else) upon which those applications will depend. Then, and only then, should the plan discuss the types of computer technology which it is anticipated will be needed to support the rest of this hierarchy. It should do so only in general terms. At this stage it is quite acceptable to say that we want to move most logic processing to the workgroup level. It might be premature to state that we will use only MBS or only MRS equipment, or both. It would certainly be premature to state here that we will acquire computers of Brand A and Brand B only. As a practical guideline, the plan should be readable and fully understandable by a high-school student. If you don't have one at home, borrow one from a neighbour who does! If your plan is not intelligible to people of this reading level it is probably either too 'professional' (maybe even pedantic or aloof-sounding), too technical or both.

Here is a sample set of goals and objectives, which you could modify to meet your specific requirements.

Goals

1 To create within ABC Inc. the capability to encourage and support the establishment of computing and communications systems which are open computing systems, able to exchange information and programs, work together and able to permit the same program to be run on many sizes of computer.
2 To assist end-users and information management planning authorities to determine which application programs are appropriate for implementation on open systems, and to support such implementation.

The specific objectives could be something like the following:

1 Monitor the situation of existing, proposed and potential open system users to determine, in consultation with line managers, those requirements which are sufficiently common to be supported centrally and regionally by IT.

2 Create one or more conceptual models (ways of planning and doing things) for information management and computer operation for each tier of processing (here define your two, three or four processing tiers), addressing both what is required locally and how best to provide it. Develop and maintain IT policies consistent with the model(s).

3 Develop and maintain specialized planning tools for use in evaluating the feasibility and actual planning of open system implementation.

4 Monitor hardware, software, communications and other technologies which are strategic to the development and maintenance of efficient and effective open systems computing.

5 Establish and maintain the means of communicating relevant technological, organizational and experimental developments to IT staff, and to paraprofessional system administrators, on a timely basis.

6 Plan, manage and coordinate the evaluation of headquarters and field lab tests, pilots and trials of special arrangements, facilities, technology and operational tactics as required.

7 Undertake liaison with governmental, industrial and institutional organizations operating, and/or offering resources in support of, open system computing.

8 Establish the means of first-line technical support and troubleshooting to reduce both downtime and dependence upon specific system vendors.

9 Evaluate and certify prepackaged applications software meeting generic requirements and provide on-request search/location/evaluation of software meeting specific user requirements.

System architecture

Without a system architecture, you will not know if a given new product you see at a trade show could even fit into your plans, much less where to put it. From the strategic plan, and from your body of information on user requirements (perhaps after appropriate studies in this area), have a system architecture produced which addresses at least the physical and either the logical or functional views. As stated in Chapter 4, there are many 'religious denominations' within the system architecture field so don't expect total agreement if you put the proponents of more than one of them in a single room. If you *lock* them in the room, you may need to return later with some of your tiger-taming tools.

You absolutely *must* have a one-page representation of the architecture understandable by the end-users, their line management and senior management. Here again, a high-school comprehension test is a good one to use.

Send smoke signals to your staff

By this time, most members of the IT staff will have at least some glimmering that you are now 'trending' in the direction of open systems. However, sending them some early and explicit messages is in your interest. Plaster the user version (and also the larger and more detailed blueprint-sized version) of the system architecture diagrams *everywhere* in the IT shop, even inside the inner sanctum of the computer room! Set up a new open systems bulletin board and keep it stuffed with articles, announcements and other items of interest! This will assist those who intend to support the change actively to get started early on learning new skills, or at least reading some new books. Populate your coffee table, magazine racks and, if you have one, IT reading room or library with a good selection of open systems publications! Initiate a zero-base budget review of all conference participation, shifting at least some resources from those dealing only with proprietary systems to those dealing with open systems!

Make provisional appointments of people to the 'watch and brief' role with respect to specific technologies of interest! Here, it is necessary to appoint avid supporters to the key technology areas. If you appoint someone who is opposed to the change to open systems to a key area, you will soon be awash in reports and clippings about how immature (even bad) this particular technology is. Finally, your smoke signals will also allow you to 'smoke out' the passive and active resistors. Some of the latter may serve themselves and you well by using the lead time to dust off their résumés and begin their job searches. They will, naturally, be seeking tranquil havens (even backwaters) where there is no intention of moving into this 'newfangled' stuff. There, they can continue plying their COBOL, JCL or similar trades until happy retirement comes along. So they hope, anyway. In such circumstances, it is almost always preferable to help them with this process, no matter how valuable you or their colleagues may think they are to the organization. Remember, a very experienced and very knowledgeable person who is also familiar with the internal petty politics may turn out to be your biggest hindrance later on.

Central technology management infrastructure

This is the time to establish a skeleton structure, perhaps even the actual organization if you can divert the people, to actually manage the inflow and support of the new technology. There are two schools of thought on this; one is to develop the capability totally within your existing structure, so it is integral from the outset. The other is to establish a discrete unit. Each strategy has its advantages. If you set up a discrete unit with volunteers and/or newcomers you will be assured of two things:

- They will make very rapid progress and will develop a good sense of purpose, and probably also a high profile.
- They will collectively serve as the 'target' for anyone in senior management, IT, userland or the vendor community who does not like your idea about moving to open systems.

If you integrate the capability, it will usually take longer to achieve critical mass, particularly if resistors are active in trying to neutralize enthusiasts. From a management point of view, it is easier to manage the leader of the volunteer army than to micromanage many minions scattered throughout your whole shop. On the other hand, if the resistors are very influential, they can engineer a we–they situation in an attempt to isolate and ridicule the new unit, forcing you to intervene constantly to clear the trees they chop down in its path.

If you elect to divide your system architecture into very distinct tiers, you may wish to organize your new unit, or indeed your whole shop, by processing tier. For example, you might have one unit handle mainframes and mid-frames and the other cover MRS, MBS, LANs, UNIX workstations and PCs plus office automation. If you have more than two or three tiers, the organization may be more complex. If you do organize by tier, however, there are several things you should be aware of:

1 While they are usually viewed as synonymous, there can be a subtle distinction between information management tier and processing tier. For example, a given application may be truly corporate, but may have security requirements which exceed those of your mainframe. Rather than upgrade the large system, it may make sense to place the application on a fully dedicated and secure MRS installed in the data centre. In such a case an MRS, which we normally associate with the workgroup tier, is used as a corporate system. There is nothing wrong with this. If you have a power user who has two PhDs and demands a workstation more powerful than the MRS

systems serving most workgroups of 50, you can agree. After all, the actual box is not much bigger than a PC and can certainly fit into the office with no discomfort. Here, the MRS is used as a personal workstation. You must therefore be very clear as to whether you are organized by processing tier or information management tier, or your troops will be genuinely confused as to who is supposed to serve the above-cited classes of clients.

2   The creation of units within the IT shop based on platform or processing tier (even on information management tier) brings with it the potential for inter-tier competition and rivalry. This may be purely internal and quite benign; after all, a certain amount of competition for a given application's place of residence may be healthy both for the users and for the IT unit. All of the pros and cons of each tier will be well aired on a case-by-case basis. However, if the rivalry becomes churlish or if senior or local line management, end-users or vendors are dragged into it you could have a big problem. Your incumbent vendors will likely side with the units whose aspirations they would most like to fulfil, while end-users may play one off against the other for their own purposes. In such circumstances you will be forced to wade in and end 'platform wars'; as in 'Father Charles goes down and ends battle!' If you sit back and do nothing, things will only get worse.

3   If platform wars erupt, end-users may be confused, frustrated, angered or even frightened by the multi-directional bombast of technocratic hyperbole (like listening to three doctors argue about what is wrong with you and not understanding a word) and simply try to find ways to acquire open or other systems without IT involvement.

4   If you intend to remain organized by platform over the longer term, not just during a transition period, you need an agreed and codified means of deciding where applications should reside. This must be seen as fair and just by all of the platform advocates, application developers (or development overseers), line management and end-users.

The above should not be taken as an indication that the adoption of open systems will necessarily cause you a lot of trouble. Many organizations have made a smooth transition; however, times of change are not only times of opportunity; they are also times of much discomfort and shuffling.

Information management (IM) planning

If your organization has not already implemented or purchased from outside consultants an IM planning capability, you will want to delay no longer in this regard. A good number of the opportunities and benefits of open systems relate to better management of information as a corporate resource. If this concept has not yet been introduced into your corporate culture, you may wish to proceed immediately to introduce it. On the other hand, you may already have a comprehensive IM plan in place. In any event, you will want to ensure that someone is responsible for regular update of the plan.

Current and planned application portfolio

Once you have a basic understanding of what information is being managed by whom, where and in what ways, you can begin to address the application architecture component of system architecture in more detail. What portion of the information will be managed by old applications in new clothes? How many can be migrated from legacy systems to open systems? Where on the portability continuum will each of them sit? How much re-engineering will be involved? For new applications, what will be the split among in-house development, contracted development, third-party vendor and recycling as sources for applications for various purposes? Will you adopt standards and form–fit–function specifications for OA and RDBMS products, or will you actually certify one or more products for each of these roles? In given circumstances, how will you decide where to source an end-user business application?

Understanding and tracking the technology

Whether or not you establish a discrete organization to lead the move to open systems, you will need people to track various technologies of interest on an ongoing basis. The 'watch and brief' people are a good start. Some of them may be candidates for elevation to a more formal technology monitoring responsibilities, while others may lose track of the ball, either accidentally or on purpose. Still others may decide that your current dominant vendor is the only source of information on open systems worth bothering with. If you are going to bring in new people, this is one of the best areas to do it, since it is just not possible to have too much expertise applied to this area. The more knowledgeable you are, the better will be the questions you can ask any presenting vendor who inundates you with claims of their long-standing tradition of openness. It will be much easier to tell if the Emperor has no clothes, whether he is a tiger in bear's clothing or a bear in tiger's clothing.

System integration

You cannot move to open systems without having the capability to at least oversee and manage the integration of diverse products from various vendors. It may or may not be necessary to have the in-house capability to perform this integration, but you *must* be able to tell when the process is finished and the system is integrated. Over the past few years a number of organizations in North America and elsewhere have become experts in providing system-integration services to their customers. This has usually been very helpful to the IT organization because it permits one-stop shopping without necessarily committing to one-vendor shopping. Indeed, you can have an external system integrator actually integrate any combination of products, sourced in any number of ways by their organization or your own. You have a single point of accountability; the integrator is responsible to you for a coherent working system, but you need to be able to settle on a contractual and, if necessary, legally enforceable description of just what that is.

Many IT organizations have developed very considerable system-integration capabilities in-house. Where such capabilities exist, you will almost certainly want to make good use of them during the tentative, early stages of your move to open systems. This should reduce by one the number of things that can go wrong. Later, if you intend to acquire a large number of systems (particularly if they are to be MBS or larger) in a relatively short period of time, you may need to supplement your own people with external assistance.

System administration and management

Open systems permit you to democratize much more of the computing power in your organization, to take it out much closer to the real users. The PC revolution has already taken us far along this path, and open systems will take us even farther. As stated in Chapter 4, open systems especially at the MBS and MRS levels are far less expansion-constrained than the DOS/INTEL standard PCs most users now have on their desktops. End-users outside our own IT field have almost always been notoriously poor in the administration and management of their desktop computers, with the exception of the far more sophisticated (from the computing perspective) power users, who tend to have UNIX or similar workstations anyway. They do not back up their working files often enough and usually pay little heed to security until something goes curiously missing. Many of them still, to this day, keep all their files on a single directory and they therefore suffer the consequences if they should accidentally enter a DOS command such as 'ERASE *.*' or similar. About the only good news in all of this is that even the most blatantly incompetent user (whom we will call 'Toby' and who will soon gain a reputation as such and will be kept off other people's PCs) can usually only take down his own personal system, no matter what he does. If he has mainframe or conventional minicomputer access, unless he is a deliberate hacker, the odds are that he is unlikely to do serious damage to the larger system.

However, what happens when Toby's workgroup gets a 50-user UNIX-based MRS which runs an OA package and also five business applications (each used by ten or twenty workers) under an RDBMS? It also provides access to the larger systems via a gateway, and all of the PCs are connected to it by a LAN. (For purposes of argument, we will assume that the system did *not* come from IT but was bought at year-end out of extra funds.) The boss puts Sue, who is a Lotus and WordPerfect whiz, in charge of the new system and she goes on a three-day course to learn basic UNIX system administration, such as how to back up the users' files to the cartridge tape, and how to restore them back onto the hard disk again. The users get training in OA and the new applications themselves, but not the database package.

Everything goes well for a while. Sue proves capable of adding new users to the system, assigning them passwords and even gets the special printer (which prints cheques for one of the applications) on-line and working well. Toby keeps volunteering to help her with the system but she politely refuses. She even helps him restore his PC to operating condition after he crashes it once more. The LAN is being used in a very simple communications mode since all of the applications running thus far employ the multi-user service model.

Then the boss says that he needs a petty cash control system. Toby says he saw one at the department store, in a UNIX version. Great, says the boss, go out and get a copy and submit the receipt for a refund. Sue was away that day and when she returns she finds the package on her desk with a note from the boss asking her to install it. She spends the next three days installing it, with lots of time on the phone to the software vendor's hot line, all long distance, of course. The package, it turns out, cannot be run from Sue's console so she brings over her old PC and plugs it into the MRS so she can run in the client/server mode required by the package. That is fine for her PC, which is now direct-wired to the back of the MRS, but when the four petty cash users who have PCs connected to the MRS by LAN try to use the software, problems arise.

Sue spends two more days reconfiguring some of the LAN server software and resetting the LAN boards on the four PCs. During this time the system was down half of the time, so now the month-end financial reports are late. Sue is very glad to get away for a skiing weekend and in fact does not even show up on Monday. She calls in mid-morning to inform the boss she has broken her leg and will be home for at least two weeks. Toby, who just happened to be in the boss's office at the time, immediately volunteers to take over the MRS and fill in for Sue while she is away.

Now the real fun starts. The users whose PCs were *not* modified (those who don't even use the new application) are wondering why the OA system behaves differently when they log on now and why one of the applications that used to be on the main menu has disappeared. Toby investigates. In the process he (sort of) learns how to use the tape drive, destroys one of the two live backup tapes and takes down the petty cash control application once again. By the end of the day, the entire MRS is back up, but now Toby has accidentally deleted the UNIX logical device which represents the cheque printer and therefore no cheques are being printed. Also, the financial report is finally complete but it is not printing properly on the other printer.

Toby works late. Next morning, things go from bad to worse. The bill comes in for $658 of long-distance telephone calls Sue made to the software vendor and now all printers except the little dot matrix are off-line. All of the E-mail in the boss's OA in-box has disappeared and so too has the financial report. In fact the directory containing not only the report but also the application which created it is gone. The system says something about 'demounted'. The two work-term university students (still completing their courses but working part-time at the firm) cannot seem to log on from their dumb terminals since their passwords are no longer valid. Toby is muttering something about 'Curses' for terminal control. Another user mutters that it is not terminal control that is cursed but either Toby or the MRS. At 11:01 am the system crashes completely. This is what we in the IT community call a 'hard crash'. Toby cannot even get the firmware diagnostic routine to run from the console. It is as dead as a dodo! Everyone is down; all 50 users. Since everyone now uses both their PC and the OA package to do word processing, many people have lost much of their morning's work. The people wanting to pump out the financial report are dead in the water; so are those waiting to print (and mail) cheques.

It's time to call the vendor, screams the boss. The vendor is very nice, but politely informs Toby that the system went out of warranty last week. Toby pleads, 'Please, oh please come. We're not even getting so much as a bleep out of it.' In lower tones, he mutters into the phone that we don't care what it costs; we just want it *fixed*. The vendor shows up at 4:42 pm and says there is not much he can do today, but promises to come back tomorrow. He asks Toby for the operating system tape but Toby has misplaced it. (Actually, it got mixed up with some video tapes in Toby's office and was deposited in a video store return chute last evening.)

The following day, the vendor gets the system back up, rebuilds the directory structure and tries to restore the crashed files. When he brings up the database package, he informs Toby that some database administration work will be required before the users can go back onto the five applications. OA can start running now, however. Toby has never heard of database administration; he doesn't even know what it is. He asks the vendor to do it, but the vendor politely replies that he didn't sell them the database so they'll have to call the vendor of that product. The vendor of that product informs Toby that they don't have a service contract in place. The computer vendor presents the boss with a bill for $1482.23 and leaves. The boss is outraged. Then Toby arrives with the glad tidings about the database administration problem. The boss calls Sue at home and orders her to hobble into the office and administer the database. She breaks down and cries, telling him her leg is too sore, Toby should never have been allowed near the system in the first place and also pleading that she hasn't even *had* the database administration course yet. He sends a taxi for her anyway. Toby and Sue spend the next couple of days trying to learn the fundamentals of database administration from a manual, with liberal use of a yellow highlighting pen. They then start reconstructing the dataset for the first application, but part of the data is accidentally loaded into the wrong directory and at once crashes the OA system again. The MRS is still up and UNIX is still humming along, but the OA users have once again lost their work, including the boss who was writing a report for *his* boss on why cheque issue is now a week behind schedule.

The users are congregating outside Toby's cubicle. It looks like a lynching party. The boss comes out of his office and announces that he has told his secretary to place a call to the Director of Information Technology, and that he intends to turn the whole thing over to those people to get fixed. He goes into his office and slams the door. The next thing audible to the assembled group are sounds of the same tonal quality as the squealings of a stuck piglet: 'What do you mean, unsupported system? Why not? It's a computer isn't it? You're supposed to be in charge of computers, aren't you? Send somebody down to fix it!'

After a few more minutes the boss comes out, and says through his teeth that he will have to sign a memo with IT for special support for a 'non-conforming' system. While the system they have is indeed consistent with the firm's overall direction of moving to open systems it is not an approved and supported type.

The point of this little horror story, surely, is clear. Unless you intend to stick to a purely mainframe and PC architecture as you move to open systems, MBS and/or MRS equipment *will* be introduced. When workgroup equipment is introduced you must think in terms of supporting workgroups. If you don't, you could face dozens or even hundreds of irate line managers just like this one. You many also end up with 50 types of UNIX MRS equipment, all from different vendors with 30 flavours of UNIX among them. Actually, you have several choices.

1 Place an IT professional at each workgroup site, or at least each facility where there are a few workgroups using such equipment. This person can be a relatively junior support specialist and can certainly be trained to handle all of the required MRS, MBS and LAN administration as well as that required for the OA and RDBMS products. The problem, of course, with this approach is that it is very expensive and involves commitment of a virtual army of IT people to the field. This also assumes that the corporate powers-that-be will authorize all this hiring or internal transferring. There is also the thorny issue of who these field people report to. Common sense would seem to dictate that since they are part of the IT unit, they should report in there, but local user workgroup line managers may have other ideas. They may feel that it makes more sense to fully integrate these valuable specialists into their own shops.

2 You can buy what are sometimes colloquially referred to as 'care and feeding' services from a firm specializing in a mix of remote and on-site system administration. These well-trained tiger feeders will keep your 'beast' well cared for and under reasonably tight control. They can also support PC users where desired. Of course, they may not be as familiar with all of your applications as you would like and may send a different person on every second visit. They are expensive, although you only pay for what you actually use.

3 Today, the technology exists to permit you to conduct virtually all system management functions (configuration management, capacity planning, etc.) and a significant portion of system administration functions remotely, from a regional data centre or even from your central IT facility or corporate data centre. This has the advantage of providing top-proficiency control of the system and also immediate reporting of problems. This approach usually requires not only that you have an implemented OSI or at least TCP/IP capable network in place, not a vendor proprietary network, and also that you have a very pro-active approach to network management. Also, you will still require someone on the ground at the site to assist with any

matters you simply cannot remote control. For example, you can download original or updated software to an MRS from head-quarters very easily, but if the MRS's operating system registers as unbootable, you may need someone to reload it from tape or to be there when the hardware vendor arrives on-site.

4 You can train and certify the administrators of MBS/LAN and MRS installations. I have referred to such paraprofessional administrators earlier in this book. The term 'paraprofessional' is used here only as it relates to the IT field. A LANA or an MRSA may well be a professional in another field, such as an engineer or a chartered accountant. In any event, this person will be trained and certified to do several things:

- Administer the workgroup system;
- Provide basic support to users for PC and MRS operating and application software;
- Know when they are 'out of their depth' and also who to call for help (IT, vendors, etc.) in what circumstances.

Networks and network management

You may already operate one network or a number of networks; for the moment, any existing network(s) will be assumed to be proprietary. Most proprietary networks have at least some capability to allow you to interface other vendors' proprietary and open systems with them. However, the level of interface is typically quite low and the 'outsider' equipment, unless it is of the 'plug-compatible' variety, is almost always treated as a second- or third-class citizen.

In many cases, it will be preferable to use MRS or MBS equipment to emulate the unique proprietary terminals, terminal controllers and other vendor-specific gear which is now interposed between the end-user and your proprietary mainframe. This varies from vendor to vendor, depending upon who built your mainframe. If you can let the workgroup system emulate all or most of this equipment, you can permit all users of simple non-intelligent terminals, X-terminals and PCs to have co-equal access to the mainframe. They simply access the MRS or MBS as an ASCII terminal. The workgroup machine emulates all of the proprietary equipment for them and they can continue accessing their mainframe applications, just as they did previously either with proprietary terminals or else from PCs emulating such terminals.

☞ You can use a UNIX workgroup system to fool your old mainframe into thinking it is still talking to its own terminals when it is really talking to users with many different kinds of terminals and PCs.

This is the theory. In reality, you will find out things like the following:

- The UNIX MRS vendor's terminal emulator and controller emulator will only provide colour to the end-user if you buy the vendor's most expensive MRS.
- The key assignments on the various PCs and terminals using the emulators turn out to be vastly different from those of the old proprietary terminal, and even from each other.

These kinds of things tend to confuse and even infuriate users who are used to seeing losses shown in red and don't want to see everything in amber.

You will also want to start moving into open system networking wherein all computers are treated as equals. Some proprietary networking topologies simply will not entertain the suggestion that a given device could be more intelligent than Level X. Such systems tend to force all processing, even much of the communications processing, upstairs to the mainframe. This is great if you are a mainframe manufacturer, but it runs directly counter to the idea that all intelligent communications devices and computers are theoretically peers.

Optimum sourcing strategies

Sourcing strategies will vary almost as much as organizations, but here the key issue is the *number* of vendor sources to be selected and ratified for a particular component of the system architecture. The three basic choices are as set out below.

Single vendor

There may be some components of your system architecture wherein it is only practical to source with one vendor. These could include optical storage devices, mainframes, high-security systems and others. The big disadvantage, of course, of sourcing an open system as though it were a proprietary one is that your vendor may have little incentive to behave like an open system vendor. There is, however, the fact that you probably *can* move to another platform if you are required or roused to do so. You have all the familiarity and confidence advantages of one-stop shopping and you also will find it relatively easy to track technology developments. None the less, this option should be used with care and only when absolutely necessary. With open systems, it is usually better to have at least two suppliers available who can meet your requirements. Even the most benevolent and non-entrapping supplier can be bought out (by someone who scraps the product line you use) or else go out of business.

Multi-vendor

For most components of your system architecture, you will have a choice of a number of vendors who make products which are both operationally suitable and which exhibit or at least promise sufficient open system standards-adherence to meet your requirements. More than likely, you will want to avail yourself of this freedom of choice, and also the various protections with which market competition provides you. For a given component, therefore, you must decide:

- How many vendors would be an appropriate number to accept, approve or certify; and
- How you should conduct such a process.

Regarding the number of vendors, you must consider the nature of the component and your present/future requirement for it, as well as the nature of the process you intend to use. If your firm will only ever buy ten or twenty MRS installations, it may not be worth doing anything more than accepting or approving a vendor on the face of his or her published materials. If, on the other hand, you plan to buy 2000 UNIX workstations, a full field trial or pilot might be highly advisable. Let's structure the consideration of these issues via a few simple questions.

1 How many of these items will you buy? The more you will buy, unless cost is no object, the more interested you will be in price/ performance, service and support. The more interested you are in these things, the more you will want to focus in on vendor current and projected future products, technology base, standards-adherence and support capabilities. The greater the value of the total anticipated acquisition, the more important it is that the number of vendors be *optimized*.

2 What process will be used to decide which vendors you want to deal with? Sometimes it is first easier to decide how to get the vendors in the door, before deciding how many to let in. You may decide to merely *accept* vendors, based on published specifications or their marketing demonstrations where the total value or importance of the component does not justify a lot of effort. For example, laser printers of various duty cycles are widely available. It is a simple matter to find several good ones. If simple acceptance is not sufficiently rigorous, you may wish to publish a requirements specification and then require vendors to show you that they or someone else has proved that they comply with all or most of your requirements. If

you think vendor claims may be a little optimistic and/or the requirement is expensive or important enough to justify the extra effort, you may wish actually to certify to your own satisfaction that the products meet your stated requirements. There are three main ways of doing this:

Lab test—you bring in samples of the competing products to your own testing lab and put them through their paces under controlled conditions, documenting the results as you go and you certify all or the top *X* number of compliant products.

Field trial—you try out the product and possibly also other products which go with it in a reasonably realistic field trial site environment, possibly also verifying support and operational arrangements within your organization, with the vendor and/or with third parties, using simulated or non-critical real production data.

Pilot—you place the product in provisional production in a situation as close to actual production as possible.

3 What is the optimum number of vendors for this component, given its priority and profundity, as well as the intended method of acceptance, approval or certification? This is a factor of two key items:

- The nature and scale of the product to be procured (it is easier to have ten PC suppliers than ten MRS or mainframe suppliers);
- Whether you intend to certify them, versus just accepting or approving them, and, if so, the method, from paragraph 2 above, chosen to satisfy yourself as to each product's acceptability.

    Clearly, if you are intending to mount full field trials to certify something even as pedestrian as laser printers, you will be able to manage only a finite number of such trials. If, on the other hand, they will just be run through a lab test there might be no problem certifying 50 brands.

In general, the larger and more complex a product is, the fewer vendors you will want to have. Also the more pervasive or universal a product will be in your organization, the fewer vendors you will desire. Fewer is often better, but one is seldom best. It is workable to have five MRS vendors and ten MBS and PC vendors but not necessarily ten OA or RDBMS vendors, for example.

Omni-vendor

There are some products for which you do not need to go to a great deal of trouble, even if certification is called for. For example, you can easily establish a DOS/INTEL-based PC286 or PC386 standard and use paper specifications, quick demonstrations or elementary lab tests to verify compliance with your specifications. Subject only to your plans for technical service, you may find that ten or even twenty suppliers are manageable, particularly if you have a third-party support vendor who has agreed to support anything compliant to your specification. In other conditions, such as when support is provided by the original vendors or their dealers, you may need to limit the field to those vendors provably capable of providing support where and when your users require it. *Within* a given UNIX RISC architecture (such as Motorola M88, MIPS, SPARC, etc.) you may be able to establish almost as basic a specification for entry-level UNIX workstations. Certainly, if you can safely do this it will allow you to concentrate your efforts more fully on the larger and more complex equipment. Many such workstations now come with their E-Net capabilities built right in, so even if you require E-Net compatibility you can still use this approach.

Big Brother, Little Brother

Each vendor, particularly each hardware vendor, will be keen to have you certify as many as possible of their products for the various component slots within your architecture. There is nothing wrong with this, providing you have open competition within acquisitions for each component and there is not too much cascading up or down with a given acquisition. For example, even if some of your MRS vendors also supply certified MBS equipment and PCs, it might not necessarily be wise to complete *all* items at one site as a block acquisition. This would defeat part of the very reason you compartmentalized acquisition by system architecture component in the first place; to get the best value for each interoperable component. This also discriminates against the smaller vendor who may make a very good and cost-effective MBS but who has no MRS to bid.

There is, however, one synergy which runs in the opposite direction and which you may want to exploit. If you have Vendor A's MBS installed with a 40-user LAN, the inhabitants of which are now clamouring for an MRS, you may want to consider the fact that even when you run your open bid Vendor A may have a built-in advantage. For example, a visionary and far-seeing Vendor A might very well have supplied you with a larger than required chassis with your MBS, knowing full well that the day would come when an upgrade to an MRS would be bid. In fact, he supplied the chassis of his low-end MRS product, de-rated to MBS performance levels and absorbed the extra cost at the first bid time. Now he is in a perfect position to bid an upgrade which involves only a few extra boards and maybe an expansion cabinet. The other vendors are forced to bid a *de novo* MRS and will almost certainly come in much higher. Assuming you buy each product on price and availability, Vendor A will win. There is, in the strictest sense, nothing wrong with this as long as you stick to an open competition policy.

Of course, even after you have approved a number of vendors for each component, you are not necessarily married to a given acquisition model. You are free to run bids on MRS equipment case by case for one-off buys and also to take formal tenders from your certified vendors for larger block buys. The same holds true for most other components. With the largest components, such as mid-frames and mainframes, you may be forced to recertify the vendor each time you acquire, since these buys are typically widely spaced in time.

Even after vendors are certified, your certification work is not done. Time and technology march on! At some interval, it will be advisable to let certified vendors propose additional or replacement products which have become available since the last product-insertion opportunity. The reason you should select an interval of no less than six months to one year is that otherwise your many vendors will continuously bombard your people with a shower of new product releases. You must carefully manage vendor expectations regarding when and how new products will be allowed in the door to join those already certified. This process is quite necessary, because without it, your entire range of certified products will steadily move towards obsolescence and eventually disappear altogether from your vendors' catalogues.

More on workgroup system building blocks

While open systems can make their presence felt from the laptop computer to the mainframe, they will have the biggest impact over the next few years at the workgroup level. The following will provide an expansion on the description of the variety of workgroup systems presented in Chapter 4. The individual descriptions define a number of possible alternatives for a basic local processing architecture. They range from MRS equipment, installed as though it were a conventional minicomputer with non-intelligent terminals through a full-function MRS accompanied by intelligent desktop equipment to a server-only device.

MRS/Terminal (MT)—UNIX mid-range system running multi-user applications under an RDBMS package with or without an office-automation package with star-wired non-intelligent ASCII terminals.

MRS/X-Terminal (MX)—UNIX mid-range system running multi-user applications under an RDBMS package with or without an office-automation package with star-wired bit-mapped X-terminals.

MRS/Diskless (MD)—UNIX mid-range system running multi-user applications under an RDBMS package with or without an office-automation package plus PC interface software allowing DOS logical access to on-board disk space with star-wired DOS/INTEL diskless PCs running both single-user applications and terminal emulators.

MRS/PC (MP)—UNIX mid-range system running multi-user applications under an RDBMS package with or without an office-automation package with star-wired DOS/INTEL disk-equipped PCs running both single-user applications and terminal emulators.

MRS/Workstation (MW)—UNIX mid-range systems running multi-user applications under an RDBMS package with or without an office-automation package with star-wired UNIX-based disk-equipped workstations running both single-user applications and terminal emulators.

MRS/LAN/Diskless (MLD)—UNIX mid-range system running multi-user applications under an RDBMS package with or without an office-automation package plus PC interface software allowing DOS logical access to on-board disk space and also functioning as a node on a LAN including DOS/INTEL diskless PCs running both single-user applications and terminal emulators as well as LAN node software.

MRS/LAN/PC (MLP)—UNIX mid-range system running multi-user applications under an RDBMS package with or without an office-automation package plus PC interface software allowing DOS logical access to on-board disk space and also functioning as a node on a LAN including DOS/INTEL disk-equipped PCs running both single-user applications and terminal emulators as well as LAN node software.

MRS/LAN/Workstation (MLW)—UNIX mid-range system running multi-user applications under an RDBMS package with or without an office-automation package and also functioning as a node on a LAN including UNIX-based disk-equipped workstations running both single-user applications and terminal emulators as well as LAN node software.

MRS/Server/LAN/Diskless (MSLD)—UNIX mid-range system running multi-user applications under an RDBMS package with or without an office-automation package and also functioning as a file server for a LAN including DOS/INTEL diskless PCs running both single-user applications and terminal emulators as well as LAN node software.

MRS/Server/LAN/PC (MSLP)—UNIX mid-range system running

multi-user applications under an RDBMS package with or without an office-automation package and also functioning as a file server for a LAN including DOS/INTEL disk-equipped PCs running both single-user applications and terminal emulators as well as LAN node software.

MRS/Server/LAN/Workstation (MSLW) — UNIX mid-range system running multi-user applications under an RDBMS package with or without an office-automation package, also functioning as a file server for a LAN including UNIX-based disk-equipped workstations running single-user applications, terminal emulators and also LAN node software.

Server/LAN/Diskless (SLD) — UNIX mid-range system functioning as a file server for a LAN including DOS/INTEL diskless PCs running both single-user applications and LAN node software.

Server/LAN/PC (SLP) — UNIX mid-range system functioning as a file server for a LAN including DOS/INTEL disk-equipped PCs running both single-user applications and LAN node software.

Server/LAN/Workstation (SLW) — UNIX mid-range system functioning as a file server for a LAN including UNIX-based disk-equipped workstations running both single-user applications and LAN node software.

The above options are seen as 'upwardly encompassing' such that if a Mini/Terminal (MT) option had even a few full-function PCs added in it would be converted to the MINI/PC (MP) option even though some non-intelligent terminals remained at the site. Likewise, where UNIX workstations were added to an MP option it would be migrated to MW even though some PCs remained. *Note that options MLD, MLP and MLW above assume that some OTHER device is acting as the LAN server, not the MRS.* Within each option there could be more than one possible generic configuration. For example, within the MT option the following configurations might be defined:

MT1 — 1 to 9 users
MT2 — 10 to 29 users
MT3 — 30 to 70 users

Each configuration cited here would include everything necessary to implement the MT option for the indicated number of users on a 5-year life cycle cost basis. Note that where a user group exceeded 70 users two or more systems could be installed. This is due to the fact that provision of an IT professional to support each installed system as system administrator/manager is most unlikely. In virtually all other support scenarios, 70 is the maximum desirable number of users to be supported on one MRS, operating in an open office environment and not supported on-site at all times by a systems professional.

You, your legacy vendor and open systems

Sometimes, your legacy vendor will honestly and openly welcome your announced plan to move to open systems, particularly if he believes that he is well positioned to help you make the transition and to capture a good share of the business you compete for purchases of specific products. True, too, some vendors will see it in their interest to maintain very cordial relationships with the IT organization. Sadly, many of the recent migrations to open systems have found proprietary vendors reacting in altogether different ways. A few of them are detailed below, along with some recommended reactions. There are a couple of rules to remember about responding to these actions by your vendor(s):

- Stay cool and mature; do not over-react or you may make things worse.
- Try to find ways to turn the vendor's energy to more mutually beneficial activities if you can.

Do not go out of your way to look for trouble with your vendor or expect that confrontation is inevitable. However, if you try to smooth the waters and avoid confrontation you are only delaying it, not averting it. In all circumstances, conduct yourself with honesty and integrity. Be firm and be fair. Treat all of the vendors the same.

The live-in 'customer engineers'

Vendor representatives who are co-quartered with your IT staff, right inside your building, may range from totally benevolent and helpful to little better than industrial spies. It depends totally on the individuals concerned, the stance being taken by their company and how your own people interact with them. Unless there is an absolute and inescapable requirement to have such people on-site, you are always better off to ask them to return to their own firm at the outset of your move to open systems. The reason is that it is very hard for you to hold council about, and debate, such things as when and how to change a certain component of your architecture if they are at the meeting, just around the corner or hanging around the coffee machine to see what they might learn. Your people will, at the least, feel constrained and may even be made to feel guilty that they are somehow deserting the long-trusted proprietary vendor. This can be expressed in quite personal terms where long-standing working relationships come into the balance. Also, their company can hardly be placed on an equal footing with outside vendors for upcoming acquisitions if they have all of the inside information about what did and did not make it into the specification.

The disinformers

A number of years ago, the Editor of *Car and Driver*, a car enthusiast publication, began an editorial with the statement that: 'BS is neck high and rising!' Some of the people who have been through a transition to open systems would be likely to make a similar statement. While your proprietary vendor may not be the only source of incomplete or misleading information, if a vendor has a strong enough incentive to induce you to remain with his closed system he may provide all kinds of blood-chilling details about the evils of open systems. Do not take at face value any statement from *any* vendor about the good aspects of their own open system products, the bad aspects of someone else's product or even the general state of open systems. This rather jaundiced approach is, in my view, the only viable one. I have heard numerous stories of vendor representatives who told their customers that the demise of UNIX or a given flavour of UNIX was just around the corner, that the firm selling system X was about to go bankrupt or that open computing systems were not really needed. By far the most frequently made inaccurate claims are the following:

1 If you adopt OSI communications and our proprietary operating system, you will never need UNIX because in a year or two operating system won't matter any more. (I was told this in every year between 1985 and 1991 and it is just not true. Canadians well remember Prime Minister John Diefenbaker, who in 1959 scrapped the Avro CF-105 Arrow interceptor because he was convinced fighter aircraft were obsolete, throwing thousands of people out of work . . .)

2 If you adopt OSI and our UNIX product you will be able to inter-operate everyone else's open computing system with ours, providing that you use our recommended approach to OSI networking. (What you can actually do, if you are lucky, is use the other vendor's lowest common denominator functionality, often not taking advantage of all the OSI and UNIX–UNIX capabilities because of proprietary baggage in your vendor's 'open network architecture'.)

Where possible, document your vendor's claims for future reference, verification or dismissal. You can also compare them to the claims they make next year. Following the open system press closely, retaining experienced experts and attending trade shows and conferences will allow your staff to ascertain rapidly who is telling the truth and who is providing a very rosy or one-sided picture. Once you have equipment from a variety of vendors in-house, you can thenceforth greet all claims of relevant and desirable (to you) interoperation capabilities with demands for on-site proof. Except where there is a clear sale in sight, most vendors will not want to become embroiled in a continuous series of demonstrations and so this response will cause them to choose their claims a bit more carefully.

The 'we have everything' claim

No matter what you ask the vendor for, they reply that it is in the lab and about to be released to beta test. They can probably get you one early next year. This is often nothing more than a tactic to dissuade you from buying it from the other vendor, whose product is released and in service. The other side of this coin is that you should not press your vendor now for a product you really won't need until much later. No vendor today has 'everything' and none will for quite a while yet. Nor has the perfect car yet been built. Don't follow up all the avenues the vendor opens up for you; only the ones you honestly believe will lead to a product you can use.

The free seminar in Florida

Probably near Disney World! If you are intending to slow or freeze the growth of your existing proprietary mainframe and minicomputer environments, it doesn't matter how nice may be the venue or how broad the agenda of the free seminar, user meeting, executive briefing or whatever it is called. You want your people attending meetings which concentrate on where you are going, not on where you've been. If the vendor responds with free seminars in Florida on open systems, then you may want to perk up but be aware that you could be subjected to two or however many days of the sort of claims discussed above. On the other hand, if you can attend two or three of these (by different vendors, of course, and even if they are held in less attractive destinations) you can start to triangulate effectively. It then becomes possible to sort out the fact, the near-fact, the pseudo-fact and the outright fiction.

The 'we integrate everything' claim

Some vendors who don't have everything, and don't even claim that they do, are pleased to claim instead that they invented system integration and they can put everything (from any vendor) together for your organization. This claim is a bit misleading for two reasons. First, if your, or any other, major hardware vendor had invented system integration then the hardware vendors would surely have monopolized the field years ago and the independent system integrators would never have gained a foothold. Second, if you believe your vendor will treat their own and their competitors' equipment with equal diligence in so far as ensuring that it is installed so as to show all its best features you are mistaken. In most cases, you will want to seek independent integrators who have no leaning towards or away from a specific vendor.

The lunching marketeer

This is perhaps one of the most widely misunderstood elements of the vendor–customer relationship. There is absolutely nothing wrong with the legacy vendor or any other taking an IT executive, manager or even supervisor to lunch to discuss any mutually relevant computer-related issue. The vendor is paying for the lunch so as to have some of the person's time and attention in a less harried and more casual atmosphere. In almost all cases, they are not doing, and should not be suspected or accused of doing, anything else. Naturally, a lot of worthwhile business is done over a good lunch. The legacy vendor who lunches regularly with senior IT officers is not, and should not be accused of, plying them with food and drink so as to obtain their support to block open systems. The IT staff themselves are just as apt to use a lunch opportunity to improve relations with an internal client. There is nothing wrong with that either.

Most medium-sized and large organizations have conflict of interest guidelines in place to assist officers in knowing where to draw the line if lunches become too frequent, gifts of logo-bearing clipboards are replaced by more substantial ones or weekend trips in corporate jets to some nice island are offered. A problem arises *only* if the legacy vendor seeks to use the privacy of the lunchtime opportunity to seek or obtain commitments or promises from the officer that something will not be done without further consultation with that vendor. Also, many of the above-cited types of vendor claims are easier to deliver over smoked salmon or roast lamb.

If you suspect that your legacy vendor is using lunchtime opportunities to thwart your move to open systems, institute a rule that no member of your staff (yourself included) will have a lunch or, for that matter, any other meeting with a representative of that vendor without a second IT person present. This not only lets the two IT people later triangulate on what happened but also provides a witness as to what was said, should a disagreement arise later.

Unless there is flagrant abuse by the vendor and/or your staff, there is usually no reason to cut this type of contact with your legacy vendor(s) just because of your open systems direction. This will help you make clear to such vendors that they will have a fair chance to survive and thrive in the new open systems regime. It goes almost without saying that you can also countenance lunch and other meetings with the new vendors. Additional advice: watch your waistline!

The trial spoilers

Sometimes a legacy vendor will participate in a lab test, trial or pilot with the sole intention of proving that open systems (even his own) simply don't work very well, or that the IT unit is off on a wild tangent and should go back to the drawing board. This is a very hard tactic to protect against because, usually, by the time you see it coming it is too late to do anything about it. The trial fails, the vendor piously screams and you are left holding the bag. About the only protection against this is to have a detailed plan, look under the hood of the product before it comes on-site to make sure it's not a Trojan Horse and have a clear memorandum of agreement (MOA) with the vendor regarding who is responsible for what. This makes blowing up the trial both harder for the vendor and more traceable for you.

The revenge pricers

These declare that they have been giving you a sweet deal on system prices or, more likely, on their service and support contract prices. This could even be true, since many hardware makers enjoy a huge profit on service and support contracts. They intimate that if you don't stop this open system nonsense, they will lose Brownie points with HQ and will be forced to raise the prices substantially. If this is a serious threat, and would break your budget, tell them you will consider their offer. Immediately go and meet with third-party support vendors, even out-of-town ones, and find one who is prepared to give you a decent quote. Then go back to your proprietary vendor and suggest that he go ahead and make your day! Most often, you will discover that they have been bluffing, since it is not in their interest to do anything which may so rile you that you move even more quickly towards open systems.

The battering-ram tactic

Not very subtle is the vendor who tries to get you fired, but when all else fails some vendors will sometimes actually try to get the main champions of open systems in the IT unit ousted or demoted, perhaps along with the CIO and maybe even their boss too. This is usually based either on a case that you are incompetently leading the organization off-track or else on the old buddy system. A vendor senior manager happens to be an old friend of someone very senior in your organization. Perhaps the only certain thing about this tactic is that it is usually used as a last resort. This is because any vendor who tries and fails at this will, at the very least, sour the relationship with the IT unit and, at worst, find the date of its ejection (or at least the open competition for a replacement of his equipment) moved closer to the present.

Off to a good start

A judicious application of the principles set out in this chapter should put in place your organization's directional commitment to open systems and should provide you with a firm foundation for moving into actual project work.

6 From paper to pilot: learning your way in

Introduction

Once you have a firm conceptual foundation in place, as discussed in the previous chapter, your organization is ready to begin the actual implementation of open systems. This chapter will take you through the steps necessary to 'ramp up' to a full production pilot of open systems. This includes the acquisition documents, internal pre-trial, main trials and finally full-scale pilots.

Qualifying, evaluating and certifying vendors

For all but the most simple components of the system architecture, a two-phase approach is recommended. Start with a paper *qualification* phase to narrow down the field of competitors to the number you are able (and actually prepared) to take to lab test, trial, pilot or whatever other means you intend to utilize to achieve certification. The second phase is *evaluation*, wherein you actually take each vendor through the certification process prescribed in your procurement documents.

> ☞ First, you want to find out who *promises* features A, B and C and then you want to look under the hood and check them out to see who actually *delivers* them.

Whether yours is a government department, an educational or scientific institution or a private company, it will be necessary to have a formal procurement document developed to describe the acquisition process through the qualification, evaluation, approval and implementation stages. Just calling up the vendor and asking over the phone for a quote, or buying out of a brochure or catalog, is not an appropriate method for the acquisition of open computing systems. If you do this two or more times, even with the same vendor, you will have problems. If you practise this with multiple vendors, a mismatch will result.

Your document must clearly set out what the responsibilities of vendors will be once they have qualified and, later on, once approved.

For example, if you are buying workstations and will simply run a lab test, the vendor may be responsible for providing two samples of their product and any requested technical support to the lab test. If you are buying MRS equipment, the vendor may have to field a complete system for a trial or pilot, possibly wholly or mostly at their own expense.

Where the acquisition is to be a substantial one, involving hundreds or thousands of units, it is often desirable to divide the document into at least three sections, as follows:

- Description of all technology requirements;
- Expected vendor standards-adherence;
- Technical service and support and other related vendor conduct.

Usually relatively equal weight will be accorded to each of the three areas. Each section (or numbered paragraph) of the actual specification describes an individual requirement with respect to equipment characteristics or performance, vendor services and support, vendor business situation or standards-adherence. Each section should contain a *synopsis* summarizing its content, a detailed *contents*, a *reference* portion indicating any standards or other references and an indication of whether its *status* is *mandatory* or *desirable*. The latter status would also connote a specific point score, of which all or some portion could be awarded to a compliant vendor. For each section one or more primary evaluation methods can be declared for use in the actual certification activity itself. These can include the following:

BEN—formal benchmark test
STD—standards-adherence certified by a recognized body
EXP—logged experience during certification
DOC—vendor-written undertaking
OBS—informal observation only
VEN—vendor statement accepted at face value without further investigation

> ☞ At one extreme, you can force the vendor to show you that an independent lab has run a standardized performance test (which makes his machine perform a series of calculations and other tasks) and has achieved a result you can live with. At the other extreme, you can just take the vendor's word that his is a great computer.

The latter is not usually the preferred method, except where the time and cost of verification would exceed the cost if the vendor claim is false.

We have already identified such important stakeholders in the open systems acquisition process as the IT community, the end-users and the vendors. Each section in your document should clearly indicate which groups would be most involved in assessing vendor performance for that section. Vendors would be required to declare whether what was promised under each section was already released and available, was under final development with a release date announced, under basic development, was merely being considered or was not expected to be available within the certification timeframe.

Where a section is *mandatory*, the vendor must be fully compliant or face disqualification. Even one such non-complicance will disqualify the vendor. Be very careful in setting items as *mandatory* as you may accidentally eliminate some or all of your vendors. Declaring mandatories is a fine art; you must balance what you need against what is available now, what is promised for release soon and what is expected to be available before your certification process ends. Nor should you allow *anyone* (IT staff or consultants or users) to choose mandatories expressly so as to include or exclude any vendor. Concentrate on your needs and on the current/anticipated total product market base. In general, the fewer *mandatory* sections, the better.

Desirable sections give the vendor the opportunity literally to 'score points' by providing something you want, but are prepared to live without if necessary. The more important the item, the higher the number of points offered for it. Total scores of *desirable* points will permit you to rank the vendors who are compliant with all *mandatory* sections. It is a good practice not to value any particular section at more than five per cent of the total of all potential *desirable* points. This prevents any vendor from 'playing the numbers' and, for example, becoming certified based on his great service and wonderful standards-adherence but presenting you with a technically lack-lustre product.

The two most widely used ways of using *desirable* points to decide whether or not to admit vendors to certification, and/or actually to certify them, are as follows:

Threshold—you take all vendors who fulfil all *mandatory* sections and have a *desirable* point score above *Y*.

Xth past the post—you will take the *X* vendors who meet all *mandatory* sections and who hold the top *X* rankings of *desirable* points.

I believe the latter to be the better approach since you can control the maximum number of vendors who will ultimately be certified. For many classes of equipment, your IT unit may not be able to support more than a very restricted number, such as something between two and five. In some circumstances, however, you can blend the two approaches together by declaring that you will take the top *X* vendors who first pass all *mandatory* sections and then accumulate a *desirable* point score above a given level. For example, you might provide that vendors who pass all *mandatories* and are awarded more than 30 000 of a possible 50 000 points will be ranked. The top three will be selected. Consider the following vendor scores:

Vendor	Mandatories	Desirables
A	Compliant	42 000
B	Compliant	36 000
C	Compliant	34 000
D	Compliant	32 000
E	Compliant	28 000
F	Non-compliant	

Here, Vendors A to C are selected. D is 'sidelined' and could enter certification if any of A to C are disqualified or withdraw. E is below the threshold and is disqualified at this stage as is F, which didn't even make the *mandatories*. This blended approach has the advantage that you can control the number of vendors to be approved, while ensuring that they also offer significant *desirable* value. It also tends to generate 'spare' vendors whom you can draw into certification if problems arise with any of the first group.

☞ This is not unlike the process you would face if trying to get onto a baseball team. First you have to 'try out'. If you cannot throw the ball a certain distance or always fail to catch the ball, you cannot even get on the team. Once on the team, your performance in practices will allow the coach to decide whether he wants you on the A Team or the B Team. The A Team gets to play against other teams, while the B Team contains the sidelined players who will only get a chance to play if one of the A players becomes incapable of doing so. There is therefore a 'double gate'. Getting past the first gate gives you a chance at getting through the second but does not guarantee that you will do so.

☞ Deciding how many 'winners' to plan for in a given procurement is part art and part science. You require a *very* good idea of how your computing requirements are evolving and what your IT group can support. Even then, there may be surprises. Perhaps you want three winners and four actually qualify for certification. However, during certification one vendor is disqualified and the single sidelined vendor decides he does not want to play after all. In such circumstances you end up with only two.

Where vendors merely promise a product or standards-adherence for the future, and cannot deliver it even during certification, you may choose to discount the number of points given under a *desirable* or to hold them conditionally compliant to a *mandatory* section. You should formally secure vendor commitment to follow the acquisition approach set out in your procurement document; make this a *mandatory* and ensure that it is the first thing checked once proposals are received. Vendors would then be evaluated on all other *mandatory* items followed by all *desirable* items.

For example, if you are dealing with MBS, MRS or larger equipment, ten or more trials or pilots would be very difficult to manage. However, it is possible that if you deploy too few vendors, and if there is high attrition during the certification process, you could end up with fewer vendors than you would like. During the certification process itself, causes of attrition may include:

- Disqualification for non-compliance to *mandatory*;
- Disqualificaton for falling below a required minimum *desirable* point score;
- Inability of system to perform in the field and/or rejection by the host-user site;
- Vendor financial or corporate difficulties force it to withdraw;
- Discovery that vendor has breached a rule of the procurement.

You want to be confident you can conclude the certification process with a large enough group of vendors to provide the desired degree of product variation, price/performance competition and corporate 'life insurance' against vendor demise. The fairest and most balanced strategy is usually to qualify only as many vendors for certification as you are actually prepared to certify and support. Therefore, there will be no problem if all of them reach certified status. On the other hand, the number you deploy must be large enough such that with attrition (and maybe replacements from the sideline) there will still be enough 'survivors' to carry on as planned. Remember also that the cost commitment to vendors for anything beyond a lab test may be very substantial. It is unfair to vendors who make a big commitment to your procurement project to deploy to certification more of them than you are actually prepared to certify and live with. Therefore, the largest acceptable number of approved vendors (the value to be accorded to X, as above) should be set *equal* to the smallest acceptable number of trial or pilot sites. Working backwards, consider that any number of sites less than five (or, at worst, three) carries undue risk (due to possible attrition) to the overall success of the program. Below three sites, you may not be seeing the desired variety of products and vendor commitment levels. However, even with three sites, you could lose a site due to a change of heart on the part of local management, a reorganization, an accident or fire, the death or sickness of a key person there or similar causes. If you are deploying anything more complex than a workstation, managing more than five sites may be a Herculean task.

There is no hard-and-fast rule for determining how many sites and hence how many certifiable vendors you should have. Key constraints are your financial resources to support parallel certification activities at multiple sites, the size and complexity of the product you are buying and the number you intend to buy. Table 6.1 provides some general guidelines on the recommended values for X; your specific circumstances must also be considered in making this determination.

Table 6.1 Recommended number of trial/pilot sites and vendors

Product	Units to be acquired	Number of vendors
PC	Under 50	2
PC	50–500	3
PC	500–5000	5
PC	Over 5000	10
WS	Under 50	2
WS	50–500	2
WS	500–5000	3
WS	Over 5000	5
MBS	Under 50	1
MBS	50–200	2
MBS	200–500	5
MBS	Over 500	7
MRS	Under 10	1
MRS	10–50	2
MRS	50–200	3
MRS	200–500	5
MRS	Over 500	5
Mid-frame	1–10	2
Mid-frame	Over 10	3
Mainframe	Any number	2

For trials and pilots, it is highly advisable to provide in your procurement document for a full formal Pre-Delivery Acceptance Test (PDAT) for each vendor to verify key operability and interface factors *before* you deploy the product to a field site. The host site will become indignant, in no time at all, if the vendor's product is dead on arrival or malfunctions so badly that it eventually has to be put out of its misery. They will not thank you for the resulting disruption and your subsequent suggestion that the replacement vendor will be better will almost certainly get you and your trial or pilot thrown out anyway.

With your procurement document, you should also provide a pro-forma of a Memorandum of Agreement (MOA) which you will require the vendor to sign, governing the conduct of the vendor and your organization during the certification process. The vendor will thus know all that is involved, up-front, and if unhappy with your approach can always decide not to bid. However, if yours is a large acquisition, the vendor is one of your legacy vendors or the market is down, there is little chance that the vendor will refuse to bid.

Many readers may consider that the above approach is only suitable for a large corporation or government agency. This is not so. Even for a procurement of 20 to 30 units, following these guidelines in creating your acquisition document, whether you call it a Request for Quotation (RFQ), Request for Proposal (RFP) or whatever, will provide an orderly, and fair, procurement. This is true even if your specification is only a few pages long. You can develop standard 'boiler plate' for use in all open systems procurements, varying it as required for scale of acquisition and the type of certification being used in each case. Your use of this approach will also send all vendors, including your legacy vendor(s), a signal that you are serious about the new way of doing business. If they choose not to play the game your way, or else to play in such a way as to seek to disrupt or topple the whole process, you have plenty of good solid grounds to curtail such behaviour. If it persists, issue a letter asking them to show cause why they should not be disqualified! You are, after all, the customer. If you wrote to five car dealers asking for a written quote by return mail on a blue car of a certain type, with certain options, you would hardly appreciate the salesperson who shows up at your door with a red one and offers to take you for a ride because this car just happens to be on special offer today.

Your document should make clear exactly what the vendor will have to do and who will pay for it. Vendor responsibilities may include any or all of the following:

- Submit equipment for a pre-test before the main trial or pilot.
- Work with vendors of complementary products which will also come on-site.
- Deliver equipment to field site and install it.
- Integrate equipment with that of other vendors and your existing proprietary and/or open communications networks.
- Train and support users and system administrators.
- Provide hot-line support.
- Provide field technical support.

Only in the largest trial or pilot, where the stakes are very high because you intend to buy hundreds or thousands of systems, is it fair to require all of this from the vendor. In most cases, responsibilities will be split between your IT unit, the host field units, the vendor, third-party vendors of complementary products and outside consultants or integrators retained by your organization. It is absolutely essential that you ensure that all vendors are not only treated equally but are also seen by each other and by your own people to be treated equally. If you hire an outside integrator to handle one site, the same firm (even the same team) should handle all of the others! If you ask one vendor for a special briefing, ask the others as well so no one thinks that the first vendor is getting unfair access to your time and attention! If you have lunch with one vendor, make time for the others! With multiple procurements, and multiple vendors, this can be hazardous to your schedule (and personal weight-control program), but vendors can be extremely sensitive to the potential for favouritism if you are not attentive in this regard.

With medium-sized or large procurements, it is often preferable to make the vendor responsible for integration of all components they bring on-site, usually with a time limit which optimizes between the vendor's need for enough time to integrate a complex system and the maximum time during which the host site will tolerate a disrupted state of affairs. Make sure that your own responsibilities to provide IT and host site staff, office facilities, tables and chairs, telephone access, electrical power for the system (verify type of power required) and similar logistical support are spelt out in the MOA. Where necessary, implement a separate internal MOA with your host sites so they are clear on their responsibilities. The last thing you want when a vendor brings ten workstations onto a distant site is a dispute over who should have brought extension cords with power bars, extra connectors or whatever. In consultation with your legal advisors, ensure that the procurement document, and especially the MOA, contains legal limitation of liability clauses. Who will cover the loss if a ladder falls onto the MRS and smashes it? What happens if the vendor's technician or the integration firm's technician falls down the stairs and breaks a leg? What if the vendor's workstation electrocutes the secretary?

☛ You must clearly set out the rules of the game, and who has to bring what equipment and make it work. Otherwise, if anything goes seriously wrong, there will be much mutual finger-pointing and, if yours is a large procurement, a lot of lawyers will end up much richer.

Lab tests

The first requirement for a lab test is to have the lab itself. For most classes of open system equipment, such a lab should include:

- Equipment representative of the major classes of system and network interface (gateway, etc.) with which the system to be tested will have to interact;
- Equipment and software to emulate any item *not* able to be itself brought into the lab;
- Equipment and software to monitor and record the performance of the tested equipment;
- An administrative system to permit recording, collation and summary of all test results;

- Electrical and electronic test equipment (meters, etc.) to verify compliance with specified standards;
- Documentation for all of the above;
- A staff of qualified experts for each aspect of the testing, including at least:
  - Electrical and electronic compliance
  - Hardware heat and sound output where required
  - Operating system and other environmental software
  - Benchmarking and other performance testing
  - Package software
  - Required application software
  - Communications software and network interfaces
  - Interoperability
- Sufficient furniture including shelving, tables, chairs, benches, etc.;
- Additional logistical items including extension cords with power bars, electrical circuit isolators (some systems in the MRS class and larger require 'clean' or dedicated power, sometimes even preconditioned power), printers and their supplies, paper, pens and other office supplies;
- Absolutely no phone lines able to be reached from the outside or able to call outside the organization;
- Appropriate physical and operational security arrangements.

For a lab test, the procurement document's detail specification can be styled as a Qualification and Test Criteria (QTC) document. This will set out the rules for bidding as above, the intended test measures and the specific technical requirements. Regarding such basic items as CPU performance, there are a substantial number of good benchmarks published upon which you can depend. Clearly, however, the nature and extent of your knowledge about your real requirements will dictate your degree of confidence in one or a given set of benchmark measures. For example, some measure mostly the purely arithmetical or logical capabilities of a processor in a very linear way. Others simulate a more balanced and, for most applications, a more true-to-life workload. The more you can learn about the end-users' intended mix of workload, the easier it will be for you to decide among one of the following strategies:

- Simply accept the vendor's statements on performance;
- Require submission of independent benchmarks of a given type;
- Specify a third-party benchmark which the vendor must run at their own facility, submitting the results for a rerun in your own lab;
- Commission a benchmark firm to develop a custom benchmark to meet your exact needs.

The cost, time and effort is least for the first alternative above and greatest for the last. So, of course, is your degree of confidence that the certified machines will do the job for you. If one or a few specific performance capabilities are crucial in some of your applications (i.e. without which trains may have head-on collisions, mixes of chemicals will explode or red cars will be built with blue doors), then seek third-party benchmarks or commission custom benchmarks for those items only.

The remainder of the testing should be somewhat simpler, once you have dealt with raw performance. However, it is important to remember to address all aspects of technology, operations and support that are relevant to your organization. If you are replacing many PCs with UNIX workstations, keyboard layout and the ease with which the workstations run DOS applications as a task under UNIX may be very important.

If some of these systems will be 'embedded' in factory or warehouse operations, in vehicles or in other 'outside systems', you may want to test for or require independent verifications of ruggedness. There are five basic degrees of robustness in the computer world:

- Requires a full data centre including raised floor and air conditioning and possibly chilled water or other cooling system, as well as dust/particulate control;
- Requires a segregated area with air conditioning;
- Office-grade equipment for use in civilized office space where it will be respected and not abused (i.e. it will not be kicked and coffee will not be poured over it);
- Ruggedized for use in factory, warehouse, on-board vehicle or similar applications;
- Military specification (MILSPEC), which generally means that it can withstand continuous cruel and unusual punishment. One firm that I know of makes a mobile computer which must be able to perform a very demanding real-time function while riding along in a military vehicle, being hit with a wooden mallet and having hot coffee poured over it.

For a given class of open system processor (for example, WS, MBS or MRS), where office-grade equipment is deemed to have a cost factor of 1, ruggedized may be priced at 2 or 2.5 and MILSPEC may range between 4 and 10. (Note that I have excluded computer room equipment from this scale.) Specify only what you will really need for each application. The good news is that many product lines based on UNIX/RISC now offer essentially the same processor and same performance for all three of the office, ruggedized and MILSPEC environments.

☞ The more robust a computer is, the more it will cost you. With open systems you can use the same kind of computer in business, operational and field/mobile applications just by specifying different versions for each application. They can all run the same, or complementary, programs and they can all talk to each other since they all run UNIX and all speak OSI.

In general, lab tests are more appropriate for smaller than for larger and more complex equipment as well as for relatively straightforward requirements. They are often more than satisfactory for PC, WS, MBS and LAN products but may be less effective for MRS or larger systems. On the other hand, if your organization will only buy a few dozen MRS installations, and your requirements are quite homogeneous, a lab test may be fully sufficient to certify two vendors.

☞ Lab tests are very effective for small computers which are not too complex, as well as for quite limited procurements of larger ones.

IT alpha tests

Where a simple lab test is insufficient, and where you anticipate use of a trial or pilot as part of your procurement, you may want to conduct an internal 'Alpha Test' of the system inside the IT organization. You can do this before, or during the early stages of, the procurement. During this test you can experiment with network interface, reliability, troubleshootability and other characteristics of the new system. You can bring in simulated (or actual) users and see if they are able to become comfortable with the system. Where you have not yet finalized your procurement document, you can incorporate the results of this valuable learning experience into it.

☞ Circus tiger tamers always make sure that the tiger knows the routine cold even before they run a preview show for a real audience. If the UNIX computer, or other open system product, is going to malfunction embarrassingly (for the vendor and for IT) it is much better that this happens before the computer is out in the user community.

Trial or pilot

This is never an easy call and it is one which must be made with the user in the loop. There are many factors to consider and they are in fact too numerous to recount here. Recall that a trial is somewhat more tentative than a pilot; a trial addresses many *if* issues such as the following:

- If the machine will work well in our environment;
- If selected packages will run well with the machine;
- If we can show real-world applications running well on the system;

- If users like the machine;
- If we and the vendor can support the machine.

A pilot usually starts with a few more things in place. Perhaps the application is already in use by real end-users and has been running for three years on VAX/VMS systems all over the company. Now it has been updated and the new version has itself been tested in the field. IT says the firm must move to UNIX and OSI so the pilot will take the revised (and almost mature, almost ready to deploy) application and run it on a UNIX machine. As soon as it is stable, the application will be made available to real users who will use it in parallel with the existing production application. They will use live data but certain checks will be in place. When IT and users are happy with both the UNIX system(s) and the application, both will become full production items. Thereafter, all of the other user groups will gradually convert to the new hardware and updated software.

If you are starting 'cold', it is almost certain that a trial is the best approach. If you have several of the technology, communications and support components already in place, then you are better off using a pilot. A trial is normally structured such that the experience gained can be used to do any of the following:

- Accept product vendors, make minor changes to the product specifications or scrap the whole procurement and start all over again.
- Institute or change user procedures, system administration arrangements or IT support capabilities.
- Revise concepts or operatives for the linking of the product in question with other products.
- Change concepts about how the product in question is to be used.
- Change IT or business operational procedures or concepts.

A pilot normally addresses only one or, at most, two 'independent variables'. In the example previously given the pilot is assessing how well a UNIX processor can run an improved version of an existing VMS production application. If the UNIX processor(s) cannot handle it (as actually tested), then IT and the users can always scrap the pilot and just continue by retrofitting the new version of the application to the existing or even upgraded VMS equipment.

> ☞ An aircraft manufacturer knows there will be a bigger challenge if it launches a new aircraft with a brand-new engine as well. Both are new and more can go wrong, so the prototyping process will have to be longer and more detailed. If the engine has only ever powered test aircraft quite unlike the one being designed, the early flights of the prototype may point to the need for substantial redesign of the engine nacelle, despite all the best engineering and planning. On the other hand, launching a new aircraft with a known engine is much easier. Indeed, it may be possible to buy the whole engine and

nacelle as one kit which is already proven in service. This should reduce the time and effort necessary to prove that the airframe and engine can work well together.

If more than one or two of the hardware, the operating system, the package (for example, RDBMS), the applicaton and the support procedures are new, a trial may be the best choice. It is always possible to move to a full production pilot *after* a trial has been successful. Conversely, if a production pilot is an unmitigated disaster, it may be some time before the users will again want to hear about open systems. The CIO and some of his or her closest advisors may also be seeking new jobs.

Pre-trials

Even where you have settled on a trial, versus a pilot, as your key means of certifying vendors, and honing your own internal support arrangements and procedures, there is sometimes a case for running a full-scale dress rehearsal before you proceed to the main acquisition. (If you have settled on a pilot, you should be confident enough already not to need a rehearsal. If you are not that confident, you should revisit your choice!) Usually, a pre-trial will also precede your issue to the vendors of anything more than perfunctory information about your acquisition plans. Sometimes, however, issue of a simple letter asking who would like to be on the bid list will provide you with an especially keen vendor, willing to risk the extra time and expense of helping you with a pre-trial in the hope of gaining experience which will serve well at bid time. The only issue you have to manage is that of perceptions; you don't want the other vendors to think you have 'pre-qualified' this vendor, because you have not done so. In most cases the cost of a pre-trial will be split between the vendor and your organization, since it is hard for the vendor's marketing staff to justify a large expenditure when you have neither enunciated your precise total requirement nor issued a procurement document.

A pre-trial can and should involve real users but should also include enough IT staff such that it can be rapidly shored up if things start to go seriously wrong. It can provide very valuable experience in planning, and overseeing, system integration even if the vendor or another outside party performs it. There may be errors or omissions in the technical or procedural details of your draft procurement document which rapidly come to light. A pre-trial can also allow you, the users and the vendor to form and refine realistic expectations about what is reasonable cooperation and support. In particular, the ideas you form about what is a reasonable response time (as measured in hours, days, weeks or whatever) for a given type of problem will almost certainly be incorporated into your certification process, providing you intend to assess vendors on their support. A pre-trial also allows you to build confidence within a group of users, who can then be used either as a model for additional user groups involved in a full-scale field trial or else dispersed among, and integrated into, the trial groups to cross-pollinate their experience to the new users. Finally, you can use the pre-trial as a showcase to management, to help them visualize what the main trials will be like and to understand why trials are important. This may be a very important factor if you must seek funding and/or further approvals before proceeding to the issue of the procurement document or the main trials.

Trials

For a trial, or a pilot, the procurement document can be styled as a Qualification and Evaluation Criteria (QEC) document, containing all of the sections necessary first to qualify, and then later evaluate and certify, each vendor with respect to technology, standards and support capabilities.

A set of documents should be developed as part of your trial planning process, quite apart from the procurement document discussed above. It is absolutely necessary to have a clear *Statement of Objectives* document which sets out the objectives of the trial. These must serve the interests of the overall organization, of the IT unit and of the user groups who will be participating. They will also be helpful to the vendors, who will see that testing and then buying computer systems are *not* the only objectives of the process.

☞ You need a clear set of goals and objectives or you cannot run a good trial.

As discussions are held between the IT unit and potential trial sites in the user community, it will become apparent what the main user concerns are. These should also be addressed in an Internal MOA signed by the IT unit and each user site. (This is not the External MOA signed by IT and the vendor.) Among other things, it should provide that:

- IT will oversee and manage the trial and will keep the vendor and other outside parties under its own supervision and, if necessary, control.
- IT will ensure that the equipment is pre-tested and ready to run *before* installation begins and will not let the vendor conduct continuous 'interface research' at the user site—if the vendor or whoever is responsible for integration cannot make the system(s)

work after some reasonable period of time, they will all be rejected and the user group will have the option of receiving another vendor or leaving the trial.

- IT will certify that the system is *ready for users* only when it really is.
- IT will ensure that end-users and administrators are trained and certified for the uses they will make of the system.
- The user group will provide the logistical support, and time of staff, necessary to accommodate the installation, integration and training.
- If there are major problems, IT will come to the aid of the users.
- The users understand they are part of a pilot in which many things are being tested at the same time (system, software, training methods, support procedures, etc.) and that sometimes things can and will go wrong.
- Any limited production or pseudo-production use of the system(s) will be made only after IT has certified such system(s) *ready for trial*—this will be done only with vendor and user agreement.
- When the trial ends, IT and the vendor will bring the system up to whatever is then determined to be the production configuration and will ensure that it runs as well as new systems then being acquired by other groups—the trial group will not be left with an 'uncompleted masterpiece' or an 'orphan'.

These kinds of provisions protect everybody and make problems much easier to resolve as soon as they occur. In very large or complex procurements, it is desirable to permit qualified vendors, the IT unit and the trial sites the flexibility to negotiate the Internal MOA after qualification and before deployment. In such circumstances, they should *all* sign it.

> ☞ Make sure the IT staff, the vendor, the trial-site users and everyone else each know what they, and each of the others, are supposed to do. The easiest way to do this is to put it in a written agreement, signed by all of them.

As cited earlier, it is very desirable to include in the procurement a *mandatory* requirement that the vendor consent to an MOA between your firm and theirs in a form given with the bid call document. Any vendor who refuses to sign this document in its basic form must, therefore, be expelled. The MOA should be written as a plan and should include who is responsible for each action, and the provision of each piece of equipment and software, from the pre-test stage through to post-trial transition of the system(s) to pilot or production status. Naturally, IT will need to ensure that the texts of the two MOAs are synchronized and contain no inconsistencies or omissions. Usually, however, you will not require the lawyers to go over the purely internal MOA between IT and each trial-site user group.

To ensure that everybody knows when a system will be considered integrated, development of an *Integration Checklist* should be considered. This checklist will enable IT staff to determine readily whether a system is ready to proceed to the next stage. Key milestones in such a document might, for example, include:

Ready for pre-test—system has been installed in a tame (IT-controlled) environment for its operational pre-test, and perhaps a full benchmark.
Ready for shipment—system has cleared pre-test, has been repacked and is ready for transportation to the trial site.
Ready for installation—system has arrived at pilot site (all shipped boxes are present and accounted for) and has been unpacked.
Ready for integration—main system components have been connected to live power and are functional—for an MRS this might mean that the CPU will turn on and boot the operating system and that all printers will come on when plugged in.
Ready for application—all packages have been installed on the system, all network interfaces have been accomplished, all local equipment has been interfaced with the system and all peripherals are connected, interfaced and working.
Ready for administrator—all intended business applications and pre-prepared user data have been installed on the system and the directory structure and end-user interfaces are finalized.
Ready for user—the administrator (to IT satisfaction) is *provably* capable of administering the system, being able to add, modify and delete user and logical devices, back up and store data, start up and shut down the system, etc.
Ready for trial—the users have been granted access to the system, and trained on it, such that they can use it in the manner anticipated in the trial plans.
Ready for test—the system has been temporarily withdrawn from daily use to permit IT staff to conduct any required intensive tests on it.
Ready for transition—the system has cleared all trial requirements, has been certified and is now ready for upgrade to production status.
Ready for production—the system has been upgraded to intended and now fully defined production status and is now available for production use by all users at the site.

☞ This is a 'staircase' of successive steps which bring the computer closer and closer to being ready for the field trial and, later, ready for conversion to production. By having the IT staff approve each step before letting anyone go to the next one, no one will trip over their shoelaces and fall down the stairs. The users will get a computer that does what it is supposed to and does only what it is supposed to. The users will not want it any other way!

If there are two or more trial sites, it is important that *from the perspective of the certification process* each vendor be given an equally 'good' trial site. The matching of sites to vendors is hardly a scientific process and there is a need for creativity and flexibility. The main issue is that no vendor must feel that the site they were assigned to did not want them or that the users are somehow less sophisticated, accepting or reasonable than those at other sites. There is no guarantee that the vendors will not compare notes (even if you contractually forbid them from doing so) before, during and/or after your certification process. If a significant difference or anomaly arises between two sites, whether it is unearthed by this or any other process, it will almost certainly be brought to the attention of the person in charge of the trials.

> ☞ Make sure each vendor gets a site which is just as good as the others, insofar as certification of their equipment is concerned. If any vendors have equipment, standards or service problems, they may start looking for scapegoats. The easiest scapegoat is to claim that their site was somehow inferior to the others.

It is important to ensure that user reactions to the installed systems, and the vendor support provided, are recorded, sorted and utilized as part of your evaluation process. A vendor who makes wonderful products but who cannot or will not service or support them, or a vendor who cannot work with the IT staff or your users, cannot be certified and your procurement approach must contemplate this. To certify such a vendor is to marry trouble! There may arise a continuous string of operational, contractual and legal problems with such a vendor. The final result may be the demise of the entire procurement program, indeed the entire open systems program if your legacy vendor is non-supportive but still very observant. In such a case, all of your good work, all of the vendors who did a good job and were certified and all of the happy users at the well-served sites will be adversely impacted.

> ☞ Make sure your procurement document does not force you to certify a vendor who cannot support the product at your field site!

If you have regional or divisional IT staffs, it is very important to involve them in the entire acquisition process. They should certainly be involved in the installation, integration overview and evaluation of vendors at the trial sites, where these are located in their domains.

If your procurement is a large one, it may be wise to establish a comprehensive on-line database (but one protected by adequate security) in which you record evaluation findings which relate to each section of your procurement document. The following process can be used to transmit specific test request to system administrators and sophisticated users at trial sites, and to obtain and record the results of such tests:

- Individual test or evaluation request sheet (for a given section or subsection) completed and validated by IT;
- Customized record format for that test entered into certification database;
- Test material transmitted to sites, well in advance of test time;
- Test time/date finalized and relayed to evaluating party;
- QEC and test materials reviewed prior to test;
- Test instructions followed by party to execute test;
- Test results recorded on hard copy and filed;
- Testing party obtains on-line access to test database in an enter-only mode and inputs test result data;
- Testing party logs test;
- Test results are assessed, interpreted and accepted or validated at first instance by IT staff;
- Primary evaluation of test results is reviewed and accepted or rejected;
- Final review and final approval or rejection of interpretation of test results.

This process includes a number of checks and cross-checks to ensure that only verified and validated data gets into the test results. The IT organization, in a full-scale trial situation, has a duty of care to everyone else involved. IT is presiding over the whole process. If test results, whether positive or negative to a vendor's position, do not get counted, and later turn up after you release the vendor scores, there will be, to put it politely, a fracas of significant proportions.

The database would be accessed on a reasonably secure, controlled basis by trained system administrators or sophisticated end-users at the trial site. IT staff would have wider access to the system, being able not only to enter data but also to extract it and interpret the meaning of it (determine its actual meaning in terms of system performance and hence rating against the QEC) and enter the resulting vendor-compliancy ratings.

You should run a separate orientation session for all of those who will be involved in testing vendor equipment, service and user support. Make available detailed instructions on how field testing will be accomplished in the form of a guidance document, along with a specific dry-run test data to be used for practice purposes and to perfect the overall evaluation system. Every test should not only be entered to the database but also recorded on paper, within a special binder provided to each site for this purpose, and kept under lock and key at all times.

Apart from this test book, each site should also keep a comprehensive log of *all* events related to the system, from its arrival in boxes until the end of the certification period. Use this log for recording virtually all occurrences of note at the site, such as startups, shutdowns, data back-ups and recoveries, service problems, service exercises, scheduled tests and other such events. Each log entry must be dated. The sites should be urged immediately to convert significant information from the log into the test book where relevant. It is wise to have the system adminis-trator be the primary keeper of this log and to ask him or her to sign each entry. In the event of a dispute with the vendor, you may find that this log is a very important piece of information, especially if the argu-ment is irreconcilable and goes to court. It may well provide the key evidence that your organization actually did fulfil its responsibilities under the MOAs and it is the vendor or even some other party who is primarily responsible for the problem.

☞ It is crucial that you carefully plan, precisely execute and scrupulously record and tally the results of each test of the product and the service/support provided by each vendor. Make sure this information is kept confidential until you are ready to tell all of the vendors their final scores.

User evaluation naturally is not confined to the formal testing process and extends to such factors as vendor promptness of response when assistance was needed, vendor conduct at the site, the performance of installed software and similar factors. Also of key interest to the sites is the ease of obtaining additional information or on-the-phone assistance from vendors, whether directly or when requests were placed via the IT unit.

It may be helpful to use a system of classification of the severity level of problems encountered at the site. The following is taken from my experience at Transport Canada, and represents a good taxonomy of problems encountered during a trial, pilot or even operational situation:

Level 1—LANA or MRSA able to solve locally at site (for example, file or directory problem experienced by end-user);
Level 2—requiring basic assistance from IT (for example, problem with use of a given UNIX command);
Level 3—requiring specialist technical expertise from IT (for example, problem with parallax created by request to a demounted directory);
Level 4—requiring vendor assistance (for example, hardware malfunc-tion or unbootable operating system).

☞ Not all problems are equal. You should be more concerned about a vendor who gives you a few major problems than one who creates many small ones.

The above guidance will assist you to plan and execute a series of trials for sophisticated high-power UNIX workstations, MBS or MRS equipment. Normally, most of the testing of mid- or mainframe equipment will be conducted by IT long before users are allowed to access it. If you intend to use field trials to certify PC or more basic UNIX workstation equipment, a number of the above measures can be relaxed or eliminated.

Pilot projects

In planning a production pilot, you must already have or create production software for your end-users. Usually, the support arrangements and some aspects of the computer systems being explored will also be well known to the IT unit. The number of independent variables or 'wild cards' is thus far less than in a trial situation. It is therefore possible to be very selective in deciding which of the measures recommended for a field trial should be utilized in a pilot. Things can still go horribly wrong, however, so vigilance is still required.

☞ In a pilot, a more mature and less troublesome set of computers and programs is used in a production environment to check out one or two new elements, which may include the computer itself, its operating system, a package, a program or something else, but usually not all of these at once.

☞ You still have to be very careful. Commanding five tigers to jump through burning hoops is fine but it takes only one not-so-well trained tiger to come around and bite you in the posterior while you are watching the others do their jumping!

At the planning stage, try to define the worst-case technology or process malfunction scenario you can imagine and write out two or three possible outcomes of this scenario, depending upon when and how it occurs and how each of IT, the vendor, the user and other stakeholders respond. Since this is a production pilot, other stakeholders may include suppliers, other workgroups inside your organization, clients or customers, regulators or others. If any of the three outcomes is unacceptable to the prospective user community (they are the ones who own 'production' here, not the IT staff) then find another pilot site. You cannot, and must not, run even a pilot in a bet-the-business situation. The failure of the pilot cannot be allowed to 'break' the organization, the IT unit or the user group. It is necessary to pay particular attention to the interfaces (both manual and automated) of the workgroup with other stakeholders and how these will function when the pilot is being ramped up, cut-over, operated and also when it is malfunctioning or crashes entirely.

It is also necessary to consider that in many circumstances the IT staff will have to put in place 'workarounds' so that any obtrusive testing is done when the system production role is off-line. Obviously, benchmark tests cannot be run on a machine which is issuing invoices, managing inventory, monitoring a process or controlling the allocation of food to thousands of hungry laboratory mice.

Conclusion

During any pre-trial, trial or pilot activity it is crucial to issue some sort of hard-copy newsletter or bulletin to keep everyone informed as to what is happening and what progress has been made recently. This will cheer users who thus find themselves 'in the news', give vendor marketing representatives something to send back to headquarters and offer your own senior management a comfortable feeling that all is well. Keep the tone very positive and never write anything which users or vendors may later say is an admission of error on your part or an undertaking to do or pay for something. Sometimes, user-group line managers, especially those with tight budgets, are prone to take comments like 'soon IT will oversee transition of the XXX trial to production status' to mean something like: 'Soon IT will pay for a machine to replace this one we now have on trial, which has given us a lot of trouble.' Once they share this interpretation with their senior management, IT management is into 'damage control' mode.

7 Hardening the framework: building from the foundation

Introduction

This chapter will attempt to provide information useful for making the transition from the exploratory and provisional world of trials and pilots to a production situation for the classes of equipment and application which you have successfully certified.

Once it is clear that the certification activities have been successful, reward the vendors as soon as possible by curtailing their (usually quite expensive) requirement to support trial or pilot sites wholly or partially at their cost. Move into an interim support contract arrangement. Also, if you are in a position to initiate at least a few procurements in the short term, do not hesitate to do so. The regional management of your vendors will have been under pressure for some time from their superiors regarding when you will *ever* start buying some of this wonderful new gear you have been trying out for so long. Give your vendors a realistic estimate of your intended purchases in the first year or quarter of the new purchasing regime and do your best, working with user groups, to stick to it. Sometimes circumstances will intervene, be they mergers, budget cuts, new managers or whatever, and usually these are outside the control of IT. However, any failure to move into 'acquisition mode' may be seen as a sign by some or all of the vendors that your commitment to their products is still not solid, despite the great lengths to which they went to accommodate your requirements.

Capitalizing on your success

This is a good time to turn the *Trial Bulletin* into the *Open Systems Bulletin* and to make it a permanent part of your IT shop's presence with its users. It is also the ideal time to recruit other workgroups for a first 'bulk buy' of systems from your newly certified group of vendors. Workgroups wanting to run the same application(s) as the trial or pilot groups, as well as those with other intended uses for the same class of equipment, may want to get together, particularly if you promise them a bigger discount on the systems.

Once you have two or more vendors certified to provide a given class of product, you can move to price competition. In principle, all or most buys will occur when you issue a very brief specification for a given lot of certified equipment to the vendors and they submit price and availability (P&A) information. Where availabilities are equal you take the lowest price as the winner for that purchase. Where timing is an issue, only a subset of the bidders may have compliant availability. In such a case take the lowest price from that subset. There are, however, conditions in which you may want to reserve to your IT unit the right to limit the field for a particular bid to a subset of the certified vendors (or even one vendor) should not all of the certified vendors offer a special, infrequently demanded but still crucial, feature required for a given site. You must, of course, contemplate such circumstances in your procurement rules. Most vendors will be prepared to go along with this, as long as there is a reasonable expectation on their part and yours that this will be used only occasionally and only for a small percentage of the total value of the procurement.

☞ Sometimes there is no point in letting all the vendors bid if only one or two have what you really need. These times, though, should remain the exception.

There is another, thornier, issue which you must contemplate at the time you set the procurement rules. Unit X wants to buy a certified MRS so IT runs a procurement just for them and Vendor A wins the P&A; his system is installed. Six months later, Unit X wants a second system and demands that it also come from Vendor A. From their perspective this is the best approach, since they do not want to get their service and support from two vendors. They also like Vendor A, who is giving them exemplary support. There are, however, two very serious problems with their reasoning, which IT must point out:

1 The whole purpose of certifying multi-vendors is to obtain the benefits of open systems, one of which is that you can substitute hardware without problems. So a Vendor B or C system is, provably, just as adequate and runs the required software just as well as a Vendor A machine.

2 If every workgroup were allowed this privilege, the vendors would engage in an orgy of ruinous price cutting right at the beginning of procurements so that each could 'stake out' enough sites to be assured of some follow-on business. The problem here is that the vendors have already invested a lot of money to become certified

and so, from the perspectives of their respective managements, they are now in a no-win situation. This may seem like a good situation for your organization (mostly free trials followed by cut-throat price competition) but it really is not. Vendors, on whom you too have spent much time and effort, may simply decide they have had enough and depart, remarking on their way out the door that you can call them when you are ready to pay full list price. Alternatively, they may resolve to make the money back from you on service contracts and adopt a service pricing strategy you cannot afford to live with.

These arguments may or may not convince the local user group but you can offer one small comfort. Your LANA and MRSA training and certification program, of course, embraces all flavours of certified systems so the administrator can certainly handle two different systems. Often, however, this is moot, since each system will have its own administrator anyway.

☞ Users cannot be permitted to play favourites with the vendors or the whole purpose of having an open system program could be thwarted.

Making trials permanent

Where a trial versus a pilot is to be transitioned to production status a significant amount of planning may be required. The trial system(s) may require an upgrade to whatever you have decided is the desirable production configuration for the user individual or workgroup. Often, the standard configurations for different purposes and different sizes of workgroups will have been modified during the certification process, based on actual experience. For example, it may be discovered that a given workgroup requires a *much* larger system than was first thought to run a given ten- or twenty-user application under an RDBMS. Also, before you can make a trial site into a production site, it is necesary to deal with some of the other issues set out below.

Extending pilots to other sites

Pilots are much easier to transition to full-scale production, since they already are in a production role. Interfaces with other systems may need to be created or improved and, here again, general or site-specific experience may point to a configuration upgrade. Often, transition provides the opportunity to deliver to all stakeholders the glad tidings that the 'disruption period' is now almost over.

It is best to complete the transition to their final state of all of the pilot sites *before* moving to implement the new open system configurations elsewhere. By first upgrading the pilot sites, and dealing with any upgrade-induced issues, you will subsequently be able to install clones (or cousins, as the case may be) of the pilot systems elsewhere with complete confidence in their maturity and stability.

Organizing for technology management

For the moment, we will ignore the issue of whether you should organize along platform lines and assume that, after the glorious conclusion of the trial or pilot, there is rising excitement and anticipation in the ranks of the users. They have read the bulletins with interest and have heard the testimonials of the happy users. They may also have seen articles about your open system program in computer magazines. If your organization is large, has started buying computers in substantial numbers, and if vendors enjoyed the trial or pilot experience, you will probably also be featured in their advertising. We will further assume that the people who first ran a lab test for UNIX workstations have now certified MBS and MRS equipment. They can, in other words, acquire and deliver open computing systems suitable for one to 100 users.

My own (albeit personal) bias is that it is best to organize a unit to oversee the inflow of open system technology along three basic lines:

1 You need a group to work with the user groups to determine what they actually need, to specify it and to ensure that it is delivered, installed, integrated and made *ready for production* in accordance with however you have decided that it should be done, based on your original planning, plus your trial or pilot experience. This group should also track the total corporate environment, noting which workgroups are likely to upgrade to which class of system within each relevant planning timeframe. For the open systems organization, this represents a 'prospect list'.

☛ You need someone to help user groups know when they should move to open systems, and to help them get started.

2 You need a group to train end-users and, more importantly, also to train LAN or MRS administrators. If you cannot train and certify good LANAs (for MBS equipment) and MRSAs (for the larger and more complex MRS equipment) you may be forced into unacceptably expensive and troublesome support activities. There is no reason why the capabilities of this unit cannot be developed, and fully tested, during the trials or pilots themselves. Then, when certi-

fication is complete, not only the users but also the user/administrator training capability can be transitioned to production. As a workgroup actually moves to acquire an open computing system, responsibility for them would pass from the first group to this one. A standardized handbook or manual should be issued for each class of certified equipment, spanning all of the various products found in each such class.

☞ You need people to train and support the 'super-users' who will actually operate the workgroup systems once they are installed.

3   With open systems, you cannot, and indeed must not, rely on one vendor as your key source of information about the state of the world. Therefore, it is necessary to have a group with the capability to monitor the state of the technology and to serve as the guardian of the certified technology base. When a vendor arrives at the agreed time with a new system to be certified to supplement or supplant an existing certified one, this group will have to decide what parts of the new system (if any) should be tested to achieve certification, or whether the system is even certifiable at all. An equally important function for this group is the translation of user requirements into generic configuration specifications derived from one of the standard configurations for the product in question, which can be put out for bid to the appropriate group of certified vendors. This group is also the final technical arbiter of a workgroup's claim that its requirements are so specialized that they just cannot be met by any of the certified open computing systems and that only Application X, which requires proprietary Computer Y, will do. For the IT staff, for administrators and for interested end-users, this group should publish a calendar of events (briefings, conferences, etc.) related to open systems. Publication of a directory of approved products as a binder, with an automatic update service, and issue of the same to all line managers will ensure that user groups are aware of what is and is not certified for various uses. The plea of 'ignorance' will be heard no more.

☞ People are also needed to keep on tracking the technology, which never stops changing. Vendors will bring in new products from time to time and these will become certified, as older ones are discontinued.

The assumption is also made here that both network management and end-user support capabilities will continue to be maintained elsewhere in the IT unit, and that these will be upgraded post-trial/pilot to include the new systems.

The group now responsible for developing and/or contracting for the development and maintenance of business applications should also be charged with a new function at this time. It should become responsible for the development of a software registry; this is discussed in more detail below. Where third-party software is to be acquired to fulfil a given requirement, it should, as a minimum, be certified for all systems of the class on which it is to be run. Where a common operating system usage definition can be arrived at for all processing tiers, and for all systems certified within each tier, a single certification test of the software may indeed serve to certify it for all OCS platforms in the entire organization.

The group with application responsibility, in coordination with the above-cited technology group, should issue development guidelines to IT staff, end-users and external contractors, specifying the operating system usage standards, and other standards, adopted and proven by your organization during the certification process. The document should make clear that all future applications *must* follow these rules and that non-conforming deliverables will be returned to contractors.

☞ It is necessary to get control of how new computer programs come into your organization, so as to make sure that they conform to open systems rules and can thus be easily carried from one computer to another.

If your organization is large and geographically distributed, it may be desirable to pre-position spare parts or even fully kitted MBS or MRS equipment at strategic points so that you can be in a position to provide very fast assistance, even in the event of a catastrophic failure of an installed workgroup system.

There are a number of other measures you can take to help support workgroup system users and their administrators, wherever they are located. They include the following:

1 Make frequent visits to all OCS sites and ensure that they are aware you are quite ready to stand behind them when problems arise. Follow up on any problems or concerns expressed in the meetings and have someone report back on what was concluded.

2 Hold an annual conference for all LANA and MRSA personnel, giving them the opportunity to take upgrade training, share experiences, seek any special assistance they may need and learn about as well as see and touch newly certified products introduced recently by the vendors. You should have no trouble convincing all of your vendors to mount displays at these meetings. For each of the MBS and MRS classes of administrators, you may want to hold a caucus for those with each certified vendor's products.

3 Ensure that your network management personnel are *thoroughly* trained in how to perform remotely those functions which they are capable of performing and permitted to perform which concern the

MBS or MRS. They must understand that a LANA or MRSA is clearly *not* a totally unsophisticated user and should not be treated like one. On the other hand, the administrator should not normally be on-call 24 hours per day. A quiet hour's monitoring of MBS and MRS equipment is highly beneficial, but having the network centre call the MRSA at home at half-past midnight just to tell him his building power is off and his system's uninterruptible power supply has also failed will not make for good relations. (There is nothing the administrator can do about it until morning, or at least until the power comes back on, anyway.) Ensure that each network management shift operator and local administrator clearly understands each other's roles and responsibilities in various circumstances.

4 For certain classes of users, it may be desirable to set up a 'premium' class of support for both the local administrator and for the system itself. This may involve an IT 'swat team' which will go into action at any time and continue working until the critical system is either returned to operational status or replaced with one that will work.

5 It is highly desirable to 'pair up' sites, particularly those with the same equipment, so that they can serve not only as the remote storage location for each other's backup tapes in the event that a system is wiped out by an accident or emergency situation, but also so that they can learn first-hand from each other's experiences.

6 Some workgroups may *insist* on a second, and identical, machine, to serve as a cold or even hot standby in the event that the main system crashes. Some of these requirements are legitimate, but make clear to the local line management that if it is going to make this case it must do so, and fund the second machine, at the time of purchase, not later. Where the requirement is then justified and funded, simply issue a P&A request for two systems instead of one; treat it as a single buy!

7 Another support strategy which will be useful in some circumstances, particularly for larger multi-user MRS applications, is to have a system within the IT organization which can, in an emergency situation, serve as a remote and temporary replacement or 'ghost machine' for a critical field system. If the local system crashes, use a pre-positioned gateway to access your peer-to-peer OSI network and simply mount the required application with the most recent backup data at your central site. Users will find the system 'sluggish' due to the impact of network overhead on local, to-screen, response time, but they will rejoice that their application can still run even though their local system is down.

8 Even if your IT unit is uncomfortable about making any aspect of MBS and MRS system administration a remote-control item, it is

essential that IT remain in control of system management. The trained/certified paraprofessionals administering the systems in the field just cannot, and will not, do it. Most of them are only part-time system administrators and they tend to be event driven. They run backups three times per week and they help users with problems. These activities differ vastly from charting disk usage over many months so as to predict when more capacity is required. Configuration management (CM) should also be handled centrally. When an administrator places new software on a system, IT will know immediately if he or she has been trained to log onto a central CM system and update the configuration. Failure to do this should be full and sufficient cause for revocation of a person's administrator certification. It is essential that IT be aware of precisely what package and application software is installed on each system. For example, if an RDBMS vendor contacts IT and announces that Version X contains a serious bug (or worse, a virus), IT must be able to determine immediately which systems have that version installed, isolate them from the network and request their administrators to take appropriate action. Use of centralized software distribution facilities whereby IT uses the network to distribute new software to workgroup systems will assist in overcoming this problem but will not remove it entirely. It is also necessary to enjoin administrators or anyone else at the site from mounting unapproved software on the workgroup system.

☞ The IT group must control, and track, what computer programs both it and the trained local administrator install on the new computers. No one else should be installing software on these machines unless pre-authorized by IT.

Software registry concept

As stated in earlier chapters, one of the most important opportunities presented by an open system strategy is the ability to create a central software 'recycling' facility. Where a local line manager asks the LANA or MRSA to find software with a given functionality, that person's first recourse would be to the organization's central Software Registry. To establish and operate the Registry, IT would:

- Make a general census of all owned and corporate site-licensed (or at least so-licensable) applications.
- Register and inventory all DOS, UNIX and proprietary operating system applications believed to be candidates for re-use beyond their current host processor and, as and when possible, cross-certify these within and among operating systems, RDBMS environments and other package environments.

- When so requested by an end-user or IT project team leader, seek one or more third-party applications capable of meeting a given requirement cited to the degree of precision found in a preliminary functional specification.
- When so requested, seek to acquire for the end-user unit the desired third-party application at a fair market value (list price, best discount, etc.) for the application.
- Simultaneously seek to acquire for the corporation at large, at some token or nominal additional cost where possible and otherwise at the firm's normal rates, a corporate site licence permitting the application to be certified on as many Registry-recognized officially approved processing platforms as possible, with or without authority to modify the source code.
- Accept and, where possible, cross-certify all applications developed *de novo* either in-house or by contractors for user workgroups or units.
- Provide advice and assistance to units seeking to evaluate registry software for possible use as is or with modifications.
- Control and oversee the modification, revision, expansion, versioning, software configuration management, release and distribution of any application held in the Registry.

☞ Because programs for open systems are easy to move between computers, you should set up a central depot for all your computer programs. Then, anyone who needs a new program can look there first. This will save your organization a great deal of money.

The first unit to buy a UNIX MBS or MRS clearly gets no or very little immediate benefit from the real or imagined existence of the Registry. The 300th unit to acquire such a system may realize a very real benefit because it may find much of the software it requires already available from the Registry, reducing its costs and offering it a wide choice of applications. There is a 'concomitance of diffusion' issue, which you must explicitly address in your planning and in your dealings with senior management and the users. If the number of UNIX workgroup system operators is expanding very rapidly, and if most are commissioning or buying at least some applications, then the pool of available applications within the Registry will rise very rapidly.

Some substantial savings can be generated. Suppose that a typical user unit might implement four applications (at an average capital cost of between $50K and $100K each). However, as the number of active MBS or MRS-operating units rose, so too would the number of custommade (as well as site-licensed third-party) applications making their way to the Registry. Thus, over time, a linear decrease can be hypothesized in the *percentage* and the *absolute number* of new unit-level application requirements which would have to be met from sources other than *registry* or *modify*, as discussed earlier. Thus, over time, the average cost per new multi-user application can be expected to fall. For any organization with a substantial user base, and at least some commonality, but not perfect homogeneity, among user-group requirements, this model will predict a significant cost avoidance due to software portability. Of course, a more complex model would be desirable, taking into account the following factors:

- Not all applications will be the same size.
- Some applications will acquire a very good or very bad reputation which will, respectively, spur or hurt their diffusion.
- Most units have at least a few requirements which are absolutely unique and for which the Registry will be of limited utility—many units have a considerable number of these.
- The success of the Registry is also dependent upon the following:
  - LANAs and MRSAs who are aware of and actively use the Registry as the first (not the last) place to look when trying to meet new user needs;
  - IT project staff who themselves use the Registry as the repository of first resort in seeking solutions for user requirements and whose actions and methodological tools in no way bias them against the Registry.

Counterbalanced against the positive aspects of the Registry is one important caution. Great care must be taken in attributing general benefits from the Registry, particularly in its early phases, since a large community is needed to make it worth while. Also, the Registry's inventory of 'product' must be considered to age just like any other inventory in terms of its relevance to the user community, and hence its value. However, one can postulate the emergence of a form of internal software 'market' within your firm. Further, even minor use of the Registry may bring large corporate and workgroup benefits.

If the Registry was seen as 'profit centre', then its manager would presumably:

- Seek to offset the incremental costs paid for corporate site (versus one processor only) licences against benefits achieved in savings from avoided purchases later on.
- Plough back some of the profits (savings) into keeping the inventory fresh and attractive to potential user units.

Suppose Unit X has found the perfect application for which the vendor charges $40K per processor licence but for which a corporate site licence can be negotiated at $70K. In budgetary terms, the Registry manager would—if convinced of the value of the application beyond Unit X—contribute the incremental $30K to the requisition and then cross-certify the product. Presumably, the cost to acquire and cross-certify would then govern subsequent 'pricing' of the applicaton out to subsequent users in the organization. In effect, the manager is running a 'used-car lot' for software.

☞ The software depot or 'Registry' operates not unlike a used-car lot. It obtains used software and returns it to circulation. Whether you make users 'buy' the software from the depot or give it to them, this is little more than an internal accounting matter in most cases.

In any event, there is undeniably *some value* in being able to join the community of users able to access the multi-user or at least client/server software available from the Registry. The problem is that if the first and 300th units to buy an MBS or MRS each intend to buy—over their respective Years 1–5—one application per year with a full development cost equivalent of $100K each, their cost profiles will be quite different. Modelling this requires some quite detailed predictions about the future software requirements of your workgroups, and is far beyond the scope of this book.

Consultations with US and Canadian officials have not produced information on the existence (much less in-service use) of any methodology, model or technique which fully addresses the Registry issue as presented above. One will probably have to be developed.

Application placement

When you can get an application from any of four generic sources (*registry*, *modify* (from Registry package), *third party* or *develop*), and can put it on a processing platform of virtually any size, anywhere in the organization, there is a tendency to lose one's bearings. In the 'good old days' it was rather more simple. PC applications came in shrink-wrap; minicomputer applications and mainframe applications came from third-party vendors or were developed in-house or on contract.

☞ You need a methodology or set of rules to help decide where to put a new computer program, since you are no longer restricted and can put many new programs on any desired size of computer.

While the subject of how to place applications among platforms of various scale and service model in an open system environment could easily be the subject of a book, in itself, this section provides some basic guidance about the factors which tend to *drive* application placement. At least, these factors should be considered when seeking to decide on what class of machine to place a non-obvious application.

1 There is an *external relationship* such that the current application is tied to another specific application or process which cannot be disrupted by the implementation of the application, nor by the subsequent movement of the application to a lower tier.

2 There is a *budgetary constraint* which forces the workgroup to remain with the as-installed system environment. The workgroup can afford neither a new or upgraded system nor to pay (presumably fully cost-recuperative) user charges levied for larger systems. The workgroup is therefore confined to its current equipment.

3 The opinions or qualitative *views of unit management* and/or *end-users* (particularly any sophisticated end-users) may affect the favour or disfavour with which one or more of the make, modify, buy or get-free software sourcing options are viewed. This, in turn, may influence all remaining elements of the analysis in favour of, or against, a candidate software solution. Where this solution has system and/or tier implications, such views or opinions will, via the process of application selection, impact tier placement.

4 The *location* of a unit's *worksite* may influence choice of tier. All other things being equal, site locations which IT staff, and technology suppliers, cannot easily support will engender approval of higher tiers.

5 Where the *workgroup* is in fact *replicative* (there are many workgroups, each distinct and each replicating the requirement for the application) there will be a tendency to push tier selection down to at least the unit level. It may be necessary to consider the minimum, median, maximum, mean and mode of site size as measured by:
   – Total *employees* at site (ultimate potential application and/or OA user community);
   – Total *system users* at site (short-term potential application and/or OA user community);
   – Total intended *application users* at site (potential application user community);
   – *Current participants* in manual system and/or users of current application at site (immediate application user community).
   Of course, each of the above measures of site population can only be compared to the same measure, across sites.

6 Where all or most members of the *workgroup* either are *not* now and/or will not in future be *co-located* at one site or facility, there

will be a tendency to employ higher tiers of processing, particularly where workspace and/or function sharing is required.

7   The degree of *security* needed by the unit or workgroup, and reflected in the formation actually managed by the application, may impact choice of processing tier.

8   Where there is a requirement for *transaction processing* there may be a restriction as to what classes of equipment are appropriate.

9   Using the 'continuum of portability' classification of the degree of *difficulty to port* (a former application to be upgraded into a new one, a current prototype or pilot or otherwise) from the source system to a conceivable target system, it may be possible to isolate tier-specific barriers to porting of a given application to or from one or more tiers. For example, these can include language, package or operating environment software versions which differ among tiers.

10   The *service model* (single-user, client/server or multi-user) desired or dictated by the unit or workgroup, or dictated by the work flow and/or application design decisions taken for the *modify* and *develop* options, will usually impact choice of tier.

11   Perhaps the most obvious, and most powerful, determinant of application tier requirements and placement, at least in so far as up-tier migration is concerned, is the *scale* of the application. In general, as these parameters increase in value, quantity or scale they push the application up-tier. The following are believed to be tier placement drivers:
   – *Lines of code* (projected or actual);
   – *Complexity of logic* (from functional specification or full design documents);
   – Number of *calls* made to other applications;
   – Degree of *interoperation* with applications on other tiers;
   – Non-vectorized total *volume of data* from disk input to, and output to disk from, the application;
   – Vectorized volume of data *input* to, and *output* from, *other processing tiers*;
   – Application-generated actual *machine* I/O including optical scanning, reading of files, writing to files, keyboard input, printing, EDI input or output, etc.;
   – Total estimated operating system *processes or instructions* and/or machine instructions;
   – Total on-line concurrent *memory* requirements.

12   The projected *degree of portability* (see continuum discussed earlier) of an application may be a determinant of whether it should be left on the tier(s) where it can run currently or considered for vertical porting to another tier. While it is obvious that this impacts

the cost to implement the application for the unit or workgroup's use, the issue does not end there, particularly if the Registry is involved. There are in fact three potentially different degrees of portability with which the project team must be concerned:

A — Source-to-target (to ensure initial application *operability*);
B — Target-to-Registry (to achieve application *normalization*);
C — Registry-to-next target (to permit application *promulgation*).

Certainly, from the perspective of the unit or workgroup, Type A is of most concern. However, IT must be equally concerned with all three unless it is prepared to preclude the application, at this stage, from consideration for the Registry. Here, IT corporate and unit/ workgroup local requirements must be balanced or traded off. Perhaps the best application for the unit will be a nightmare for the Registry; in such a case the application may simply be exempted from the Registry. In other cases, particularly where two essentially equivalent *third-party* applications are the final candidates, Types B and C (as well as the assistance and corporate site licensing policy the vendor is prepared to offer to IT) may be tie-breakers in both technical and economic terms. The application emerging as winner of this particular comparison may, in its present manifestation, be entirely tier-specific, at least in so far as the unit (which always wants to implement as soon as possible) is concerned. Thus, selecting an application which demonstrates excellent portability characteristics for the future may be a tier-limiting choice in the immediate context.

13   The 'family history' or *pedigree of the application* in terms of specific source (vendor), tier/platform history, links or ties to languages or packages, operating system/operating environment and various other factors may be important in determining choice of tier. Formerly, packages such as ADABAS, NATURAL, SAS and others were tier-limiting factors, usually invoking the main- or mid-frame class of system. While this is now far less often the case, there are still circumstances where the requirement for a package, a specific version of a package or a specific package functionality may dictate a choice of tier.

14   The intended *future* of the application can impact the choice of tier for the immediate placement. Where such a future use connotes a change of application scale (as defined above), role and/or user community nature/size, it may be desirable or even mandatory to make provision for these changes at the outset, even in the version supplied to the initial user community. In these circumstances, such a provision may in turn determine tier, or at least push the appli-

cation up- or down-tier. The provision could affect not only scale but also such areas as package-dependencies, I/O, transaction processing, real-time requirements, security and other requirements.

15 Application *support requirements* are an important determining factor of tier, since each tier, by definition, has unique support capabilities. In general, the following are the support characteristics of the tiers and specific component systems:

Workplace—self-service by end-user;

Unit—MBS—basic paraprofessional service by LANA covering PC, PC connectivity, LAN, WAN access, server and client portions of application and any packages such as client/server OA if available—may also include application and/or database administration and OA administration;

Unit—MRS—enhanced paraprofessional service by MRSA covering PC, PC connectivity, LAN, WAN access and usage, multi-user application(s) running on MRS and any packages such as OA—usually also includes application and/or database administration and OA administration;

Mid-frame/mainframe—comprehensive professional support by IT unit, including support and administration of all hardware, software and communications environments.

The above list is not a comprehensive one, although it should provide enough information to assist your organization to decide what the important placement determinants are. As stated earlier, it is possible to take a common law or a codified approach to placement. Certainly, the latter is preferable if you can devise a sufficiently flexible (and perhaps automatable) method.

8 Fact and fiction: two case studies

Introduction

To provide a balanced case study chapter, I have elected first to share some of my experiences during my approximately two-and-a-half years as Director, Intermediate Informatics at Transport Canada (TC), and then to provide a more general, private sector-oriented, hypothetical case study. The latter is based on a paper delivered at the May 1991 North American Conference on Open Systems, sponsored by the Corporation for Open Systems (COS). While both are drawn from the transportation field, the first case study details many issues which are common to all public agencies, while the second is set in a private firm and should be quite applicable to many other areas of business and industry.

The Transport Canada Unit Level System (ULS) program

Disclaimer

It is always much more difficult to write dispassionately about an activity in which one was integrally involved over a significant period of time. For this reason, and because I do not at the time of writing represent or speak for Transport Canada, it should be pointed out that the views and opinions expressed here are my own and do not necessarily represent those of any Canadian government department or agency.

Transport Canada background

The origins of the Canadian federal Department of Transport (DOT) are found in 1936 legislation which brought together various previously independent activities and concentrated, as much as practically possible, responsibility for integrated national transportation planning in one minister. While they reported to Parliament through the same minister, many related agencies (most notably the Air Transport Board and the Board of Transport Commissioners, which were respectively concerned with the economic regulation of aviation and the economic/technical regulation of rail and interprovincial motor vehicle traffic) remained independent from the department.

With rapid growth in air and motor vehicle transportation demand and services after the Second World War the department expanded quickly and its responsibilities, particularly with regard to airport and airway operation and coastal protection, were broadened considerably over time. Various other departments and agencies with mandates in such areas as communications and meteorology were ultimately formed from core groups which had evolved within the department. A Ministry concept was developed and implemented in 1967, the organization's name was changed to Transport Canada and economic involvement in all modes of transportation was increased. With the advent of Canadian transportation deregulation in the 1980s, some of the former functions of the Canadian Transport Commission (successor to both the Air Transport Board/Board of Transport Commissioners) were transferred to the department.

By the mid-1980s the department consisted of the following major elements (called 'Groups'), each under an Assistant Deputy Minister:

- *Aviation*, with responsibility for aircraft, air carrier and pilot certification and technical regulation as well as air traffic control, flight paths, navigational aids and aviation information system planning and operations and most other matters related to experimental, civil and general aviation as well as the provision of air transport services to various government agencies;
- *Airports*, with responsibility for the planning, construction and operation of virtually all large, medium and small airport facilities and related infrastructure in Canada;
- *Marine*, with responsibility for vessel, water carrier and marine personnel certification and technical regulation as well as the operation of the Canadian Coast Guard;
- *Surface*, with responsibility for motor vehicle standards and certification, provincial highway funding collaboration, dangerous goods transportation and later rail technical regulation;
- *Policy and coordination*, with responsibility for most non-operational transportation issues such as information base, research, coordination among modes and tiers of government, international coordination and similar matters;
- *Finance and administration*, with responsibility for financial planning, implementation and managing administration, all common

service manual and automated information management, internal cost recovery and management consulting activities;
- *Personnel*, with the corporate personnel function;
- *Review*, with responsibility for comprehensive internal program review and assessment.

Smaller units, also reporting directly to the Deputy Minister, addressed issues such as public affairs and security/emergency planning.

Application of advanced technologies

The Aviation Group (which, as the Canadian Air Transport Administration, had earlier also overseen airports) was one of the largest Canadian users of relatively advanced communications technology in each decade from the 1940s onwards. As automated information-processing systems became available (in the form of tube technology and solid-state computers) in the late 1950s, the Aviation component of the DOT was quick to adopt them. The importance of aviation in Canada's post-war economy cannot be overstressed and DOT played a leading role in promoting, and supporting, general and civil aviation, not least by developing a very advanced air traffic control and air navigation system. DOT was among the earliest organizations in Canada to use a strong communications experiential background as a foundation for the use of computers in a wide variety of planning, engineering and operational roles.

In parallel with these developments, the implementation of commercial 'EDP' was in progress throughout the 1960s with the implementation of IBM and other equipment for financial and administrative purposes. This occurred largely, but not entirely, within those elements of the then DOT now forming part of the Finance/Administration Group of TC. Of course, the earliest systems were batch-oriented using tape and punched cards and forcing the organization of all computer-related work so as to minimize the actual use of expensive machine time. At TC headquarters an evolution through IBM 360, 370 and eventually 30XX technologies occurred in parallel with a progress to more usable forms of high-level languages and the move towards on-line computing. Motorola Four Phase mid-range system equipment was also acquired along with IBM System 8100 computers.

In the early 1980s it was decided to attempt to decentralize to TC's regional organizations a percentage of the 'information system' computing; i.e. that conducted under Finance/Administration Group auspices and not directly supportive of the operations of the modal Groups. The latter were themselves already, in large part, decentralized and used DEC PDP-10 and PDP-11 equipment, many DEC VAX systems and various types supplied by other vendors. The decision led to the acquisition of IBM 4331 mid-frame systems for nine regional offices and the expansion of the IBM System Network Architecture (SNA) network, which had already been providing terminal/controller-based timesharing access throughout Canada. This network became known as the Distributed Data Processing Network (DDPN). None the less, most serious medium- and large-scale application development remained under headquarters EDP auspices, being performed in COBOL and targeted for the IBM MVS environment.

This situation, which was in no way unique to TC, being a classic phase in information technology development in most large organizations, resulted in excessive centralization and an increasing backlog of application development requests at the central EDP complex. Many local user units felt that the EDP human and physical resources were oriented largely towards meeting corporate and not small group or individual requirements; this led many of them to venture into the world of computers on their own initiative, with varying results.

By the early 1980s, TC also faced an explosion of PC acquisition and use — with little centralized coordination or standardization being provided. Individual units simply acquired whatever types of equipment they found most easily available. In many cases, what seemed like a small programming problem expanded greatly and ultimately resulted in the need to summon professional informatics assistance. Life cycle costs, particularly related to training and software maintenance, were almost always underestimated by end-user units acquiring computer equipment for the first time. As more and more small, independently operated systems were acquired, the pressure on the central EDP unit for support and assistance escalated rapidly. A separate organization was created to address these requirements by providing standards, guidance and actual assistance with acquisition and application development; it was ultimately known as Integrated Office Services (IOS) and was soon merged with the Communications and Informatics directorate. Its mandate also came to include the study and fulfilment of Office Automation (OA) requirements within TC.

In response to a rapidly increasing demand upon limited central computing resources, and to provide maximum flexibility for future demand growth, the resulting Director General Information Management Services (DGIMS) organization within TC initiated a review of network and processing requirements. Called the Network Processing Strategy Study, this review pointed clearly to the need to identify four levels of information management (and information processing) within TC.

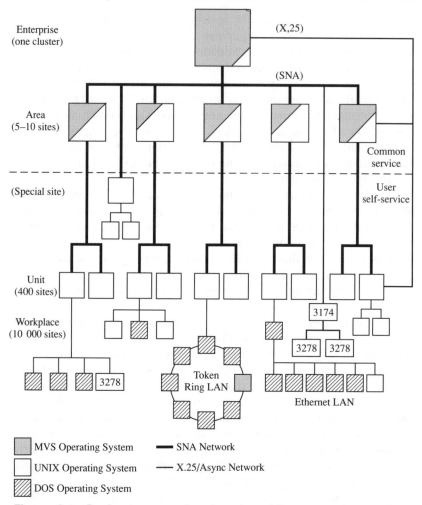

Enterprise
(one cluster)

(X,25)

(SNA)

Area
(5–10 sites)

Common
service

(Special site)

User
self-service

Unit
(400 sites)

Workplace
(10 000 sites)

3174

3278   3278

3278

Token
Ring LAN

Ethernet LAN

MVS Operating System   ━━ SNA Network

UNIX Operating System   ── X.25/Async Network

DOS Operating System

Figure 8.1 Business, operational and mobile computing environments.

These were:

- Enterprise (corporate—mainframe);
- Area (regional—mid-frame);
- Unit (branch or directorate—minicomputer/mid-range system);
- Workplace (desktop or workbench—personal computer or similar).

At each level, managers are responsible for the management of information and may wish to pursue manual and automated information processing in accordance with their business mission and operational requirements (*see* Fig. 8.1).

The ULS program

A 'Unit' is a section, branch, directorate or facility under the line control of one line manager and which has a user community of between five and fifty. A Unit Level System (ULS) is a multi-user computer system which is owned and operated by the unit, in accordance with DGIMS functional guidance. At the unit level, the study identified a requirement for the supply of up to 400 mid-range computer systems for use in information system, operational support, engineering, scientific and technically embedded computing environments. The ULS Establishment Program, set up to establish the standards, certification, acquisition channels and support mechanisms for ULS equipment, was mandated to provide support for the acquisition of ULS equipment where appropriate and to ensure that only appropriate applications were run on such equipment.

While not the first large Canadian government procurement program to cite open systems as an objective, the ULS program represented some important firsts:

- It specified a common operating system *Use Profile* and a comprehensive open system approach as described below, permitting programs and data to be carried from one make of system to another;
- It contemplated initial qualification, a comprehensive field trial and ongoing post-trial competition among five approved hardware vendors, based on price and availability, for each individual system acquisition; and
- It planned the use of specially trained paraprofessionals as local system administrators.

The ULS Establishment Program began in 1988 with a further internal review of TC processing needs which highlighted a significant number of pending and outstanding requests for mid-range equipment, for which no DGIMS guidance or standards had yet been promulgated. At that point the DGIMS Intermediate Informatics Branch was established to take responsibility for the overall mid-range computer program within TC. Interim Guidance on Mid-Range Systems was soon issued, limiting all future purchases to those which could run a UNIX operating system derivative, could interface with the IBM SNA network and on X.25 network, and also support an Ethernet or Token Ring LAN interface.

Previously, the Treasury Board (TB) had recommended the POSIX operating system interface standard as a preferred direction for open systems development, and consideration was given to using POSIX alone as the means of promoting portability among computer platforms. However, TC desired to exercise data environment, application software and data portability on three axes:

Vertical portability among different sizes of computers at the Enterprise (mainframe), Area (mid-frame), Unit (five- to fifty-user mid-range) and Workplace (PC/workstation) levels;
Horizontal portability among similar computers within one level; and
Forward portability to replacement computers at any level, and probably from a different vendor.

It was readily determined that use of POSIX alone would not permit this to occur. A common operating system was still believed to be required and UNIX was seen as the only viable common operating system if a multi-vendor price- and performance-competitive acquisition strategy was to be followed. None the less, UNIX itself was not monolithic and various strains existed. It was decided not to specify everything that an operating system should or should not contain but rather what part of it would actually be used and thus must be present. This would restrict TC software developers and users somewhat but would permit vendors using either UNIX family to supply equipment while safeguarding portability. Vendors were free to include third-party products to make up any deficiencies against the specification. This approach was called 'Greater UNIX' or 'GX', because it attempted to homogenize the differences among UNIX variants by setting a common 'how we will use it' profile. It is discussed in more detail below.

A multi-vendor strategy was believed superior either to a single-vendor approach or one permitting many vendors to supply such equipment, as it would prevent undue vendor dependence and permit price/performance competition among a manageable number of suppliers in terms of hardware/software support and software portability certification. Naturally, the specification of a common way *of using* the operating system was not, in and of itself, sufficient to guarantee the degree of portability required by TC. Common languages and a common RDBMS were also specified and further procedural and protective measures were evolved during the subsequent national ULS Field Trials.

TC first conducted a Demonstration and Evaluation Project (DEP) to prove key concepts and permit staff to gain experience with advanced open system-based mid-range equipment; AT&T 3B2 computers served this purpose, installed at the Ottawa headquarters and also at Montreal/Dorval. This was followed by a full-scale pre-trial activity, involving 50 users at the Moncton regional Air Navigation Office, using IBM RT equipment. The pre-trial allowed considerable refinement of administrative and operational procedures. A full ULS program workplan was meanwhile developed and specific acquisition categories were established for ULS hardware, database packages, office-automation packages, system-integration services and application-development services.

A Request for Proposal (RFP) was developed based upon a Qualification and Evaluation Criteria (QEC) document which set out the parameters not only for paper qualification of vendors but also for full evaluation in the field trials. The requirements document placed considerable (and equal) stress on equipment performance, on vendor support and on vendor commitment to present and future standards adherence. It was necessary for the ULS equipment to integrate with local PC/LAN environments as well as with the IBM SNA network in the present, as well as a future, X.25 network. A parallel specification was also developed for the Office Automation (OA) package to be run on the ULS. The resulting materials were approved by a TC national task force and an interdepartmental Procurement Review Committee prior to release to industry in March 1989.

Ten responses were received by the September 1989 deadline resulting in a full qualification analysis, including visits to nine vendor facilities in North America and Europe. Vendors were qualified, and their sites were selected from TC Groups and vendors were assigned as follows: Vancouver/Finance (UNISYS), Montreal/Airports (AT&T), Moncton/Aviation (DEC), Dartmouth/Marine (BULL) and Sydney/Personnel (HP).

After the vendors had integrated and made operational their systems a series of user evaluations, formal benchmarks and vendor service, technology development and standards-adherence assessments were conducted over a seven-month period. During this time vendors were not permitted to upgrade the installed technology; this provided a stable basis for evaluation against the QEC. Vendors' original qualification ratings against each requirement were modified as necessary based on actual experience. The QUADRATRON (CLIQ) and UNIPLEX OA products and ORACLE relational database were also evaluated in service.

At the conclusion of the evaluation the five surviving vendors were each awarded a Departmental Individual Standing Offer (DISO). Subsequently, each mid-range system acquisition was competed only among the five DISO holders, on a price and availability basis.

In parallel with the system specification, acquisition and integration phases, it was necessary to train and certify a Unit Level System Administrator (ULSA) to operate and administer each local ULS installation. This person may have had some previous computer expertise but would probably come from an administrative or support background—they might even be a professional in another field but would *not* be a systems professional. The ULS RFP contained many requirements aimed at making the administration of the ULS as simple and easy as possible.

Field trial vendors were largely responsible for training the ULSAs for their respective sites, but on a one-time basis only. TC has developed a comprehensive ULSA Course which is delivered at the Transport Canada Training Institute (TCTI) in Cornwall, Ontario. The course covers ULS and ULSA role orientation, UNIX, system adminstration, OA and ORACLE basic administration, LAN orientation and other subjects.

There was, in strict principle, nothing which confined the GX concept to UNIX; it was thus decided to broaden the definition potentially to include non-UNIX operating systems; any operating system which can be modified to operate according to the GX specification could be declared compliant. To reflect this change and the possible move towards a more generalized definition of a system executive, as an operating system is sometimes called, the term *General Executive* was substituted for Greater UNIX. The GX acronym was retained.

The Transport Canada GX approach to open systems

Portability can be promoted by commonality not just of operating system but also of database environment, development tools and procedures, and by user conventions. However, given the rapid technological advancement within the mid-range system marketplace, forward portability was seen by TC as by far the most important. When a given ULS is replaced by a successor machine, *all* of the software and data on that machine must be carried forward and commonality of operating system is thus a cornerstone of portability in general. Horizontal portability is also very important at the unit level because there are fewer opportunities for horizontal portability at the enterprise/area levels (where fewer lateral peers exist) and much lower initial custom application software investment (with much more use simply of generic packages such as LOTUS and DBASE) at the workplace level. The UNIX operating system, developed by AT&T/Bell Labs in New Jersey, had been widely heralded as offering the best potential for supporting portability among varying hardware architectures. Indeed, UNIX is now running on computers manufactured by more than 100 vendors and offers a reasonably high degree of commonality in operating system, application interface and communications among most such systems. It was therefore decided that UNIX offered the highest potential for supporting portability and that a UNIX-based approach should be pursued. It was also recognized that UNIX had a strong reputation for being an operating system not at all suited to novice users, often offering challenge even to those with many years of computing experience.

The three leading versions of UNIX at that time (System V, XENIX and Berkeley) were in fact being merged into System V Release 4 and this development was viewed as a favourable one by TC. During the development of the TC ULS specification, however, a potentially serious problem arose when a number of major computer vendors joined together to form the Open Software Foundation (OSF), which proposed to develop yet another version of UNIX that would not necessarily be compliant with UNIX V.4, as discussed above. This heralded a reversion to a 'multi-UNIX' situation even before the vaunted merger of the above three was fully consummated, which was hardly the desirable outcome from the user perspective. The AT&T UNIX community quickly responded by forming a consortium of its own – UNIX International (UI) – to fortify and protect their own UNIX V.4. These were the classic ingredients for potentially long-standing commercial product *and* standards battle, or at least rivalry, which could both confuse users and complicate equipment specification and acquisition. Further, the OSF product was at such an immature and ill-defined stage that comprehensive specification of this product in an RFP was not, at that time, possible.

After due consideration, the strategy selected was *not to specify everything that an operating system shall or shall not contain but rather what part of an operating system is to be used and how it is to be used*. This permitted, for example, specification by TC of features A, B, C and E, where UI might provide features ABCDEFGH and OSF features XYZABCEKL. Thus, TC developers, system administrators and users would utilize only those features which fell within A, B, C and E no matter what else was provided. Whatever else was supplied would be simply ignored and not used; indeed it would be locked out or blocked wherever this could be done on an unobtrusive basis. Conversely, a vendor was compelled to provide features ABCE as mandatories. Thus, the operating system use profile which, in this example, consists of ABCE plus any required minor additional capabilities represented a small enhancement of the key features found in the common (overlap) area of the functional map of the UI and OSF operating systems and was therefore an enhanced subset of each. Vendors were to be free to include third-party products to make up any deficiencies against the specification. This concept and approach was called 'Greater UNIX' or 'GX' because it attempted to homogenize the differences among UNIX variants by setting a common 'how we will use it' profile. GX did not dictate creation of a new operating system version or variant nor did it necessarily exclude any existing one. It merely set out the features (and the *only* features) that TC would utilize (*see* Figs 8.2–8.4).

TC's initial contacts with industry on the GX approach produced somewhat mixed reactions; some firms did not believe the approach was

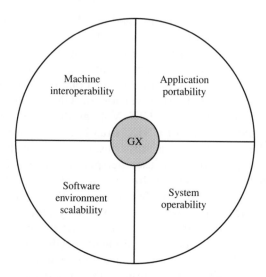

Figure 8.2 GX operational objectives.

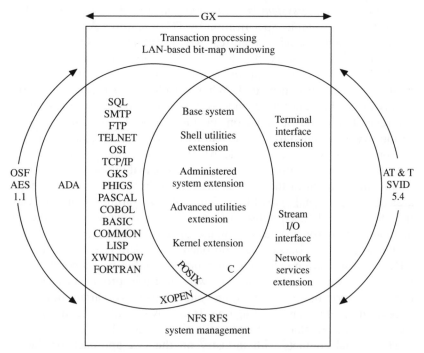

Figure 8.3 Standards conformance.

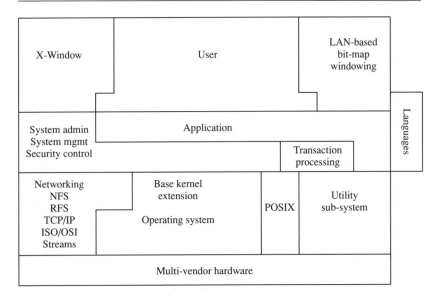

Figure 8.4 GX open systems architecture.

possible or viable while others stressed the superiority of a specific UNIX variant (i.e. their own) and still others suggested that the entire open systems approach was incorrect, recommending instead that TC select a closed system, again presumably their own. No outside organization, however, was able to point out a fundamental flaw with the intended approach. Indeed, it soon became clear that the GX approach would offer TC several advantages, because it:

- Did not confine the department to the UI UNIX family (which represented the dominant UNIX vendors with the most UNIX mid-range computer installations) nor to the OSF UNIX family (which included the dominant vendors in the market at large with the most mid-range, and other, computer installations of proprietary types) and thus permitted management the risk of the failure of one of the two groups. There was particular concern about OSF which, despite being backed by major vendors:
  - Was starting relatively late and faced a two-year development cycle; and
  - Was seen by some as a way to slow overall progress of UNIX while the biggest vendors caught up;
- Permitted implementation of a competitive procurement strategy *without* awaiting the outcome of the UI–OSF standards and market battles—this was because GX could be described in sufficient techni-

cal detail that the remaining partially defined elements could be leveraged by invoking the various vendors' own stated commitments to either UI or OSF compliance;

- Permitted selection of a full range of language and communications standards appropriate to TC requirements;
- Could be used with POSIX, which TB had already elected to support.

Naturally, the specification of a common way of *using* the operating system was not, in and of itself, sufficient to guarantee the degree of portability required by TC. Common languages and a common RDBMS were also specified and further procedural and protective measures were evolved during the subsequent national ULS field trials. *Taken together, the GX operating system use profile, POSIX and the implementation and control measures evolved during and since the field trials represent a means of establishing and protecting the portability of software and data among operating system variants and hardware types.*

Thus, GX is a specification for *how an operating system and related features will be used.* This information permits a vendor to provide an operating system accommodating such uses, and preferably only such uses. Technology vendors can only be held responsible for the integrity and operability of the products they provide; the implementing agency itself has a responsibility to do its part to maximize portability. The GX Master Specification document also sets out the accompanying mandatory and desirable measures an agency using the GX specification can employ so as to ensure that portability is promoted and protected.

TC representatives have presented a number of papers throughout North America on the ULS program, and the GX concept and specification. They also attended early meetings of the User Alliance for Open Systems, an association of the largest user organizations aimed at removing barriers to open systems. Canadian Government Treasury Board representatives have on several occasions reported on the progress of the ULS program at meetings of committees in North America and Europe under the auspices of Joint Technical Committee 1, an international coordinating body.

Current status

The program reached full operational status in 1991 and although financial constraints have slowed acquisitions, ULS equipment began to be purchased by user groups within TC during the 1991/2 fiscal year. During the subsequent fiscal years, the pace of acquisition may accelerate.

Cascade Transportation

Overview

Within a transportation firm, whether single- or multi-modal, there are three distinct processing environments: the *business* environment (marketing, sales, orders, billing, planning, general administration, etc.), the *operational* environment (vehicle and traffic dispatch and control, loading/unloading and trans-shipment) and the *mobile* environment (on-board vehicle and field-installed systems). In the past few years the advent of reasonably priced, and powerful, single- and multi-user UNIX processors as well as open system communications has made these systems viable not only for business processing but also for operational and mobile processing environments. Now, for the first time, it is possible for systems within each of these three information management realms to treat each other as peers: technically possible, at least.

However, when a transportation company actually seeks to implement this new technology—to gain the benefits which a move to open systems so clearly promises—there may be a number of challenges:

- The need to link open systems to business objectives;
- The need to 'wean' system suppliers and the in-house MIS organization from mono-vendorism and to end internecine MIS feuding and parochialism;
- The need to forge conceptual and practical links between the business, operational and mobile computing environments and to permit evolution of a peerage among them.

It is necessary first to examine the totality of information management within the organization plus the interfaces with shipper customers, interline transportation companies and all suppliers. This goes beyond EDI and beyond just casual or even formalized networking. It addresses adherence to advanced technology *and* transportation industry standards. At a Transportation Research Board committee meeting in 1991 in Los Angeles the two galaxies of standards bodies—the SAE, AASHTO, etc., in transportation and ISO, ANSI, IEEE, etc., in advanced technologies—came face to face in trying to address Intelligent Vehicle Highway Systems (IVHS) standards issues. They clearly spoke different dialects of 'standardization'.

There will be advocates and resisters within the company and each will have a sideline-cheering section. There will also be many fence-sitters. It is necessary to have an information management plan and a technology inflow plan. There must be a systems architecture, an acquisition/support program and top management must send everyone a signal that it is serious about open system computing. Otherwise, there will be many detours. Also, user and local system administrator support are crucial.

Background

At the 1995 Annual Shareholders Meeting, the Chairman and CEO of the company, which we will call 'Cascade', recounts the history of what he considers the three phases of their transition to open systems by tying them to three reasonably well-known clichés:

- The *initiation phase* is best remembered, he remarks, by the old farmer's comment to the totally lost urbanite: 'You can't get there from here . . .';
- The *understanding phase* is perhaps best recalled by transmuting the remarks of Canadian Prime Minister Mackenzie King about conscription during the Second World War: 'Not necessarily UNIX but UNIX if necessary';
- The *commitment phase* is best considered in the light of a transmutation of George Orwell's remarks about equality, part of his jibe at Communism in his classic satire *Animal Farm*: 'All vendors are committed to open systems but some vendors are more committed than others.'

Cascade is a large railway operating in the US Pacific Northwest but with two rail subsidiaries, one in British Columbia and one in Alberta. It offers general freight, piggyback and single/double stack container service and operates some 1700 road and switcher locomotives with more than 80 000 of its own railcars. It runs a contract commuter passenger service for three states and one province. Last year it purchased Blue Ox Trucking, which has 3500 tractors and about 10 000 highway trailers. Combined revenues are about US$3 billion with about 20 per cent of that coming from Canadian traffic. Since the last year has been spent in trying to develop a strategic Information Management (IM) plan, no actual integration of Cascade rail and Blue Ox truck systems has yet occurred as of early 1991.

The rail system operates a large IBM 370/MVS environment with three computer centre installations, an SNA network and a large number of home-grown systems, written mostly in COBOL and running under CICS. The company's business offices also have an unknown number of PCs (they are not capitalized but are bought out of operating money) of at least 40 different brands. Train dispatch and crew call are run at 12 locations on DEC VAX/VMS machines, some of which have Ethernet LANs while each of 40 major classification yards has its own

DEC PDP-11 running a yard management system. All major operational sites have IBM 3278 terminals for mainframe access. Recently a new loco maintenance software package was purchased, complete with eight AS/400 systems. About 200 DEC Rainbow PCs running CP/M and DOS are in service at operational sites; most user package software is under DOS but there are at least 2000 small CP/M applications. Fifty new-generation locomotives are participating in an Advanced Train Control System (ATCS) pilot project on three subdivisions; they each have a 16-bit on-board microcomputer.

Believe it or not, things are somewhat *less* homogeneous at Blue Ox! They have four IBM S-38 systems with three of them co-located. Unfortunately, an earthquake recently put the main truck data centre out of commission, so they have been renting S-38 capacity from a timeshare house at outrageous rates for the past two months. The key issue is whether to rebuild the previous environment or move to a new one, perhaps AS/400 which IBM highly recommends. They have about 470 PCs in office use plus many Token Ring LANs. There are seven dispatch systems; these are Burroughs 1800s linked by a commercial store-and-forward system (which charges by the kilocharacter and is costing the company $400 000 per year). The Burroughs machines are two years past their nominal service lives and three of them are on death row, according to their erstwhile maker. A 'spare' was bought used and is held in storage ready to replace the first fatality. Since dispatchers are frustrated with frequent non-synchronization among systems (and attendant data loss) they frequently confirm complex dispatches with voice calls and/or faxes; ringing up another $150 000 in communications costs! Each of 180 truck terminals has a DG Nova system which runs terminal management software and maintenance management. (All truck tractors have a home terminal.) There are also 300 Radio Shack TRS-80s which run a licence management system; they are matched to groups of trucks depending upon truck make, year of purchase and licence jurisdiction of the home terminal! The license system was developed by the past head of Blue Ox MIS (who was previously an accountant and who is now deceased); it is not extensively documented. Two hundred truck tractors have 8-bit trip computers purchased by the Vice-President Maintenance. Over half of them are barely operable and have software problems, especially when uploading data to the dedicated PCs used to read them. One of these special PCs was recently quarantined, having come down with a virus. The truck computer troubles are believed to have something to do with the Vice-President Maintenance; he got a 5 per cent discount from the supplier in exchange for no user support! It should also be noted that the S-38 and Burroughs fraternities within Blue Ox hate each other—they are mortal enemies and have been feuding since at least 1982. Two years ago the Burroughs central support manager was fired for allegedly trying to sabotage one of the IBM machines.

The CEO set up an IM Committee just after the merger and this visited many sites trying to assess overall IM requirements. It also made many tentative mentions of open systems during this period. They were greeted thus:

- The rail IBM data centre manager and staff said that open systems lead to UNIX, and UNIX is proprietary to AT&T ... we would rather stick with tried-and-true IBM than buy our computers from a telephone company.
- The DEC computing community said they were all for it; after all, their VAXs might some day be used to run ULTRIX and they were already using Ethernet—they liked the OSI model and they were in favour of *peer-to-peer* communication with the corporate systems which would help cut those data centre guys down to size.
- The people running the rail pilot were too busy trying to keep the loco computers up to have time to talk about open systems.
- The truck IBM people said they favoured an immediate EDI trial and that was more important to them than general commitment to OSI products, many of which they felt were not mature yet.
- The Burroughs supporters said that all existing systems were working just fine (except for hardware) and money should be spent on more spare Burroughs 1800s and more spare parts for existing 1800s rather than on new systems.
- The DG Nova supporters said much the same thing and the guy supporting the TRS-80s wasn't sure what open systems were.
- The truck Vice-President Maintenance didn't have time to meet with the committee; he was too busy negotiating a 5 per cent discount on a big buy of spare wheels.

Senior management commitment

The CEO sat in stunned silence as his committee recounted the state of his empire with respect to computing. The Chair of the committee ended by saying that calling it a horror story would be altogether too kind. It was disaster incarnate! Something had to be done, and very soon.

Although he had lived in the United States for ten years, the CEO was an expatriate Canadian. As he leaned back in his chair he thought out loud for a bit. He recalled a phrase from many years ago. When Lester Pearson became Prime Minister of Canada in the early 1960s he had embarked on what he called 'Sixty Days of Decision', wherein he identified all of his most major problems, jumped into the middle of the bullpit and began blasting furiously away in all directions; not all of the resulting solutions stuck but many of them did. Maybe the same basic approach was needed here. A many-faceted initiative would have to be launched because the time for partial solutions had passed. If Cascade couldn't manage information efficiently it couldn't stay competitive. If it couldn't stay competitive it was eventually doomed. They would have to look at the firm's business mission, the totality of how they handled information and how changing the latter could help to accomplish the former. His first act would come right now.

He pointed at the Director of Rail MIS:

> Since you are the systems mogul with the largest empire, and since truck systems are in even worse chaos than rail systems, I am hereby appointing you as Chief Information Management Officer (CIMO) of this corporation. You're now a Vice-President. Furthermore, we're going to join that User Alliance thing and we're going to move to open systems interconnection and open system computing as part of our fix to this mess. I've had it with being told what to do by computer companies. I'll pull a lot of money out of the capital budget for next year and ask the Board to float a special stock issue to replace it. If they won't then we'll just have to buy fewer new railcars and truck trailers but we are *going* to fix the information management problem. We have to get the different computers—and the people who run them—working together. We'll probably have to start with the people! I want to meet you and the V.P.s in Palm Springs to set objectives in two weeks and I want the whole plan together in sixty days! Okay?

The new Vice-President and CIMO—after recovering from shock— agreed to *try* and pointed out that if the company was to become truly integrated (and intermodal), the information systems should themselves be as intermodal as possible. He would therefore set about inventorying and classifying every system owned by Cascade not by mode but rather as being one of:

- *Business*, which involves marketing, sales, order entry, service tracking, commercial documentation, invoicing, collection, accounting, general administration and finance and all related areas;
- *Operational*, which involves the acquisition, preparation, maintenance, dispatch, operation, recovery, repair and retirement of vehicles, vehicle systems and infrastructure elements;
- *Mobile*, which involves the field or on-board vehicle handling of route and traffic authority, pickup/delivery, passenger and freight tracking, customs, licence and other regulatory documentation, billing and collection authority, en-route and out-station goods and services acquisition, operating environment and infrastructure observation, census or survey.

The results shown in Tables 8.1 and 8.2 were compiled over the next

Table 8.1 Transportation information management environments

	Business	Operational	Mobile
Air	Marketing Rating Sales Order entry	Routing Air traffic control Flightcrew management Dispatch Manifest Fleet management Licensing Vehicle maintenance	Communications Avionics A/C system management Cabin management Load management
Rail	Service tracking Documentation Insurance Invoicing Collection Accounting	ATCS (train control) Crew call Dispatch Classification Train operations Fleet management Vehicle maintenance Maintenance of way	Communications Loco management Train management Consist management Crew management

Motor vehicles

General administration
Finance
Personnel
Executive information
Other

IVHS
Crew call
Owner settlement
Dispatch
Load management
Fleet management
Licensing
Vehicle maintenance

Communications
Navigation
Truck management
Licensing/taxes
Driver management

Marine

VTMS
Port clearance (regulatory)
Load management
Manifest
Fleet management
Licensing/certification
Overhaul/drydock

Communications
Port clearance (self-dispatch)
Navigation
Ship management
Load management
Crew management
Unit business management

two weeks. He then developed a working paper on open systems and why they are important.

Open systems

The CIMO and his immediate working group met with seven vendors in five days! It was a torrent of account executives, customer engineers, open systems gurus, strategic product architectures, soon-to-be-released products, coffee, vapourware and long expensive dinners. Every vendor, it seemed, was totally committed to open systems; you could buy their UNIX box, their OSI network, their GUI, their terminals and their LANs and then (wonder of wonders) you would be able to inter-operate with other vendors' UNIX boxes and straight ANSI C language applications . . . Of course, this assumed you didn't do anything unusual with their operating system or communications software. However, at the end of the week the Cascade crew was able to rank each vendor as being one of the following:

1 Pays lip service (i.e. his own open system products are not compat-ible even with *each other*);
2 Getting started (i.e. has released the same OSI communications products for his proprietary and UNIX products and can show that his open systems folks are 'out-releasing' his proprietary folks); and
3 Away to the races (i.e. he has actually been integrating communica-tions products and CPUs from different sources into his product line and they actually work—or at least they seem to at the demo stage . . .).

Open systems and business objectives

At the Palm Springs meeting one Vice-President was fired and one resigned. It was far from pleasant but it did establish several things:

- The CEO was *in charge* of the company and the Executive Committee.
- Carrying programs developed on one system to another system would almost always save the company money over redeveloping the program again and again.
- If the same systems and standards were in place everywhere there would not only be fewer suppliers in total but also it would be easier to move MIS staff around.
- Adding OSI to otherwise proprietary systems was seen as a distant second-best choice, since many systems were obviously going to have to be replaced anyway—adding OSI, to the extent possible, to

Table 8.2 Current system environments

	Business	Operational	Mobile
Rail	IBM 309X/MVS (3) SNA network 372X/327X CICS COBOL (Most business systems and all support systems) PC/DOS (??) WordPerfect LOTUS DBASE (Local application)	DEC VAX/VMS (12) (Crew call) (Train dispatch) Ethernet LANs DEC PDP-11 (40) (Yard management) IBM AS-400 (8) (Maintenance management) DEC Rainbow/CP/M DOS (Local application)	Loco computer (16-bit) (ATCS pilot) (50 locos)
Truck	IBM S-38 (4) (business systems) Token Ring LANs PC/DOS (470) LOTUS MS WORD	Burroughs 1800 (7) (Dispatch) DG NOVA (180) (Terminal management) (Maintenance management) TRS-80 MICRO (300) (Licence management)	Truck computer (8-bit) (Vehicle maintenance data) (Service hours) (200 trucks)

all intended surviving proprietary systems and replacing the rest with UNIX/OSI systems seemed the way to go.

- There would be an Open Computing System Task Force (OCSTF) chaired by the CIMO with an Executive Sub-Group and a Technical Sub-Group—each local workgroup of 20 or more would have a rep on the task force's Council.
- The CIMO would head a new IM Services (IMS) organization and all those who worked full time on computers or communications or managed manual records were now part of it . . . paper to follow. . . .
- Cascade would join COS and the User Alliance and would commit not only to open systems but also—to the extent possible—to the UNIX operating system for corporate, workgroup, personal and vehicle processors.

Open Computing Systems Task Force

The OCSTF decided at its first meeting that it would have to determine the *current*, *interim* and *target* architectures and would also have to establish the means to certify vendors and their products as meeting OSI and Cascade's own standards. They would have to provide IMS with the capability to oversee integration of diverse products (from various vendors) and train/certify many more 'super-users' to administer and operate systems in the field. Certainly, they wished to decentralize as much processing as they could to field sites; a repeat of the S-38 data centre disaster (or worse, a similar one at the MVS site) was too horrible to contemplate. Also, since they could at least begin to use UNIX processors and OSI communications in all three environments (business, operational and mobile) they could now allow these systems to treat each other as peers. Applications could be developed with this in mind. Application developers might as well start learning about open systems, about UNIX, about C language and about modern relational databases *now* since that was to be the company direction.

It was decided to meet with the key 'computer person' within each workgroup and to have them complete a requirements survey form jointly with a member of the OCSTF leadership. They would then become a member of the OCSTF Council, a mailing list contact and later would be encouraged to evolve into a paraprofessional IM support person within their workgroup. The results of the survey indicated that user needs were even more diverse than expected.

Well before the 60 days had elapsed, the OCSTF held its third meeting, followed by a full Council meeting. At that time the following initiatives were put in place:

1 Since some sites were desperate for new workgroup applications, and since futher development without a Relational Database Management System (RDBMS) was considered nonsensical, ORACLE was selected as the corporate standard. ORACLE is not perfect but at least it would run under MVS, VMS, DOS and, most importantly, UNIX. All future application development (except for purely personal use) would be under ORACLE. An interim truck business system, based on ORACLE, would be bought off-the-shelf as soon as possible. Later, a bimodal corporate system would replace it. All developers who could be pried away from the now almost all-consuming chore of maintaining the millions of lines of old code were sent on courses.

2 Since the trucking division was in the worst shape, a few pilots would be run there, not only to put up some urgently needed new applications but also to develop a new dispatch application to allow all Burroughs 1800s to be 'shot dead' within 9 months. The purchase of more spare Burroughs was expressly forbidden! This was the CEO's absolute deadline. Technical proposals would be solicited and the best three vendors would be invited to lend Cascade minis at their own expense in exchange for certification as standard suppliers. Thereafter, all of several hundred Mid-Range System and several thousand workstation buys would be bid competitively but only among the certified vendors. This would limit the number of flavours of UNIX that Cascade had to contend with while preserving some price/performance competition and preventing vendor lock-in. For the MRS and power user workstations XPG and POSIX were specified along with UNIX SVID V.4.

3 Since office automation was viewed as a high-payback application in most places (particularly phone management and local/corporate E-mail) an OA package would be chosen and run on all three pilot machines. Each trial site would get a new-generation PABX which would be tied to the MRS. The trials would also be used to determine corporate standard desktop equipment as well as terminal emulation and communication software.

4 The trial minis would also have to prove they could run emulation software to serve as gateways to the IBM mainframes.

5 After the trials, all MVS, VMS and UNIX multi-user systems would be connected to a backbone leased line X.25 network. X.25 was viewed as an imperfect solution but was felt to be a good starting point. X.400 messaging and (when mature) X.500 addressing would be implemented. The OA package would have to take this into account.

6 The AS/400-based rail maintenance system was too new to touch so

installation of OSI-based communication handshaking and data exchange with other contemplated systems was all that could be accomplished in the short term.

Towards the future

The Executive Committee greeted these results with satisfaction but actually pushed things a little further. They wanted the mainframe tied into the open system trials too. Therefore it was decided that one of the IBM 3090s would be traded for a 390 machine which could dynamically repartition MVS and AIX. Thus, it would run the UNIX OA package for any users not yet served by new-generation local workgroup systems. As local systems came on-line, local OA users would be offloaded. The desire to use the pilots to determine desktop processing was short-circuited and a 386/UNIX standard was imposed from the top, even over the objections of the CIMO that this might be overkill. It was felt that eventually full open networking would extend right to the desktop, not just the MRS, and it was decided to err on the side of purchasing too much—rather than too little—desktop power. Ethernet was made the corporate LAN standard and the Token Ring people were given one year to convert. (It was acknowledged that Token Ring can support some OSI elements but with three MRS types the local administrator training was going to be complex enough without two LAN types.) The MRS processing tier would be used as the open systems beach head. These systems would be in place everywhere within one year. They would initially provide X.25-based access to mainframe applications (replacing dumb terminals) and host local OA. As workgroup applications were developed or converted, the workgroup processing platforms would already be in place and their power could be easily expanded as required. Within 18 months, the SNA network would be confined to the premises where the mainframes existed as well as to intermainframe links. SNA would thus be islanded within an X.25 sea. All networking was placed under a new Director in the IMS shop, which was reorganized into Applications, Networks, Systems and Human Development units.

It was also soon decreed that, barring major unforeseen problems in the trials, the overall *target* architecture would be generally as shown in Table 8.3. The IBM mainframes would keep the older applications but would also run AIX for the RDBMS. A second 390 would soon follow the first. Over time, these systems would take on the corporate server role, far more than being logic processors. Most new application logic would reside at the workgroup level on UNIX-based MRS equipment, probably based on the 'ABU' standard, named for AT&T, BULL and

Table 8.3 Target system environments

	Business	Operational	Mobile

Rail	IBM 309X/MVS (1)
	SNA and X.25 gate
	CICS/COBOL
	  (Old business systems not moved
	   to RDBMS environment)
	IBM 390/MVS/AIX (2)
	  (Redeveloped and new business
	  systems)
	  (Corporate server)
	ORACLE
	UNIPLEX OA
	X.25 network
	X.400/X.500
		DEC VAX/ULTRIX (2)
		  (Crew call)
		X.25 network
		X.400/X.500
		Ethernet LANs
		ABU MRS/UNIX (60)
		ORACLE
		X.25 network
		X.400/X.500
		  (Train dispatch)
		  (Yard management)
		  (Maintenance management)
		UNIPLEX OA
		PC386/UNIX (300)
			ABU MICRO/UNIX
			  (Communications)
			  (Loco management)
			  (Train management)
			  (Consist management)
			  (Crew management)
			Satellite link
			AM/VHF link
			  (1200 locos)

Truck	ABU MRS/UNIX (150)
	  (Redeveloped and new business
	  systems)
	  (Workgroup processor)
	ORACLE
	UNIPLEX OA
	X.25 network
	X.400/X.500
	PC386/UNIX (4200)
	ORACLE
	  (Local application)
		ABU MRS/UNIX (250)
		ORACLE
		UNIPLEX OA
		Ethernet LANs
		X.25 network
		X.400/X.500
		  (Dispatch)
		  (Terminal management)
		  (Licence management)
		PC386/UNIX (500)
		ORACLE
		  (Local applications)
			ABU MICRO/UNIX
			  (Communications)
			  (Vehicle maintenance data)
			  (Service hours)
			Satellite link
			AM/VHF link
			  (2000 tractors)

UNISYS, the three vendors who qualified for the trials. MRS equipment would run most new business system logic (except where scale of logic and/or data prevented this) and virtually all operational logic for both the truck and rail modes. Where/when a UNIX MRS was installed, an Ethernet LAN would also be installed and a paraprofessional (and backup) would be trained to administer the local equipment. All computer hardware, software and communications products would be certified centrally and cataloged on-line. Henceforth, it would be a sacking offence to purchase something not on the list without an IMS exemption. Desktop systems would run a to-be-determined flavour of UNIX which would run DOS as a task under it. However, common DOS application packages such as LOTUS and WordPerfect would also run on the MRS equipment under UNIX and DOS itself would be supported but only for two more years. Vehicle systems would be based on 32-bit UNIX processor technology with PLCs or real-time controllers treated as modules or subprocessors. All communications with vehicles would adopt the OSI model as soon as possible.

Conclusion

While UNIX and open systems are by no means synonymous, there exist strong links and synergies between them. Organizations that embrace OSI usually find themselves embracing UNIX too, and vice versa. What is most profound, however, about the gradual (or in this case shotgun) transition to open systems is the advent of architecture/standards-driven computing. This in turn begets the need for certification and a central registry not only of approved products but also of application programs which have already been produced in-house and are available for all to use. It also begets much more decentralization, which brings the need to train and certify those who will support the new technology locally.

9 As old as the industry; as modern as the hour

The title of this chapter is taken from the motto and slogan of the latter-day Riley Motor Car Company; it seemed the most appropriate way to sum up a book on the very timely challenges of dealing with constantly evolving open systems.

The pace of advancement of electronics technology since the mid-1960s has been nothing short of astounding. We have reduced by almost a million times the cost of storing or processing a piece of information since 1965. The fact is, though, that our ability to assimilate change has certainly not increased by a million times; far from it! It wasn't very long ago that people were marvelling over the transition from tube-based to solid-state computers, and from the latter to the modern digital computer. It is also worth noting that some of the people who founded Digital Equipment Corporation in 1957 left IBM because of resistance to change and because nobody would support the contention that digital computers were the way of the future.

As we begin to move away from the era of the computer room, and the wizardries that were always arrayed round about it, we must surely come to see that the role of what we now call the IT fraternity is henceforth to be the guardians of change and the keepers of the gate. We must ensure that technologically driven change does indeed continue to occur in the organization, and that the rate of inflow of the new technologies is consistent with what can be assimilated. This, it would seem, is a very potent challenge and one requiring much of St Francis' 'wisdom to know the difference', as cited earlier.

I personally believe that, historically, looking back from 2020, 2030 or beyond, the coming into prominence of UNIX, OSI *et al.* will be seen as a critical turning point in the application of technology to the management of information. It will be seen as the point at which the technologies of computing and computer communications finally began to serve us far more than we had to serve them; the point at which the 'balance of effort' shifted in favour of the users, and away from the wizards (i.e.

the 'computer experts'). Oh, make no mistake, the IT discipline is *not* going to disappear. Even in 2020 or 2030 there will still be those who are charged with overseeing the inflow and assimilation of new technology, although by then the process will be seen as more routine and somewhat less discomforting.

There is an interesting parallel in the automotive world. While all of the components necessary to construct the Model T Ford were in existence by about 1885, it took until 1908 (more than 20 years) for someone to put the right combination together, in the right way. Finally, someone made a horseless carriage that was truly *reliable* and which we could make do what we wanted most of the time. How like the computer industry of today. It could be debated whether we have spent 20 years wandering in the wilderness, but it bears some thinking that the 'PC revolution' taught MIS a thing or two about what users really needed from the technology. Are we not all users? Why was MIS unable to discern this for itself?

In future, the IT unit will be very much the gate keeper and the pacer of change. It will decide which 'wild beasts' to let loose within the organization and will have to take at least the initial steps in collaring them and bringing them under some semblance of control and, later, domestication. The users will take it from there, often coming up with applications and permutations never dreamed of by the systems professionals.

Back to the present! The challenge for today is to implement open systems as rapidly as possible, while still moving slowly enough both to permit the majority of the IT staff to keep pace and to avoid inducing 'future shock' in the users. Improving our ability to do our business in a world of bewildering changes and challenges demands that we do our best to ensure that something with as much to contribute to the bottom line as open systems does not take forever to be adopted.

We are in a period of transition. We are moving from a period when major changes in technology have been, to say the least, revolutionary, with all of the attendant disruption, to a period wherein they will be evolutionary, incremental and (almost) smooth. Certainly, we can see the beginnings of that now. To replace an existing MRS or MBS with a newer or larger model is to disrupt the users for only a day or two and to then return them to the humdrum of before. Five years ago, the replacement of a 30-user system was accompanied by much shouting, cursing, gnashing of teeth and ripping out of proprietary wires. There was the need to learn new stack registers, a new operating system, new terminals, new printers, new packages and, most probably, new business applications. (The existing ones, you see, and all the learning and careful honing incorporated into them, were thrown into the dustbin.) It is called three steps forward and one-and-a-half back. With open systems, three (or more likely ten or a hundred) steps forward will be just that!

Some readers may have found this book a bit vexing to read. IT professionals may have scoffed, along the way, at the triteness or simplicity of the ☞ paragraphs. Non-IT readers may have marvelled at the apparent arcaneness of some of the others. All readers will, perhaps, have found my tone a bit jaundiced towards the proprietary vendors. My bluntness, however, is based not only on my experience as an officer of a large purchaser but also on my work with a system-integration firm, two aerospace firms and as the technology czar of a medium-sized transportation firm. My abiding interest in railways also contributed.

When mass-production diesel locomotives appeared on the North American scene late in the 1930s they began, rather imperceptibly, a process of change in the railway industry which took more than 20 years to complete. The first response to that statement will undoubtedly be that yes, of course, diesels were more efficient than steam locomotives and they eventually crowded the latter off the rails entirely. However, diesels also did something more profound. They unlocked the design of railway locomotives from geography. In the steam age, the ruling gradients and most plentiful types of coal worked together to have a large impact on the boiler design and wheel arrangement of steam locomotives. This tended to make home-designing, and in some cases actual home-building, of locomotives economic for most of the larger railways. However, the advent of the standardized diesel locomotive, units of which could be ganged together under the control of one man, changed all of that. The difficulty was that it took railway managements a very long time, almost a generation, to realize the implications of this development. Many railways (such as the Norfolk and Western) and some loco builders (such as Baldwin Locomotive Works) did all in their power to fight these developments. Both, alas, are with us no more.

Open systems are not unlike diesel locomotives. They have already begun to change profoundly how the game is played but many of the players have yet to realize that the rules are not the same as they were. Some of the biggest vendors are, like Baldwin, building a few diesels and meanwhile pushing bigger and better steam locomotives as hard as they can.

This book will not give you *all* of the conceptual and practical tools you need to convert your particular railway from steam to diesel, but it will make you sufficiently well acquainted with the latter that you will not fear it, nor curse it for not having big driving wheels or belching coal smoke. It will, I believe, provide some building blocks and some initial tools you will require to start asking the as-yet unasked questions. It is my sincere hope that it will give you the desire to find out more and will, thereby, lead you to the point where taming the tiger will be no more forbidding than stroking your pet cat. Both are tameable, but the scale and nature of the challenges are quite different. Good luck.

Index

Access:
  to UNIX applications, 75
  to mainframe, 94–95
ADA Language, 36
Application development,
  collaborative, 99
Application software, 52

Benefits of open systems, 48, 92–106
Business process:
  control of, 103

C language, 31
Canadian Open System Application
  Criteria (COSAC), 32
Cascade Transportation, 233–246
Champions, requirement for, 158
Client-server service model, 17
Closed systems, 7
COBOL, per ANSI, 30
Compatibility, 21
Competitiveness, enhancement of, 72
Compliance, with standards, 22–23
Configuration management—unified, 80
Conversion, application/data, 64
Costs of open systems, 48, 49–68
Costs—operational, 62
Customer engineers (proprietary
  vendor), 178–179

Data:
  restructuring, 67
  sharing, among applications, 99
Development environment, 75
Discard, of interim solutions, 68
Disinformers, of proprietary vendor,
  179
Disruption, avoidance of, 95
Downsizability, organizational, 87

Efficiency:
  workgroup and individual, 68
  IT staff, 103
Electronic data interchange (EDI), 36

Ergonomic impacts, 72
Expansion opportunities, exploiting, 73

Failure risk, 57
Features, foregone, 56
French, Canadian, 31
Frustration, of user, 59
Functionality, 57

Graphical user interface (GUI), 78, 88
Greater UNIX (GX), 35, 228–232

Hardware, computer, 49
Home workplace, 81

Information management planning
  (IM), 163–164
Installation, integration and
  commissioning, 52
Installed life, of product, 105
Insurance, liability, 56
Interoperability, 80
  environment, 89

Layers of OSI, 13
Local area network administrator
  (LANA), 94
Learning period, 57

Mainframe, UNIX, 59
Marketeer, lunching, 181–182
Mergeability, organizational, 87
Micro-based server (MBS), 15
Mid-range system (MRS), 15
Mid-range system administrator
  (MRSA), 94
Misbehaviour—proprietary vendor, 65
Motivators, user group, 156–158
Multi-user service model, 17

Network:
  management, 170–171
  consolidation, 92

Office automation, 93

Open computing systems, 10
Open software foundation (OSF), 24
Open system interconnection (OSI), 10,
  12
Open systems, 9
Opportunities of open systems, 48,
  68–92
Organization:
  knowledge-based, 102
  for technology management, 208–212
Orientation and training, 52–53
Overhead, communications/processing,
  54–55
Over-pricing, OSI products, 56

Package software, 51
Personal computer (PC), 14
Pilot projects, 203–204
Placement, of applications, 84, 215–219
Policy and standards, 60
Portability, 12, 79
  continuum of, 40
POSIX (of IEEE), 10, 34
Predictability, of IT, 104
Pre-trials, 196–197
Price/performance:
  installed net benefit, 95–96
  selection on basis of, 70
Processing tiers:
  advantages/disadvantages, 146–152
Products, introduction of, 76–77
Profiles of standards, 25
Progressivity, in UNIX licensing, 71

Re-engineering, software, 82
Relational Database Management
  System, 28
Requirements:
  corporate, 154–156
  information technology, 156
Response time, reduction of, 74
Retirement of proprietary system, 56
Revenge pricers, proprietary vendor,
  182

Scalability, 12, 79
Security, 71
Seminar, free, in Florida, 180
Service model:
  single-user vs client-server, 116–121
  single-user vs multi-user, 121–124
  client-server vs multi-user, 124–146

Sharing, work item/workspace, 69–70
Shopping, one stop, 64
Software registry, 215
Sourcing strategies:
  single-vendor, 171–172
  multi-vendor, 172–173
  omni-vendor, 173–174
Standards:
  early bird syndrome, 66
Structured query language (SQL), 28
Success, capitalizing on, 205–207
Support, software and hardware, 53
System administration, 54, 165–170
  remote, 80–81
Systemic architecture, 160–161
  definition of, 107–109
  driven approach, 86
  importance of, 109–114
  planning, 60
System software, 49

Tactics, battering ram, of proprietary
  vendor, 183
Technology:
  lag, (of UNIX), 64
  tracking, 63, 164
  management, 162–163
Telecommuting, 81
Tests:
  alpha, 194
  laboratory, 191–194
Time, freed up, 69
Transport Canada (TC), 35–36
Trial spoilers, proprietary vendor, 182
Treasury Board Information
  Technology Standards, 27–37
Treasury Board (TB) of Canada, 26
Trials, 197–203

Unit level system (ULS), 225–228
UNIX, 14, 24
UNIX International (UI), 24

Vendor:
  qualification, 184–204
  evaluation, 184–204
  certification, 184–204
  reorientation/re-education, 58
  lock-in, 66
  independence, 100

Workstation (WS), 14–15